Selznick

THE MAN WHO

PRODUCED

GONE WITH THE WIND

Other New Millennium Titles by Bob Thomas:

Biography:
King Cohn: The Life and Times of Hollywood Mogul Harry Cohn
Thalberg: Life and Legend
Astaire: The Man, The Dancer
Clown Prince of Hollywood (Jack L. Warner)

Also by Bob Thomas:

Biography:
Winchell
Marlon: Portrait of the Rebel as an Artist
Walt Disney: An American Original
Bud & Lou: The Abbott and Costello Story
The One and Only Bing
Joan Crawford
Golden Boy: The Untold Story of William Holden
I Got Rhythm: The Ethel Merman Story
Liberace
Building a Company: Roy O. Disney and the Creation of an
    Entertainment Empire

General:
If I Knew Then (with Debbie Reynolds)
The Art of Animation
The Massie Case (with Peter Packer)
The Secret Boss of California (with Arthur H. Samish)
The Heart of Hollywood
Howard, The Amazing Mr. Hughes (with Noah Dietrich)
The Road to Hollywood (with Bob Hope)
Reflections in Two Worlds (with Ricardo Montalban)
Disney's Art of Animation

Fiction:
The Flesh Merchants
Weekend 33

For Children:
Walt Disney: Magician of the Movies
Donna de Varona: Gold Medal Winner

Anthology:
Directors in Action

Selznick

THE MAN WHO PRODUCED
GONE WITH THE WIND

Bob Thomas

NEW MILLENNIUM PRESS
Beverly Hills

Design: Susie Dotan
Typeface: Garamond Book

Original hardcover publication in 1970 by Doubleday & Company, Inc.
First New Millennium Press edition 2001

Library of Congress Cataloging-in-Publication Data

Thomas, Bob, 1922-
    Selznick / by Bob Thomas.--1st New Millennium Press ed.
        p. cm.
    Originally published: Garden City, N.Y.: Doubleday, 1970. With new foreword.
    Includes bibliographical references and index.
    ISBN 1-893224-27-9 (trade pbk.)
    1. Selznick, David O., 1902-1965. 2. Motion picture producers and directors--United States--Biography. I. Title.

PN1998.3.S395 T45 2001
791.43'0233'092--dc21
[B]

00-55040

New Millennium Press
A Division of NMWorldMedia, Inc.
301 N. Canon Drive
Suite 214
Beverly Hills, CA 90210

Printed in the United States of America

Dedicated to
Everett and Elizabeth Sadler,
gratefully

CONTENTS

FOREWORD

By Peter Bart
VARIETY *Magazine*

Hollywood's old-time moguls were a fearsome lot, but few if any had the polish or the "cool" to survive at today's bottom-line oriented studios.

David 0. Selznick would have been the exception, as Bob Thomas' deft 1970 biography now reminds us. Ruthless but well-spoken, Selznick understood the rules of the game and adapted brilliantly to them. Remembered today as the man who went from producing rather staid film adaptations of *David Copperfield* and *Anna Karenina* to risking the store on *Gone With The Wind,* Selznick was a smooth operator, but hardly the erudite filmmaker who dedicated himself to the art of the cinema. He was a gambler and bully who lived beyond his means and habitually popped Benzedrine and random barbiturates. He married the boss's daughter — Irene's father Louis B. Mayer, was the monarch of MGM — and, in recruiting John Hay Whitney as his partner, revealed a talent at exploiting the fascination of Old Money with New Hollywood. The plethora of memos that flowed from Selznick's office reminded filmmakers and artisans alike of his insistence on quality, but also underscored the fact that he often simply missed the point. In producing a dreadful movie called *The Garden of Allah*, Selznick rhapsodized, "This script is poetry. I want to hear every syllable on the sound track, every consonant, every vowel." The film would have been better off if the audience hadn't distinguished a single line of dialogue.

If Selznick had his rough edges, he also was a sophisticated businessman. He knew he could get away with considerable liberties when it came to adapting Charles Dickens, but since virtually everyone in America had read Margaret Mitchell's *Gone With The Wind,* he understood he had to hew close to the text, irrespective of cost. The risks were considerable. Selznick had only recently joined Whitney in founding Selznick International

Pictures and debts were mounting up. He had left a safe perch, working for his father-in-law at MGM, but wanted more autonomy. He also bridled at comparisons with Irving Thalberg, the town's golden boy, who cast a big shadow over that studio.

In fact, Selznick had to be prodded into making *Gone With The Wind*, rather than plucking it out of the air, as the myth-makers later suggested. His New York story editor, Kay Brown, hammered away at him to read the newly-published best-seller. Finally succumbing, he read only a 25-page synopsis, but it was not until John Hay Whitney, of all people, announced that he would personally write the check and buy the damned book for $50,000, that Selznick closed the deal. When he finally repaired to Hawaii to read the long tome, he realized that he had bought both a best-seller and a hot potato. "If this picture fails, I'll lose everything," he fumed. "That's just what L. B. (Mayer) wants. He'd like me to fall on my ass so I'd have to crawl back to him at Metro."

Much has been made of Selznick's search for Scarlett O'Hara — a brilliant publicity stunt — but Bob Thomas also relates the details of Selznick's search for a script. After his first writer, Sidney Howard, turned in a five-hour screenplay, Selznick went through virtually every top writer in town in an effort to compress it to viable length. He even anointed F. Scott Fitzgerald, who complained bitterly that he'd been instructed simply to re-arrange words written by Margaret Mitchell, and not to add his own.

The producer agonized even further over the choice of Clark Gable to play Rhett Butler. Gable was under contract to the dreaded Louis B. Mayer, so the stubborn Selznick ricocheted between Gary Cooper (he was under contract to the also dreaded Samuel Goldwyn) and Errol Flynn (who was under contract to the equally feared Jack Warner) before capitulating to a killer deal with Mayer. In the end, of course, Gable played opposite an English girl, Vivian Leigh, thus inflaming many of the novel's Southern readers.

Gone With The Wind went famously over its absurd $2.5 million budget, which sent Selznick traveling for additional money from A.P. Giannini of the Bank of America as well as the Whitney family. In the process, he drove his director Victor Fleming crazy, ultimately finishing the movie with Sam Wood, along with filmmakers like Sidney Franklin and William Wellman, who directed selected scenes.

At the end of these agonies, Selznick collected more Academy Awards than any other film in Oscar history. Yet, Oscar in hand, he still paused to blast his publicist because Gable didn't get the best actor award.

Gone With The Wind haunted Selznick for the rest of his life. Since he was only 37 at the time he made the film, his later years were spent trying to top himself. The obsession caused almost everyone who worked for him to have nervous breakdowns. The famous screenwriter, Nunnally Johnson, turned down a writing contract with him because "my understanding is that an assignment from you consists of three months of work and three of recuperation."

He made some other noteworthy movies, such as *The Song of Bernadette* starring Jennifer Jones, then known as Phylis Isley, with whom he ultimately became involved. By 1949, turkeys like *The Paradine Case* and *Portrait of Jennie* all but ruined his once-successful company. His friends deserted him in droves.

The press regularly ridiculed Selznick for announcing so many projects that never got made. By the time he finally got *A Farewell to Arms* off the ground, Selznick's myriad memos were the subjects of jokes throughout the industry. The failure of the film left him broke and tired. His final grand scheme was to launch a Broadway musical of *Gone With The Wind*, but he failed to get the financing.

Selznick's death at 63 occasioned abundant tributes, but Thomas reminds us that the producer once delivered his own best epitaph when, in 1959, the set for "Tara" was dismantled. Selznick watched the scene sadly and commented, "Once photographed, life here is ended. It is symbolic of Hollywood."

That remark in itself was enough to inspire a final memo, but it didn't.

PREFACE

This is the final volume of a biographical trilogy dealing with power figures and creative forces that helped bring forth the Golden Age of the American film. The first book concerned Harry Cohn, a rough-and-tumble rogue who epitomized the pioneering spirit of the founders of the movie industry. An unabashed vulgarian, he nevertheless advanced the art and sophistication of the Hollywood film to an astonishing degree.

Next came the biography of Irving Thalberg, an entirely different kind of man, revered as a saint, yet as human in his motivations as was Cohn. Thalberg was a dedicated, almost obsessed filmmaker, an innovator who developed the major studio to its peak of creativeness.

Now, Selznick.

It is a dynastic saga, concerning a profligate father and his two compulsive sons. Both David and Myron Selznick conquered the film industry and in the end were defeated by it, as was their father before them.

As with *King Cohn* and *Thalberg*, I am indebted to many persons for sharing their memories with me. Among them:

Ingrid Bergman
Pandro Berman
Russell Birdwell
Whitney Bolton
Harry Brand
Kay Brown
Ruth Burch
Tom Carlile
Robert Carson
Anita Colby
Stanley Cortez
Joseph Cotton
John Crosby
George Cukor
Olivia de Havilland
D. A. Doran
William Dozier
Douglas Fairbanks, Jr.
Arthur Fellows
B. P. Fineman
Joan Fontaine
John Ford
Henry Ginsberg
George Glass
Willis Goldbeck
William Golden
Frances Goldwyn
Samuel Goldwyn
Ruth Gordon
Helen Hayes
Leland Hayward
Alfred Hitchcock

Al Hix
John Houseman
Mervyn Houser
Rock Hudson
John Huston
Frances Inglis
Arthur Jacobs
Nunnally Johnson
Louis Jourdan
Garson Kanin
Hal Kern
Henry King
Raymond Klune
Mervyn LeRoy
Joshua Logan
Myrna Loy
Clare Boothe Luce
Ida Lupino
Paul MacNamara
John Lee Mahin
Sarah Mankiewicz
Fredric March
Ann McCall
Marjorie McDougall
Dorothy McGuire
Lewis Milestone
Agnes Moorehead
Daniel O'Shea
Gregory Peck
William Pereira
H. C. Potter
Marcella Rabwin

Carol Reed
Dore Schary
Budd Schulberg
Leon Shamroy
Joseph Steele
James Stewart
Howard Strickling
Dimitri Tiomkin
King Vidor
William Wellman
Dwight Whitney
John Hay Whitney
Henry Willson
Daniel Winkler
William Wright
Collier Young
Loretta Young
Darryl F. Zanuck
Bennie Zeidman

I am also grateful to Leonard Maltin and R. E. Braff for preparing the list of Selznick films and to Earl Anderson and Philip K. Scheuer for their review of the manuscript for accuracy. The Larry Edmunds Bookshop, Raymond Lee, and Ray Stuart were helpful in tracking down the photographs. And my gratitude, as always, goes to my wife and three daughters for their support during these long projects.

I

BEGINNINGS

*Selznick Pictures Make
Happy Hours*

David Selznick, executive of Select Pictures

WHEN DAVID SELZNICK WAS SEVENTEEN,
and his brother Myron was twenty-one,
their father provided them with
unconventional weekly allowances:
$750 for David and $1000 for Myron.
Lewis J. Selznick told his sons:
"Spend it all.
Give it away.
Throw it away.
But get rid of it.
Live expensively.
If you have confidence in yourself,
live beyond your means.
Then you'll have to work hard to catch up.
That's the only fun there is:
hard work.
Never try to save money.
If you do, then you have two things to worry about:
Making it,
and keeping it.
Just concern yourself with making it.
The rest will take care of itself."
David and Myron never forgot the lesson.

D.O.S....

Over the initials went the memos, millions of words each year issuing caution, praise, chastisement, advice, reflection, warning, and instruction to those who worked for him in the making of motion pictures.

David 0. Selznick . . .

Under the name appeared the movies, a succession of carefully wrought entertainments that ranked with Hollywood's best achievements during its period of dominance in the film world.

The name itself was fraudulent. Selznick's parents had failed to endow him with a middle name. The youthful David, analytical in all things, reckoned that greatness was his destiny. The important figures of the film world bore middle initials: Cecil B. De Mille, Louis B. Mayer, Jesse L. Lasky, Nicholas M. Schenck, Irving G. Thalberg, etc. David Selznick needed a middle initial to give his name a more imposing look and sound.

But which initial? He tested each one for effectiveness:

> David A. Selznick
> David B. Selznick
> David C. Selznick
> David D. Selznick
> David E. Selznick
> David F. Selznick
> David G. Selznick
> David H. Selznick
> David I. Selznick
> David J. Selznick
> David K. Selznick
> David L. Selznick
> David M. Selznick
> David N. Selznick
> David 0. Selznick

That was it! The 0 provided a harmonious link between his double-syllabled names. But what would the 0 stand for? David

Lewis J. Selznick

cast about for a name and happened upon Olive Thomas, a star in brother Myron's movies. And so the official name became David Oliver Selznick. In later years many Americans thought of him as that Irish movie producer, David O'Selznick.

His father was a Russian Jew whose name was Zeleznick when he was born in Kiev on May 2, 1870. Being one of eighteen children, young Lewis learned to scramble for himself at an early age. Perceiving no opportunities for a Jewish boy in tsarist Russia, he emigrated to England at twelve and worked as a factory hand until he could earn passage to America. Lewis J. Selznick, as he now called himself, settled in Pittsburgh and attended school only long enough to perfect his English. He became a jeweler's apprentice and learned the trade fast. He was scarcely in his twenties when he was operating his own jewelry store.

It was time to begin his own family. Florence Sachs was seventeen, a gentle, pretty girl who listened attentively to his dreams of wealth and glory. Her parents were Orthodox Jews who recoiled at the fast-talking, irreverent Selznick. But he was an irresistible salesman, and Florence Sachs became Mrs. Lewis J. Selznick.

"That young man will never amount to anything," muttered Florence's conservative friends, but he seemed to prove them wrong. By the time he was twenty-four, Lewis J. Selznick had organized three jewelry stores and a national bank. His family began to grow; Myron was born on October 5, 1898, and David on May 10, 1902. There was also a third son, Howard, a sunny, ineffectual boy who was to spend his life being protected and supported by his family.

Myron and David soon developed the characteristics they bore through their lifetimes. Both were brawlers, eager to impose their wills; this led to innumerable fights with playmates and with each other. Myron was closest to his father, whom he resembled in stocky figure and bullheaded drive. David was more like his mother, whom he adored. He had her Germanic looks and her devotion to literature.

Pittsburgh could not hold Lewis J. Selznick. He was eager to broaden his horizons, to take on the challenge of New York City. He moved his family there in 1910 and opened "the world's largest jewelry store." It was a fiasco. Selznick's high-powered ideas didn't fit into the New York jewelry market, and he lost interest in such a backward business. Impulsively, he auctioned his entire enterprise.

But he retained a handful of large diamonds. L.J. liked diamonds. They were compact, glittery, and immensely valuable. A man could never tell when they might come in handy.

Carl Laemmle

"I am going into the picture business," Lewis J. Selznick announced one evening to his astonished wife and their three sons. "Today I met my old friend Mark Dintenfass. He is the dumbest man I ever knew. If he can make money in pictures, anybody can."

Dintenfass had been a Philadelphia boy who gave up his father's salted herring business to open a movie theater, then began producing his own films. In 1912 he became one of the investors in Universal Pictures, and he soon found himself caught in the crossfire between forces seeking control of the corporation. The opposing generals were Patrick A. Powers, a wily Irishman, and Carl Laemmle, a Bavarian Jew of immense cunning. Both were capable of unruly tactics, legal or extralegal, and the beleaguered Dintenfass sought escape from the conflict.

But neither Powers nor Laemmle was willing to buy out Dintenfass' interest in Universal. Whenever the matter came up, Powers glanced furtively around his office and indicated it wasn't safe to talk about it there. "Meet me in the washroom," he whispered. Dintenfass waited in the washroom for hours, but Powers never appeared.

Lewis J. Selznick agreed to take on Dintenfass' problem. One day L.J. called at the Universal Pictures office in the Mecca Building on Broadway and asked to see Mr. Powers. No, he would not state his business, and he would talk to no one but Patrick A. Powers. When L.J. was admitted to the presence of Powers, he mysteriously took an envelope from his vest pocket and spread an array of diamonds on the desk. Powers was suitably impressed, and he made a purchase. Then L.J. sprang his question:

"Why don't you buy my friend Dintenfass' stock in this Universal Company? He only wants seventy-five thousand."

Powers smilingly declined.

Next L.J. applied the same technique to Carl Laemmle. This time it worked. Laemmle purchased the Dintenfass stock, making himself the largest stockholder in Universal. Laemmle withheld news of his purchase, preferring to wait for Powers' next move.

Lewis J. Selznick decided the time had arrived for his own move into the picture business. During his visits to the Mecca Building, he had recognized the chaos created by the internecine war within Universal. Laemmle, Powers, and other dissident factions had planted their own operatives within the company, with the result that no one knew exactly what was going on. Without a word to anyone, L.J. commandeered a desk in the corner of the main office and began busying himself by reading the files and papers of the corporation. The more he studied, the more excited he became about the picture business. Not that he was movie-mad. He thought that motion pictures were silly and stupid, aimed at the lowest denominator of the American social structure. What intrigued him was not the low-brow entertainment, but the power and riches which could be swiftly acquired in the youthful, fast-growing industry.

Soon the presence of the well-dressed man in pince-nez glasses was accepted by the Universal workers. Laemmle, Powers, and other warring executives failed to question his occupancy of a desk in the company's headquarters; each suspected that a rival had appointed him to a position. None had, so he appointed himself. Poring over the company records, he noted that Universal had no general manager. He commandeered a secretary and ordered some stationery reading:

Universal Pictures Corporation

Lewis J. Selznick, General Manager

He placed himself on the payroll and began supervising all purchases and expenditures.

The Laemmle-Powers war intensified. Powers came to the realization that he required more ammunition. Laemmle was acting strangely confident, and Powers decided he needed Dintenfass' stock to combat whatever Laemmle was up to. But now Mark Dintenfass was strangely aloof.

"What's the matter with your friend Dintenfass?" Powers complained to Selznick. "He won't speak to me."

Selznick feigned surprise. "I will see if I can't make an appointment for you—in the washroom," he said.

Powers decided to take the offensive. Seeking to satisfy his claims against Universal, he took a gang of movers to the company's New York studio and began loading movie props into trucks. Furniture was removed from sets while actors were performing before the cameras. The studio manager reported the raid to Universal general manager Lewis J. Selznick.

"Call the police and then report again to me in half an hour," Selznick ordered.

A half hour later came the report: "The police arrived, and they're getting along fine. They're helping Pat Powers load the trucks."

Selznick sought to ingratiate himself by acting as mediator between the two factions. That was his mistake; both sides distrusted the erstwhile peacemaker. Laemmle was further disturbed by Selznick's claim of a $39,000 commission for delivering Dintenfass' stock. One day after Laemmle had departed for Chicago, his secretary handed Selznick a letter.

"Your resignation has been accepted," wrote Laemmle.

Selznick, who had not offered his resignation, cleaned out his desk and exited, smiling.

"Less brains are necessary in the motion picture business than in any other," Lewis J. Selznick told a Congressional committee investigating the film industry in 1917. For proof he offered his own experience of starting as a movie entrepreneur with $1000 and clearing $105,000 within ten weeks.

Indeed, there was quick money to be found in the film industry, and it was being exploited by a number of enterprising men. Most, like Lewis J. Selznick, were immigrant Jews with a minimum of formal education. All were brainy in the ways of putting together deals and supplying entertainment for the masses. The most astute of the new breed was tough little Adolph Zukor, the Hungarian furrier who was building the Famous Players Company into the giant of the industry. The ice-hard Zukor disliked anyone who interfered with his concept of a tightly controlled (by Zukor) film industry. Hence he would inevitably collide with an upstart named Selznick.

Clara Kimball Young

After his "resignation" from Universal in 1914, Selznick had joined the World Film Corporation, adding his modest savings of $1000 to the company that sought to release movies made by independent producers. One of his first acquisitions was a film called *Whom the Gods Would Destroy*, which was available for $4250. Lacking the necessary capital, Selznick ventured into Wall Street, where he cajoled and browbeat ninety-nine bankers into providing $42.50 apiece to finance the purchase, adding the hundredth share himself. The investment paid off handsomely for all investors.

Convinced that the play was the thing, L.J. next blustered into Broadway to make arrangements with the Shuberts and William A. Brady for the movie adaptations of hit plays with the original stars. Among his prizes: Lew Fields in *Old Dutch*; Alice Brady and Holbrook Blinn in *The Boss*; Wilton Lackaye in *Trilby*; Lillian Russell and Lionel Barrymore in *Wildfire*. An impressive array. But the most important asset of World Films proved to be Clara Kimball Young, a buxom, appealing beauty with dramatic skill.

Selznick began advertising his product with the slogan "Features Made from Well Known Plays by Well Known Players." This was an unabashed steal from "Famous Plays for Famous Players," the motto of Zukor's prestigious Famous Players Company.

Mr. Zukor was not pleased. Nor was he pleased when Selznick announced a profit-sharing plan for directors who joined World Film. The plan drew a hearty response from directors, who were piqued at the immense salaries Zukor was paying Mary Pickford and other stars.

L.J. came into his own at World Film. He issued statements to the trade press at the slightest inclination and signed his name to advertisements in the same journals. He introduced each of his films with a special hoopla, creating the institution of the press preview, always with a hotel party afterward. He was indefatigable in promotion, although some of his critics questioned whether he was promoting World Film or Lewis J. Selznick.

His bankers raised the same question, and one day Selznick

Adolph Zukor

found himself relieved of his position. To their consternation, they discovered that he had relieved World Film of its most valuable asset, Clara Kimball Young.

Selznick formed the Clara Kimball Young Film Corporation with himself as president and general manager. He raised a million dollars in stock and began charging theater men four times the usual rental for her films. Oddly, they did not rebel. They were delighted to book the Young pictures, even at the inflated rental; they knew they could make a profit on her popular films. The major companies, principally Zukor's Famous Players, made the theaters buy a flock of losing movies in order to acquire those with audience-drawing stars.

The all-powerful Zukor was incensed.

"Selznick is a menace!" the little man raged. "Like a fool he has tossed aside the old contract and program system. The presentation of the Young pictures as a separate proposition and the greatly increased charge to the exhibitor for the product will disrupt the industry."

Zukor did not like disruption of the industry, which was largely his own creation. His vow to destroy Lewis J. Selznick became common knowledge.

Trade paper reporters asked Selznick about this.

"You take him too seriously," L.J. answered airily. "Mr. Zukor has a peeve on. He's sore because I took the jump on him. He intends to do with several of his stars precisely what I am doing with Clara Kimball Young. This talk of my being 'a menace to the industry' is ridiculous. The intelligent exhibitor is only too glad to pay four or five times what he now pays for big features if he can eliminate the rest of the trash on the program and double his receipts. And Mr. Zukor knows it is impossible for one firm to put out fifty-two or more good pictures a year."

Selznick had set a trap that Zukor unwittingly fell into. To hold onto the screen's most valuable star, Zukor had been paying Mary Pickford a million dollars a year. Now she wanted more. Zukor's solution was to distribute her films through the newly created Artcraft Pictures, giving Mary a half interest in the company's profits.

The Pickford movies had to be sold on an individual basis, instead of being lumped together with the rest of the Famous Players product. Zukor was careful to leave his name off Artcraft Pictures. But his connection with the company was impressed on the trade through an advertisement signed by Lewis J. Selznick. He congratulated Mary on adopting the same plan he had devised for Clara Kimball Young. He concluded with a reference to Adolph Zukor, "a man so broadguaged that neither false pride nor shortsightedness can deter him from the adoption of an excellent plan, even though conceived by another."

L.J. was having a glorious time. He formed the Selznick Company and sought other attractions to augment the Clara Kimball Young specials. He found a powerful ally in Marcus Loew, the fun-loving financier who had built a huge chain of vaudeville-movie theaters. Loew enjoyed pitting Selznick against Zukor, a onetime associate and now Loew's competitor. When L.J. needed backing for his grandiose schemes, Loew often provided the funds. Loew also convinced his associate, Joseph M. Schenck, to use the Selznick Company for the release of films starring his wife, Norma Talmadge.

Alla Nazimova was one of the great names of the theater, and L.J. sought the Russian actress for a screen version of her vaudeville success, *War Brides*. Nazimova sniffed at the presumption of the movie maker. She would consider his proposition only if she were paid a thousand dollars a day.

To her surprise, Selznick answered: "I'll not only pay you a thousand dollars a day, but I'll pay it to you at the end of every working day!"

Mrs. Selznick with David, Howard and Myron

Amid much publicity, L.J. handed to Nazimova a thousand-dollar bill daily for thirty days. *War Brides* earned ten times what L.J. had paid her.

During this period, a newspaper interviewer called at the Selznick office and wrote this description:

"A movie magnate at his work is a surprising sight. L. J. Selznick, for example. An office of solid sumptuousness. Sumptuous, that is, but simple. Not a contradiction. To enter it one must pass guards galore. The outer chambers are like a monastery. Long stone corridors. Managers. Secretaries. Assistants. Finally into the sanctum. Nothing of the conventional. No series of telephones. No series of baskets. Just a magnificent desk and some chairs. The work is done by conferences. Prepared for him in summaries. He decides. While we were there one of the staff came in sadly. The cost of a production the worry. Answered the magnate, 'I like it. Go the limit. It's a good picture and what does it matter if we lose on it? Anything done by stinting shows it. If you do it as well as you can, it has a better chance for success."'

L.J. played publicity like a master organist. He was the first to emblazon Broadway with movie advertisements; usually the name of Selznick appeared in larger electric lights than that of the star or the movie title. L.J. conceived a slogan for his company and spread it everywhere: "Selznick Pictures Make Happy Hours."

He seized every opportunity to reap publicity benefits. When he learned of the overthrow of the Russian tsar, he fired off a cable in his native Russian:

NICHOLAS ROMANOFF
PETROGRAD, RUSSIA
WHEN I WAS A POOR BOY IN KIEV SOME OF YOUR POLICEMEN WERE NOT KIND TO ME AND MY PEOPLE STOP I CAME TO AMERICA AND PROSPERED STOP NOW HEAR WITH REGRET YOU ARE OUT OF A JOB OVER THERE STOP FEEL NO ILL WILL WHATEVER YOUR POLICEMEN DID STOP IF YOU WILL COME TO NEW YORK CAN GIVE YOU FINE POSITION ACTING IN PICTURES STOP SALARY NO OBJECT STOP REPLY MY EXPENSE STOP REGARDS YOU AND FAMILY
SELZNICK
NEW YORK

There was no reply to the cable, which Selznick had been careful to release to the press.

L.J. worked his wiles in other, more subtle ways. His ace salesman for World Film had been Al Lichtman, who had left to handle Mary Pickford's movies for Zukor. Lichtman had disagreed with Selznick on business matters, and he was surprised when L.J. presented him with a handsome gold watch bearing the inscription in diamonds: "To Al Lichtman from Lewis J. Selznick-Selznick Pictures Make Happy Hours." As L.J. had anticipated, Lichtman was extremely proud of the watch, and he displayed it every time he visited exhibitors. Thus he provided an advertisement for Selznick while performing the work of Adolph Zukor.

Zukor seemed unable to escape the crafty ex-jeweler from Kiev. One day Zukor gazed out the window of his luxurious office and winced as he read the brilliant sign: "Selznick Pictures Make Happy Hours." Zukor looked out the opposite window and saw the same message: "Selznick Pictures Make Happy Hours." And to the rear of Zukor's desk, the same words appeared on the opposite building. It was too much for Zukor to bear.

One day when L.J. was recovering from an illness at the Hotel Astor, Adolph Zukor paid him a call. The little Hungarian was not concerned with his rival's health. He offered a proposal: "Lewie, I will pay you five thousand dollars a week for life if you will go to China and stay there."

No one knew if Zukor had been serious, but he was a man who rarely spoke in jest. At any rate, L.J. would not consider going to China or anywhere else. He was having too good a time where he was, in the heart of the film world.

Not the least of his pleasures was the opportunity for romance which his position afforded. Since he masterminded the career of Clara Kimball Young, there were rumors that he directed her offscreen life as well. The rumors seemed to be confirmed when her husband sued Selznick for alienation of affection. L.J. tried to offset such reports by having his wife accompany Miss Young to public events and on trips. But the whispers continued.

Florence Selznick realized that her husband was as profligate with his affection as he was with his money. She knew that Clara Kimball Young was her chief—but not her only—rival. A break with Lewis was out of the question; Florence's Orthodox upbringing did not permit her to consider it. In any case, she was still madly in love with her erratic, exciting husband. She had a Jewish wife's patience and forbearance with her husband's wanderings from the family bed. She was firm in her conviction that Lewis would return to his monogamous life after the fancy passed.

That time came, she believed, when Lewis presented her with a $20,000 sable coat. He was given to impulsive gestures, but never like this. Florence Selznick was convinced that he meant it as a peace offering, a plea for forgiveness of his transgressions.

"He loves me after all; I'm still number one!" she exulted.

Her joyfulness lasted until L.J. escorted her to the premiere of one of his new movies. Florence Selznick's heart sank when she saw Clara Kimball Young—wearing an identical sable coat.

Florence Selznick continued her role as the long-suffering wife. She had much to occupy herself because of the family's new-found wealth. L.J. had moved his wife and three sons into a lavish, twenty-two-room apartment on Park Avenue, and there was a staff of servants to manage. L.J. had little time to devote to his growing sons, and Florence saw that they were outfitted and schooled.

L.J. bought anything that struck his fancy, including a Rolls Royce to drive himself to work in the morning. He gambled all day on stars and movies and sometimes all night on poker hands. Florence Selznick often sat behind him as he played for high stakes, and she offered words of caution as his bets went higher: "Now, Lewie, don't forget you have to meet the payroll tomorrow." L.J. scarcely listened. In one year his gambling losses amounted to a million dollars.

There started to appear small, nagging indications that his luck with the movie world was beginning to tarnish. Or could it be that by overextending his fortunes he was setting himself up for revenge by powerful men, especially Adolph Zukor, to whom he was a clownish irritant, a threat to control of the industry?

Clara Kimball Young defected. Whatever feelings she had for

Myron Selznick in a publicity photo depicting his function as production boss of Selznick Pictures Corp.

L.J. were superseded by considerations of money; she sued him for breach of contract, claiming he owed her a $1000-a-week increase in salary. Significantly, she signed a contract for a series of movies with Adolph Zukor.

L.J. dispatched a pack of lawyers to inform Miss Young and Zukor that she still had a contract with Selznick. Zukor moved his own lawyers into action. Peace was achieved when Zukor relinquished his claims on the star—on condition that Selznick release her future films through Zukor's Artcraft company. L.J. agreed. Adolph Zukor had successfully concluded his first move against the upstart Selznick.

Meanwhile Joseph Schenck suspected that L.J. was misusing the popular Norma Talmadge pictures which Selznick was releasing. Schenck appointed a young assistant, Henry Ginsberg, to look into the matter. Whenever an exhibitor sent in a cancellation for a Talmadge film, Ginsberg sought the reason. Inevitably the theater owner replied that the Selznick salesman insisted that he also buy lesser films before he was allowed to have the Talmadge specials. Schenck removed his wife's movies from the Selznick company.

The net was being laid around the empire of freespending Lewis J. Selznick.

Functioning in an industry that considered nepotism a way of life, L.J. quite naturally brought his boys into the business early. Myron came first. He attended Columbia University for a desultory two months, then became bored with education. He asked his father for a position in the company, and L.J. agreed. In a rare instance of parental discipline, he put Myron to work in the film-examining room. From seven in the morning until late afternoon, the boy scanned film for defects.

Myron learned fast. He served as shipping clerk, assistant purchasing agent, purchasing agent, studio manager, and then production manager. His brother Howard acted as his assistant.

David also started early. Throughout his boyhood, he had spent his spare time in the Selznick offices, absorbing the sound and excitement of the movie business. L.J. permitted the boy to sit in on conferences and contract negotiations and sometimes deferred to his judgment. Once producer Carey Wilson brought a movie to L.J. in hope of acquiring a Selznick release. "Show it to David," L.J. instructed. "If he likes it, it will make money." David, who was sixteen years old, liked the Wilson film, and L.J. accepted it for release.

While a student at Hamilton Institute for Boys, David began keeping a card file that listed the successes and failures of every director and writer in pictures. This rating system proved valuable to L.J., who consulted it before making assignments to film makers. L.J. was not entirely oblivious to his son's education. Noting David's appreciation of literature, he insisted that the boy study the works of Dickens, Thackeray, Scott, Shakespeare, Byron, etc., and make reports on plots and characterizations. This, L.J. believed, would prepare David to discover screen stories and evaluate scripts when he joined the Selznick empire.

That happened soon after David's graduation from high school. He enrolled at Columbia University, but, like Myron, he didn't stay long. Instead of stuffing his mind with useless facts, David wanted to be doing things. L.J. put him to work as editor and publisher of the weekly house organ that circulated to the company's twenty-eight film exchanges in the United States and Canada. It was suitable work for David, who had ambitions of becoming a writer and even dreamed of operating a publishing house. He called the newspaper *The Brain Exchange*. Later David was placed in charge of the newsreel and short subjects.

L.J. pressed forward with his ambitious program, signing new stars to appear in his films and taking on more producers to release through his company. But his pace of spending and gambling accelerated, and for once his ambitions outraced his resources. No one knew this better than Adolph Zukor, who kept himself informed of everything that was going on in the industry.

Zukor sent to L.J. a plenipotentiary, a powerful theater magnate of Chicago who did business with Selznick. The theater man earned $50,000 for carrying the message: Zukor was ready to deal.

The two old enemies sat down to discuss a merger of their

interests. After long conversations, they arrived at an agreement. Zukor would pay Selznick a much-needed half million dollars for a half interest in the Selznick company. Selznick would be allowed to make his movies at the Lasky studio in Hollywood, thus effecting a considerable saving. In an appeal to parental pride, Zukor also proposed that Myron Selznick would be installed at the Hollywood studio to learn production under the expert tutelage of Jesse L. Lasky and Cecil B. De Mille. This part of the plan never eventuated.

Zukor stipulated that the name of Selznick would not appear on the new corporation. No more electric signs on Broadway proclaiming, "Selznick Pictures Make Happy Hours." The Zukor-Selznick firm would be called Select Pictures Corporation. The proposal struck deeply at the Selznick ego, but he was in no position to argue.

As half owner of Select Pictures, Zukor suggested that the company could profit by making less expensive movies instead of trying to compete with the major studios. Selznick agreed. Select did prosper by offering exhibitors much-needed films at lower prices. This had two salutary effects for Zukor: he profited from his investment in Select, and he eliminated another competitor of his more expensive Famous Players-Lasky movies.

Lewis J. Selznick rankled under the stricture against use of his name on pictures. But if he couldn't use his own name, what about his sons? After all, Myron was an extremely bright boy with a liberal education in the making of movies. L.J. was convinced there was no great mystery to fashioning film entertainment for the masses; it was child's play.

All of a sudden Myron Selznick blossomed out as a producer. He was still underage and his mother had to sign the checks for him; otherwise he functioned like any other producer. He wooed the Ziegfeld Follies beauty Olive Thomas, and she was intrigued with the idea of working for such a youthful and attractive producer. One day a sign brightened Broadway:

SELZNICK PICTURES-OLIVE THOMAS

Adolph Zukor was livid. All his efforts to bury the name of Selznick had been thwarted by a boy not old enough to vote.

Zukor realized that Myron was not operating entirely on his own, and he complained mightily to the boy's father. L.J. replied that he had no control over his headstrong son.

The argument was carried on in the trade press. Zukor declared that L.J. had broken his word and he grumbled, "Selznick gives too much advice to his son and too little attention to the time clock."

L.J. retorted, "If that's the way Zukor feels, I'll buy out Select, time clock and all."

Eventually Zukor did sell his share in Select—at a profit, as usual. L.J. met his price of one million dollars.

At the age of twenty-one, Myron Selznick found himself the head of a huge production enterprise. His father appointed him vice president in charge of production of the Selznick Pictures Corporation. While L.J. devoted himself to the distribution activities of Select, Myron bore responsibility for the product of five studios—Selznick, Biograph, Peerless, and Solax in the east, and another studio in California, all of them supplying films for distribution by Select. A magazine article pointed out that Myron controlled more producing units than any other film maker. Myron took time out from his busy day to tell the interviewer:

"I heard photoplays talked all my life. I guess my father has marketed some five hundred pictures. What could be more natural than that I should enter the game? . . . Please make it clear that I direct Selznick Pictures. Dad hasn't been over to our studios twice in a year. True, I frequently talk over things at night with him, as is quite natural. But I manage my own companies in every sense of the word . . . My methods? Nothing more or less than to make entertaining photoplays and to build up and maintain the best organization with that end in view . . . We're one big family and there is no red tape in our organization. Anyone can get to see me at any time. That's why I have my office in my studio rather than in Times Square . . . I've made something like fifty productions so far. I know their faults. But I'm learning and I think we are steadily working ahead. Anyway, it's great fun!"

L.J. had full confidence in Myron, as well as in David, who became a vice president in the company. The future looked so sunny that L.J. refused the blandishments of moneymen who wanted to buy into the enterprise. James Cox Brady tried to purchase a share for $5,000,000 and William Randolph Hearst made an offer of several million. L.J. turned both down. He was building an empire for his sons to rule when he himself stepped out of the picture. As a symbol of his solvency and a reminder of his beginnings in the world of commerce, he continued to carry in his pocket a quarter million dollars' worth of diamonds.

By 1922 Lewis J. Selznick had survived a decade in the film industry and by his very longevity was considered one of the pioneering leaders. He began to abandon his pose as jester and assume a more statesman-like stance. He shared with his fellow moguls the concern for the industry's image in the wake of a series of much headlined scandals involving movie figures. When the public's censure caused film stocks to tumble—Famous Players from 90 to 40—drastic action seemed imperative.

The film leaders discussed hiring of a czar to police the industry. Selznick had his own candidate: Will Hays, the Hoosier lawyer who had become President Harding's Postmaster General. Selznick convinced the other corporation presidents of the wisdom of his choice. Selznick and Fox attorney Saul Rogers visited Hays in his Washington hotel and offered him the post as film czar at $100,000 a year. Hays, who was earning $12,000 as Postmaster General, accepted.

While Lewis Selznick was busy with industry matters, monopoly-minded Adolph Zukor was maneuvering against his bothersome competitor. A new film company called Realart sprang up, and it offered inexpensive pictures aimed at the same market as Selznick's Select releases. Many of Realart salesmen had been lured away from the Selznick employ, and they convinced many exhibitors to abandon the Select films.

The Selznick empire began a precipitous slide. Sensing impending disaster, the company's stars began to depart for other producers, especially Zukor. Creditors made nagging demands. L.J. remained calm as always; he had uncannily removed himself from tight situations before.

But this time it was different. When he sought help from his fellow leaders in the film industry, they turned their backs. For once his ingenuity had failed him.

L.J. stepped out of Select and Selznick Pictures and turned over the management to Myron as president and David as vice president. But the Selznick creditors failed to see the wisdom of entrusting company affairs to a pair of young men who had been trained in extravagance by their father. In 1923, when L.J. failed to meet a three-thousand-dollar obligation, he was forced into bankruptcy.

Gone was the sumptuous apartment on Park Avenue. Gone were Florence Selznick's hand-picked furnishings, sold at auction. Gone was the handful of diamonds L.J. enjoyed fondling in his pocket. He and Florence moved into a three-room furnished flat and once more she did the cooking and housework.

In 1925, L.J. went off to Florida to try his hand at the land boom. But his gambling nerve had vanished, and he failed once more. He and Florence moved on to California, where they spent the remainder of their years being supported by their sons. It was painful for Myron and David to see their once-vigorous father broken and dispirited. What had happened would profoundly affect the lives of both sons, each in his own way.

II

STUDIO YEARS

The Search for
Independence

David O. Selznick, studio executive, before a portrait of his father.

WHEN DAVID SELZNICK WAS TWENTY-NINE,
he became restless with studio control
over his activities as producer at Paramount.
He composed a memo to his bosses
urging them to grant autonomy
so he could make movies his own way.
He reasoned:
"A motion picture is like a painting.
Instead of oil paints, it uses talents and personalities
to tell its story. But each artist must paint his own picture
and sign it."
The Paramount bosses remained unconvinced.

After the Selznick empire had crumbled, Myron Selznick fled to Hollywood to start anew. David remained in New York. He had some ideas on how to make money, based on his experience in supervising the short subjects for Selznick Pictures. He had been an innovator, especially with the newsreel, to which he introduced fashions and other new subjects. He also convinced Will Rogers, then a star in the *Ziegfeld Follies,* to contribute humorous comments on the news events, replacing the dull titles that usually accompanied the reels. Rogers agreed to write the jokes for no fee, figuring he would earn good publicity.

David began scouting ideas for movie subjects. The talk of the sports world in August of 1923 was the forthcoming heavyweight prizefight between champion Jack Dempsey and Luis Angel Firpo, the Wild Bull of the Pampas. David borrowed two thousand dollars from a friend and called on Firpo.

The Argentine understood little English until money was mentioned. The young film maker offered to pay Firpo to appear in a short movie to be titled *Will He Conquer Dempsey?* Firpo quoted his appearance fee of a thousand dollars per day. David purchased an afternoon.

David hired a camera and cameraman and filmed the fighter jogging through Central Park and exercising his famous right hand on punching bags and sparring partners. David hastily put the film together and sold it to a distributor the following day. Besides Firpo's fee, the movie had cost him $875. He sold it for $3500.

His next project profited from Rudolph Valentino's pique with Paramount. The star had jumped his contract and was touring the country making personal appearances. One of them was to judge a beauty contest in Madison Square Garden, sponsored by a face-cream maker. David Selznick proposed a movie short based on the beauty contest, and the face-cream company agreed that it would be worthwhile advertising. David paid only for camera and film and enough lights to photograph inside the Garden; Paramount's $5000-a-week star performed for the camera without charge. Since the feud had kept Valentino off the

Some of Hollywood's elite pose in 1926, the year of David Selznick's arrival in California, at a beach party given by Norma Talmadge and Joe Schenck. (left to right) Top row: Fatty Arbuckle, Mae Murray, Ward Crane, Virginia Valli, Ronald Colman, Bessie Love, Jack Pickford, Rudolph Valentino, Pola Negri. Middle row: Maitland Rice Lederer, Chris Goulding, Louella Parsons, Lila Lee, Carmel Myers, Allan Forrest, Bert Lytell, Claire Windom, Al Hall, Mrs. Jack Mulhall, Mrs. John Robertson, Julanne Johnston, Agnes Ayres, John Robertson, Mrs. Charlotte Goulding, Marquis Henri de la Falaise de la Coudray, Marshall Neilan, Howard Hughes. Bottom row: Antonio Moreno, Prince David Mdivani, Charles Lang, Edmund Goulding, Marcel de Sano, Manuel Reachi, Harry D'Arrast, Doris Dean Arbuckle, Ivis Goulding, Eddie Kane, Mrs. Edward Sedgwick, Christine Francis, Alister MacInosh, Kitty Scola, Blanche Sweet

screen, exhibitors clamored for the Selznick short. David's profit on the venture was $15,000.

David used part of the money and borrowed more to produce his first feature, appropriately enough titled *Roulette*. He used every means possible to hold down expenses, even persuading Henry Hull to play a role in return for a new dinner jacket. The total cost was $17,000.

Now it appeared that David should follow his brother and go west.

New York remained the financial center of the film world, but the real excitement in movie making was taking place in Hollywood. By the time he paid off his obligations, David had $5000 left. He sewed the cash inside his clothes and boarded a train for California.

Hollywood of 1926 was a dazzling sight to young David Selznick; almost immediately he was convinced of the wisdom of his trek west. Here indeed was the creative heart of the film business. Hollywood itself seemed like a bucolic community after David's life in New York City. But there was no mistaking the dynamism that was in the air. It was a boom town, with studios rising everywhere — in Culver City, in the San Fernando Valley, all over Hollywood. The town had already developed its own elite, headed by the near-royal couple, Mary Pickford and Douglas Fairbanks. It was David Selznick's vow to become a commanding figure in that elite.

But he quickly learned, as his brother had before him, that Hollywood was hostile territory for anyone named Selznick. At studio after studio, David was told, "No openings." Having served in positions of responsibility with his father's company, he sought important production jobs. Gradually he lowered his ambitions. In the end he took the only position he could find, as assistant story editor at M-G-M for fifty dollars a week.

The prospect of working for M-G-M held great excitement for David Selznick. The amalgam of three film companies had been formed only two years before, and it seemed destined to be the titan of the industry. This was due to the curious partnership of Louis B. Mayer, the bullheaded ex-junk dealer from Minsk by way of Nova Scotia, and Irving G. Thalberg, a fragile, esthetic Brooklyn boy with a will of iron. Mayer was the skilled money-man, and Thalberg was the creative production boss; David Selznick looked forward to learning from both. Within less than a week he was fired.

"Nobody named Selznick will ever work here!" the imperious Mayer decreed.

Louis Mayer had his own reasons for detesting the Selznick name. He had been distributor for Lewis J. Selznick's Select films in Boston, and their association ended amid name-calling and accusations of dishonesty.

David Selznick refused to accept the Mayer firing. He learned of the arrival in Los Angeles of Nicholas M. Schenck, president of Loew's, the parent company of M-G-M. A few years before, young Selznick had been able to do a favor for Schenck, who promised to repay David in the future. The time for repayment had arrived. David was restored to the M-G-M payroll, over the furious objection of Louis Mayer.

When David Selznick went to work at the Culver City studio in 1926, he was a well-fed, apple-cheeked twenty-four. Although youth was not unrecognized at M-G-M—Thalberg was only three years older—David realized that few would listen to a youthful assistant story editor. So he began submitting his ideas in memo

Dorothy Sebastian and Tim McCoy on location for Wyoming

form. He explored all areas of the studio operation, seeking ways of improvement. Delving into the scenario department, he discovered dozens of writers engaged on projects that had long been abandoned. He composed a memo on the subject, and the Writers' Building was swept clean of the futile scenarists. David's reward for this economy was the position of story editor.

His astuteness with stories, born through his study of scripts in his father's office, led to a position as assistant to Harry Rapf, who supervised the inexpensive films for M-G-M. One of David's provinces was supervision of the Tim McCoy westerns, program pictures that were produced for the lowest possible price. In 1927, David went off on location with the assignment of making a Tim McCoy western. He came home with two.

"How did you do that?" Mayer demanded.

"Easy," said the resourceful David. "I took along two scripts and two supporting casts. I moved McCoy back and forth between the two plots."

The achievement helped alter Mayer's opinion of L.J. Selznick's aggressive young son. *Wyoming* and *Spoilers of the West* were no worse than other westerns made by M-G-M, and Selznick had produced two for $120,000 instead of one for $90,000.

David felt encouraged to speak out on matters concerning production. He was assigned to assist Hunt Stromberg, who was supervising a South Seas saga, *White Shadows of the South Seas*. David was pained to learn that Stromberg wanted to sprinkle the tale with Polynesian sex and had no interest in the sociological aspects of the islands. The two men engaged in violent arguments.

As was his custom in areas of dispute on production matters, Thalberg offered to mediate. David was no less vocal in his protestations to the production boss. Thalberg felt offended and asked for an apology. David refused. He was fired.

Myron Selznick was enraged by the reception that greeted him in Hollywood. It ranged from indifference to active hostility.

Myron managed to gain entrance to the office of Carl

Monte Blue (center) in WHITE SHADOWS OF THE SOUTH SEAS

Myron Selznick, talent agent

Laemmle at Universal City. Laemmle blanched at the proposal that he hire the son of Lewis J. Selznick as a production aide.

Laemmle turned on his most avuncular smile and counseled: "Myron, my boy, let me give you some good advice. Get out of the picture business. You don't know anything about it, and you'll never get anywhere in it."

Having simultaneously operated five studios, Myron was incensed by the advice.[1] He became more and more frustrated and angry as every other studio boss turned him down. Only Joe Schenck, who had released the films of his wife, Norma Talmadge, through the Selznick company, gave Myron a job. Myron was assigned as assistant to producer John Considine at a hundred dollars a week. But Myron clashed violently with the domineering Considine and was discharged.

Myron was out of work for a long period, then Joe Schenck hired him to produce *Topsy and Eva* with the Duncan Sisters. It was an unsuccessful film, and Myron's combativeness again caused his release.

Recognizing Myron's ability, Bernard Fineman, general manager of F.B.O. (Film Booking Offices, later RKO), sought to put him on the payroll as a producer. But the president of the company dispatched a stern telegram closing with: "Under no cir-

---

[1]Ten years later, Universal Pictures had suffered reverses, and Carl Laemmle was threatened with loss of the company. Desperate for cash, he applied for a loan with a California bank. The bank officer remarked: "It would help get you the loan if Myron Selznick would put in a word for you; he's one of our largest stockholders." Laemmle failed to get the loan.

cumstances can you hire Myron Selznick."

Both Myron and David found themselves broke and out of work. They continued to live in the Selznick tradition, with their friends footing the bills. The two brothers moved into the Santa Monica beach house of Lewis Milestone, the Russian-born director, and Bennie Zeidman, an associate producer. David ran up enormous telephone bills, and Myron helped himself to the bootleg whisky. They swam in the ocean and played furious games of tennis at the homes of Florence Vidor and Matt Moore. At the Moore house David became acquainted with Louis Mayer's daughter Irene, a dark-eyed, vibrant girl with strong physique.

Because no one would hire him to make movies, Myron Selznick decided to become an agent.

In 1928 the agent occupied one of the lowest positions in the Hollywood scheme of things. During the earliest years of films, the agent was unknown. Actors, writers, and directors offered their services on the open market. If they were in demand, their salaries rose. If not, they worked for whatever the producers would pay them. During the 1920s some of the talented film workers began to feel they were too often at the mercy of the studio bosses. They began hiring agents to seek pictures and negotiate contracts. Many of the agents were flashy hustlers who sold talent like patent medicines. The producers tried to keep agents on a lower social stratum and to prevent the talent from adding to their bargaining power. A star who jumped his contract with one studio found all others closed to him. The producers honored a gentlemen's agreement not to lure stars or directors from other studios with the promise of larger salaries. It was a comfortable arrangement—for the producers.

This was the system Myron Selznick aimed to smash. Nothing would give him greater pleasure than to wreak financial harm on the men who had ruined his father.

Myron set up his own agency and soon found his first opportunity to confound the producers. His friend and sometime host, Lewis Milestone, had become embroiled in a dispute with Warner Brothers and refused to report for work. The studio sued him for breach of contract and sought $200,000 damages. Milestone submitted to the claim and next day filed for bankruptcy. It was a clever ruse to escape both the payment and his contract, but Milestone discovered no other studio would hire him.

The blacklisted Milestone made plans to return to Europe in search of film work. As he was packing, he received a telephone call from Myron Selznick.

"Where the hell have you been?" Myron bawled.

"Why?"

"Because we got an important phone call."

"We?"

"Yeah. I'm your agent."

"Okay, you're my agent. So what was the phone call?"

"Neil McCarthy wants to see us. It's about a contract."

Milestone and Myron visited McCarthy, a prominent Beverly Hills attorney who said he had a client who was looking for a young and promising director. McCarthy studied the legal papers involving Milestone's departure from Warner Brothers and assured himself that the director was contractually free. The attorney proposed a three-year contract with annual options at a salary greater than Milestone had received before.

"We accept," said Myron. Only then did he and Milestone learn that McCarthy's client was an eccentric young Texan named Howard Hughes.

Myron searched for other clients whose economic status he could improve at the expense of a studio. William Wellman seemed a likely prospect. He was a maverick young director who had drifted into films after serving with the Lafayette Flying Corps in France. Because of his wartime experience, Paramount (formerly Famous Players Lasky) assigned him to direct *Wings,* starring Buddy Rogers, Clara Bow, and Richard Arlen, with Gary Cooper in a small role. Myron suspected that Wellman was dissatisfied with his lot, and Myron was right. He learned that Wellman was being paid a mere $250 a week while directing Paramount's most expensive production. In addition, the studio had apparently overlooked the fact that his contract had expired.

"I'm supposed to go on a long location at San Antonio," said Wellman. "What'll I do?"

"Go on the location," Myron replied. "Take all the time you need. Make the picture you want. You've got 'em where it hurts." Wellman went off on the Texas location and filmed *Wings* according to his own tastes. He was under constant pressure to hurry up the filming, but he resisted all entreaties. He kept fliers, planes, and an entire film crew waiting for thirty days until the Texas skies produced the right background for a massive dogfight.

He finally completed the picture amid much acrimony from the Paramount hierarchy. Such was the feeling against Wellman that he wasn't invited to attend the New York preview of *Wings*. Opinions changed after the preview. *Wings* thrilled the audience and created a new star, Gary Cooper.

Wellman was invited to B.P. Schulberg's office. The Paramount production boss said with paternal indulgence that Wellman had proved himself with *Wings* and would next be given the privilege of directing Gary Cooper in *Legion of the Condemned*. Wellman was amused by this, since he himself had suggested *Legion of the Condemned* as a movie vehicle.

"But there's just one problem, Mr. Schulberg," said Wellman.

"What's that?" Schulberg asked.

"I've been working for Paramount many weeks now, and I haven't received a cent."

Schulberg was incredulous. But he learned from the legal department that Wellman's statement was correct.

Schulberg switched off the speaker and turned to Wellman with a forced smile. "Well, Bill, you've got great talent, and we have big plans for you," he began.

Wellman interrupted: "Yes, I've got great talent. And there's a guy outside who will talk to you about it. His name is Myron Selznick. Sound familiar? "

Schulberg's smile vanished. He signaled his secretary and said grimly, "Send Selznick in."

Myron heard the message and said to the secretary, "Tell Schulberg I don't have time to talk to him; I've got to take Mr.

Kay Francis, William Powell, STREET OF CHANCE

William Powell, Clive Brook, Theodore Von Eltz, Richard Arlen,
FOUR FEATHERS

Wellman to see some important men."

Outside the officel Wellman began to feel qualms. "Do you know what you're doing?" he asked Myron.

"Hell, yes," Myron said. He took Wellman to see three visiting Paramount backers—Otto Kahn, Sir William Wiseman, and William Stralem, millionaires all. Myron ran Wellman's $250 a week into four figures.

Myron gloried in his triumph, especially since it had been accomplished against the hated Paramount, of which Adolph Zukor was president. There would be more such victories, Myron vowed.

"I'll break them all!" he exclaimed. "I'll send all those thieves and fourflushers crawling to the poorhouse. Before I'm done, the artists in this town will have all the money."

Broke and unemployed at twenty-five, David decided on a bold course: he would storm the bastion of his father's old enemy,

Adolph Zukor.

Early in 1928, David applied for a job as assistant to Bernard
Fineman at Paramount. Fineman, who had tried to hire David at
F.B.O., was now assistant to the studio boss, B.P. Schulberg.
Schulberg agreed to Fineman's proposal, despite the run-in with
Myron.

One day Schulberg and Fineman were viewing film in a projection room when the telephone rang. "I said I didn't want to be
disturbed," Schulberg snapped.

"I'm sorry, Mr. Schulberg," said his secretary, "but Mr. David
Selznick is here to see you."

"Tell him to wait."

"He says he doesn't want to wait. He wants to know what his
salary is going to be."

*The wedding of
Irene Mayer and
David O. Selznick*

Schulberg muttered, "Why, that goddam—"

"Why don't you see him?" Fineman suggested. "If you were starting a new job, you'd want to know what your salary was going to be."

Schulberg stormed out of the projection room and confronted David. "You are the most arrogant young man I have ever met," Schulberg snapped.

David was unperturbed. He started to discuss salary, and the exasperated Schulberg said he would pay him three hundred dollars a week "against my better judgment." He emphasized that the employment would be on a two-week trial basis.

Faced with the deadline to produce results or get out, David first thought of duplicating his M-G-M feat of pointing out inefficiencies in the writing department. But he found all the

Paramount writers to be engaged in potentially worthwhile projects. No waste there. David peered into other departments of the studio and discovered to his dismay that all were being conducted in a smooth, efficient manner.

Time was running short and he still had not proved his value to Paramount Pictures. As the fortnight neared an end, he received a memorandum asking studio employees to submit new titles for seventeen films in progress. David made his suggestions and all seventeen were selected. He had assured his employment.

The astute Schulberg quickly recognized the creative abilities of young Selznick, and David became Schulberg's own assistant. David enjoyed being close to the seat of power once more, but he was impatient to make his own decisions instead of assisting the production boss. William Wellman knew of David's ambitions, and he taunted Schulberg, "You're afraid to make David a producer because his name is Selznick."

Schulberg prided himself in his independence from the control of Zukor, and he assigned David to produce westerns. David planned to impress his employers by repeating his M-G-M stunt of producing two westerns at once. But his planning went awry this time, and when he assembled the two pictures, they made no sense.

"My God," said David in tears, "my career is ruined." But with the help of Wellman and an expert cutter, David was able to juggle scenes, rearrange titles, and gain a semblance of order out of the two films.

David sought new challenges. As Schulberg's assistant, he had been charged with the responsibility of hiring and assigning writers. He retained his youthful reverence for words and realized that writing was the lifeblood of the movie business. He cultivated the Paramount scenarists, listened to their woes, and often suggested Myron's services as a solution to their financial problems. He also pumped them for ideas.

A new writer, Oliver H. P. Garrett, mused one day about a movie based on the murder of Arnold Rothstein, notorious New York gambler. "Write it!" David said. Garrett turned out a story

The wedding of Myron Selznick and Marjorie Daw

concerning the big-time gamblers who bet fortunes in Broadway's traveling crap games. *Street of Chance* held great appeal for David, who had learned the love of gambling at his father's elbow. Howard Estabrook wrote the script, and David cast William Powell and Kay Francis as the leads. The picture advanced the careers of all those associated with it.

David began drawing more important pictures to produce. One was *Four Feathers*, which had been made in Africa by Ernest Schoedsack, a gifted cameraman who had once shot newsreels for David, and Merian C. Cooper, a soldier of fortune. The project had begun as a silent, but additional footage was filmed at the studio under David's supervision to add dialogue and sound. *Four Feathers* was one of the distinguished pictures of 1929, and it began an association that was later to prove highly successful.

Both David and Myron were now making important strides in rebuilding their careers. They were once more living as a family—L.J. and Florence had moved to California, and the Selznicks shared houses that increased in size as the sons' fortunes improved. David and Myron had been accepted, somewhat grudgingly, as members of Hollywood society. Round-faced, bespectacled David was an amiable escort for the town's beauties, particularly Jean Arthur, with whom he was infatuated. Women were attracted to Myron, because of his appealingly tough manner, as well as for the increasing power he could wield over careers.

In 1929, Myron was thirty-one and David was twenty-seven, yet both seemed like overgrown boys. They arrived home at night to recite like schoolboys their triumphs of the day. Mama Selznick cooked huge meals, which the boys gulped down— both were inclined to overweight. She never knew how many guests the boys would bring to dinner, so she provided accordingly. After dinner, David often fell asleep on the thick oriental rug, to be awakened later by a kick in the ribs from Myron. This could touch off a brotherly tussle, and they overturned furniture and rolled on the floor until exhausted. Sometimes their fights were more in earnest, as when Myron made a pass at Jean Arthur. David took offense, and a slugging match ensued. Often Myron and David arrived at parties with bandages on their faces, the result of an early-evening fight.

Recovered from his infatuation with Jean Arthur, David began paying attention to the dark-eyed daughter of Louis B. Mayer, Irene. This alarmed the protective Mayer, who raged at Irene:"Keep away from that schnook! He'll be a bum, just like his father."

Mayer did everything he could to discourage his daughter's interest in young Selznick. One night when David called at Irene's home, Mayer became abusive and insulting. David stalked out of the house, telling Irene, "I'll be damned if I'll stay and let him talk to me like that!"

The father's opposition seemed only to deepen the attachment between Irene and David. She appealed to him, after all the flighty actresses he had escorted. Irene had her father's sagacity in business matters, and she could offer sound advice on how to implement David's dreams. For hours she listened attentively as he spun designs for his future achievements in Hollywood.

One evening David drove along Washington Boulevard in Culver City and parked opposite the studio once owned by Thomas Ince. He gazed at the white colonial facade of the main building and said to Irene, "Some day my name will be above those columns." Irene was impressed by the intensity of his resolve.

Louis B. Mayer was able to bend the biggest stars and directors in Hollywood to his will, but he could not control his daughter's heart. On March 29, 1930, Mrs. Mayer announced that her daughter Irene Gladys, twenty-two, was engaged to marry Mr. David 0. Selznick, twenty-seven, executive and assistant general manager of Paramount studio.

The wedding was to be held on April 29 at the Mayers' Santa Monica beach house. A small, select group of Hollywood society arrived and waited for the ceremony to begin. The wait extended beyond the normal period, and the guests began to grow restive.

Irene Mayer was frantic. Her father had taken David into the library and had locked the door behind them. For forty-five minutes the two men remained inside, engaged in heated conversation. Then Louis Mayer emerged stern-faced and told Irene, "You may start the wedding." Neither he nor David revealed what had been said behind the door.

The bridal pair posed for an official photograph against a wall of flowers, she in an Empire-line white satin gown with bouquet of white orchids, he in white tie and tails. They were flanked by a half-smiling Myron Selznick, the best man, and the father of the bride, unable to force a smile. To his right was daughter Edith, a recent bride; Myron's wife, Marjorie; Edith's husband, William Goetz; and writer Oliver H. P. Garrett. To Myron's left were a Mayer relative, Marjery Strauss, and Janet Gaynor, bridesmaids; M-G-M executive Paul Bern; and David's boss, B.P. Schulberg. Looking on with approval were Mrs. Mayer and Irving Thalberg and Norma Shearer. Rabbi Edgar F. Magnin performed the ceremony.

Zasu Pitts, Skeets Gallagher, Nancy Carroll, HONEY

The wedding night was spent at the Santa Barbara Biltmore, and it was not a success. David was distraught by his failure, and when Irene awoke in the morning, she discovered he was gone. She found him striding up and down the beach in an agitated state. "Irene, we must face the fact that it's no good," he declared. "Let's go back to Hollywood and admit that we made a mistake."

Irene would not give up so easily. She argued that her father had given them a three-month tour of Europe as a wedding gift and it would be a mistake not to take advantage of it. David reluctantly agreed.

The pair took the train east and stopped in Washington to dine at the White House with her father's good friend, President Herbert Hoover. Then they sailed to France. During the European honeymoon, David and Irene were able to achieve the harmony that had eluded them on their wedding night. When they returned to Hollywood, they formed a satisfactory marital partnership. Theirs was not a storybook romance. Both seemed motivated less by love than by the prospect of uniting two movie

Ruth Chatterton, Fredric March, SARAH AND SON

dynasties. In time both profited from their interdependence. He appreciated her stability, her excellent sense of taste, her ability to assist him in sound decisions. She was stimulated by his creative drive, his boyish gaiety and gusto.

From the outset, David was determined not to play the son-in-law game. Louis Mayer had offered to buy the newlyweds a honeymoon house. David declined. "We'll buy our own house," he told Irene firmly.

On January 23, 1929, Myron had been married by a city clerk in New York's Municipal Building to Marjorie Daw, a winsome young actress he had known since she had been a child performer. The newlyweds boarded a train for California, and Myron carried his bride across the threshold of his parents' house. He and Marjorie moved in with Lewis and Florence Selznick.

Marriage did little to change Myron's obstreperous ways. A few months later, newspapers reported a fistfight between Myron and John Barrymore.

Gary Cooper, Fay Wray, THE TEXAN

"Yes, I think I won the fight," Myron commented airily to reporters. "And I don't think Mr. Barrymore will be seen around for a while."

Myron gave this version of the battle: "I was giving a supper party at a meeting of the Little Club at the Ambassador Hotel when Owen Moore asked me to excuse myself for a few minutes to talk business with Lionel Barrymore in one of the Ambassador bungalows occupied by him and John. In the bungalow John Barrymore made a number of remarks that I considered insulting. I asked him to stop. He invited me to fight. I told him he was too old a man for me to fight him (Barrymore was forty-six). That angered him and he struck me. I didn't strike back then, but continued to remonstrate. When Owen and I left, he followed us out and struck me again. Then I began to fight. We fought for about ten minutes, with Mr. Moore dancing around us. Then Moore and I went back to the supper party and Barrymore returned to his bungalow."

Myron made the newspapers on another occasion when he playfully tossed a ball of hot candle-wax onto the dance floor of the Embassy Club one evening. It struck the cheek of Mary Pickford's niece, who was dancing past with William Bakewell, the actor. Bakewell was incensed and started for Myron, but Lewis Milestone and other friends interceded with an apology. Miss Pickford told reporters she had accepted Myron's apology and considered the whole thing a tempest in a teapot.

Myron had ambivalent feelings about his brother's growing success at Paramount. On one hand Myron felt a familial pride because David was ascending to a position of power in the movie business and restoring the name of Selznick to its former eminence. Myron felt no qualms about using David's position to secure new clients.

But Myron's troubled spirit was also upset by David's success. His younger brother was doing what Myron once did and yearned to do again: to make movies. Myron submerged his ambition and devoted his energies to revenging his father's name. He envisioned his agency as an instrument to conduct a vendetta against the power structure of the film business. Myron expressed his feelings to his client, William Wellman: "I hate all producers—except my brother. And I even hate him, when he's acting like a producer."

Myron formed a partnership with Frank Joyce, a former New York hotel manager who entered the agency business by managing his sister, Alice Joyce. Because of their aggressive manner in acquiring better terms for movie talent, Selznick and Joyce attracted dozens of big names as clients. Myron was unsatisfied. Agents such as himself still had to enter the back doors of studios and sit in anterooms until the studio bosses deigned to see them. Myron was anxious to maneuver a single audacious deal which would impress the producers with his power.

William Powell's contract was expiring at Paramount. The actor had developed into a serviceable leading man, and his agent, Myron Selznick, believed there would be no difficulty in achieving better terms at another studio. But whenever he offered Powell elsewhere, the salary proposed by other producers was the same the actor was being paid at Paramount. Myron sniffed out the conspiracy: the studio bosses would not bid against each other for Powell's services.

Myron saw in Warner Brothers a chance to break the trust. Warner Brothers had grown in importance through its pioneering of talkies, but the company had difficulty getting playing time for its pictures in the theater chains, which were controlled by the major film companies. Also, Warner lacked enough important stars to support its production program. Myron arranged a meeting with Jack Warner, head of production.

"Jack, you got no guts," Myron muttered.

"What do you mean?" Warner demanded.

"Those bastards at Paramount won't play your pictures, but you don't have the guts to take their stars away from them."

Warner's interest was aroused when he learned that the contracts of William Powell, Kay Francis, and Ruth Chatterton were soon to expire at Paramount. As their agent, Myron was willing to deliver them to Warner Brothers—at a considerable rise in salary. Jack Warner telephoned his brother Harry, president of the company, and they agreed to the deal.

Katharine Hepburn, John Barrymore, A BILL OF DIVORCEMENT

Myron added another proposal. Constance Bennett could make two pictures at $150,000 apiece during her ten-week vacation from her Pathe contract. Jack and Harry Warner gulped—and accepted the proposal, which meant a $30,000 weekly salary for Miss Bennett.

The news of Myron's coup struck Hollywood with immense force. The acting community was delighted that someone had finally broken the stranglehold on salaries, and the Selznick-Joyce agency signed many new clients. The producers were incensed. B. P. Schulberg growled, "In a year people will be saying, 'Whatever happened to Myron Selznick?'"

Aware of the distress Myron had caused Paramount, David offered to resign his position. But his boss, Schulberg, decreed that David could not be held accountable for his brother's transgressions.

The emboldened Myron continued playing one studio against another to escalate salaries of stars, directors, and writers. One studio boss told Myron bluntly that the companies had amassed three million dollars to run him out of business.

"Three million bucks!" Myron gloated. "Why don't you just give me two million? Then I'll leave town voluntarily."

Adolph Zukor tried to talk sense to the eldest son of his one-time partner. "Myron, Myron, be reasonable," Zukor cautioned. "You have cost the industry fifty million dollars this year."

Myron grinned. "I haven't started yet," he replied.

After three years at Paramount, David Selznick's ambitions had outrun his opportunities, and he was restless for change. He had been able to produce his own pictures, including such creditable films as *Sarah and Son* with Ruth Chatterton and Fredric March, *Manslaughter* with March and Claudette Colbert, *Honey* with Nancy Carroll and Lillian Roth, and *The Texan* with Gary Cooper and Fay Wray.

But he was eager to establish his own production unit at Paramount, and he made several entreaties to the company management. The Paramount officialdom was deaf to his pleas. The factory system was working wondrously well, manufacturing

Joel McCrea, Dolores Del Rio
BIRD OF PARADISE

Fay Wray and friends
KING KONG

pictures which enjoyed automatic playing time in Paramount's vast network of theaters.

On June 18, 1931, David O. Selznick submitted his resignation to Paramount studio. He was twenty-nine years old, and he felt that he was ready to assume a position of responsibility. He sought his own independent producing company, with which he could make his own pictures and sign them with his name, the name of Selznick. He wanted that name once more to draw attention and respect in the motion picture industry.

His plan ran headlong into big-studio opposition, especially from his father-in-law. Louis B. Mayer and the other bosses had no intention of allowing film makers to operate outside the major studios. That would erode the studios' power and upset the system of a controlled product and a controlled market. David made no headway with his proposal for his own independent company. So he decided to operate within the big-studio framework, this time as the man at the top. David Sarnoff's Radio Corporation of America had recently acquired control of RKO studio and was sweeping out the previous regime. Newcomer Sarnoff was not beholden to Mayer and other industry powers. He hired David as the new studio boss.

At last, David had a studio of his own! It wasn't exactly what he wanted; he had to seek approval for major decisions. But for the most part, he was autonomous. Sarnoff and the RCA people knew nothing about making pictures, and they generally nodded assent to his suggestions.

David first began to build his own production staff. One of those marked for firing was Pandro Berman, nephew of an RKO founder. As was the Hollywood custom, all relatives were ordered swept out in a studio change-over, but David declined to fire Berman. "You can stay on as my assistant if you want," said David, sympathetic to Berman's position as a second-generation film maker. Berman stayed on.

Enjoying his new-found power to do his own hiring, David began to assemble associates who were to play important roles in his future career. One of them was George Cukor.

They had met at Paramount, where Cukor was a dialogue

Jean Parker, Frances Dee, Katharine Hepburn, Spring Byington, Joan Bennett, LITTLE WOMEN

director. Through Myron, David had arranged for Cukor to work as dialogue director with Lewis Milestone on *All Quiet on the Western Front.* Cukor returned to Paramount and began directing Maurice Chevalier in *One Hour With You* under the supervision of Ernst Lubitsch, who was busy on another film; later Lubitsch took over and finished *One Hour With You.* B.P. Schulberg wanted to put Lubitsch's name on the film as director, and Cukor sued to prevent it. Selznick used the impasse as a means of luring Cukor to RKO.

David had inherited as his secretary at RKO an attractive young girl named Marcella Bennett, and he was quick to recognize her uncommon faculties. She could take dictation as fast as he could talk, something most secretaries could not manage. She could distribute and file the memos he broadsided to all important workers in the studio. Her sense of order brought organization to his work day, which otherwise might have fallen into chaos. She shielded him from time-wasting appointments and relieved him of routine functions, even to the buying of his underwear. She learned to edit his angry letters and memos so the message didn't make an enemy of the recipient. She sent gifts to stars and directors who were in need of special attention. She anticipated his every need. When she noticed him drowsing in a conference, she brought him orange juice, a chocolate bar, or a Coca-Cola. His associates believed David dozed out of boredom, but Marcella knew that he had hypoglycemia, low blood sugar. After he consumed something sweet, his alertness returned.

Another important figure who entered David's life at RKO was Daniel O'Shea.

He was an Irish Catholic, a New Yorker who came out of Harvard Law School at the depth of the Depression and could find work only with the trouble-ridden film company, RKO. One of his early negotiations was for a contract with Lewis Milestone and David O. Selznick, who proposed an independent company to release through RKO. David went to New York to negotiate the deal with the young law graduate. Green at the job, O'Shea introduced a host of clauses to protect the company. David, who showed a surprising knowledge of the law and delighted in debate, combatted him on every point. They failed to arrive at an agreement, and Milestone left for another studio.

Months later, O'Shea received a telephone call from an RKO executive who asked him, "How would you like to go out to Hollywood as legal aide to the new studio head, David Selznick?"

"I'd like to go," said O'Shea, "but I don't think he'll have me. Not after the fight we had over Milestone's contract."

"He asked for you," said the executive. O'Shea moved to California and began a working relationship that lasted twenty years.

David acquired as his assistant Merian C. Cooper, with whom he had been associated on *Four Feathers* at Paramount. Cooper proved an excellent choice. An adventurer who had traveled throughout the world for wars and film projects, he was outspoken and imaginative.

Lionel Barrymore,
Billie Burke,
Edmund Lowe

Madge Evans, John
Barrymore (with director
George Cukor)

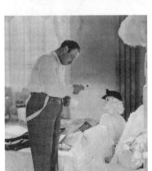

Wallace Beery, Jean
Harlow

David O. Selznick's
all-star cast of

DINNER AT EIGHT

Marie Dressler

William Gargan, Clarence Brown, Myrna Loy, NIGHT FLIGHT

Having gathered a skilled staff about him, David began building a program of pictures for RKO. He started to develop the traits that characterized his mode of operation throughout his career. He delved into everything that concerned the making of motion pictures. He queried every craftsman about his work, looked into every studio department. Memos were fired off in staggering numbers. He composed them during every waking hour, in his office, his projection room, his car, his bedroom—even the bathroom. One sleepless night he pondered ways to improve the studio operation. He fumbled for writing paper, found none. The next day he brought to the studio long memos to department heads, written on a roll of toilet paper.

After taking over as production boss, David reviewed the RKO product awaiting release. One of the films showed unrealized promise. It was an airplane picture starring Richard Dix and Mary Astor, *The Lost Squadron.* David ordered it back into production, an unknown practice at cost-conscious RKO. His judg-

Production number, DANCING LADY

Publicity photo, Joan Crawford, Ted Healy, and The Three Stooges
DANCING LADY

ment was justified when the improvements helped make *The Lost Squadron* a success.

Cukor was assigned to direct *What Price Hollywood?* with Constance Bennett and Lowell Sherman; it proved to be a witty film, the first to deal with the film capital in a realistic manner. Berman produced *What Price Hollywood?*, as well as *Symphony of Six Million* with Irene Dunne and Ricardo Cortez. John Barrymore gave two of his best performances in *State's Attorney* and *Topaze*. Other RKO films made during Selznick's regime included *The Conquerors* with Richard Dix and Ann Harding, *Rockabye* with Constance Bennett and Joel McCrea, *Westward Passage* with Ann Harding and Laurence Olivier, and *Animal Kingdom*, a smart comedy with Leslie Howard, Ann Harding, and Myrna Loy.

Selznick searched about for new stars to match the galaxies enjoyed by M-G-M, Paramount, and the other big companies. He viewed test after test of acting hopefuls, and one of them was an angular young woman who spoke in an accent that hinted of Back Bay and English drawing rooms.

"My God, that's the worst scarecrow I ever saw," Selznick exclaimed. "If we need someone to play *The Witch of Endor*, she'd be the one."

George Cukor, who had seen Katharine Hepburn on Broadway in *The Warrior's Husband,* urged David to sign her for *A Bill of Divorcement* despite the mannered test. David agreed, and the bony-faced actress was brought out from New York to appear with two veteran stars, John Barrymore and Billie Burke. As the rushes began coming in, David recognized Miss

Wallace Beery, VIVA VILLA

Gary Cooper visits William Powell and Clark Gable on the set of
MANHATAN MELODRAMA

Hepburn's ability to keep up with the older professionals and surpass them. She electrified audiences with a style and beauty all her own. After *A Bill of Divorcement*, David immediately cast her in *Christopher Strong* and then in *Morning Glory*, for which she was awarded the Academy Award for best performance by an actress in 1932-33.

RKO owned the screen rights to a stage melodrama of the South Seas, *Bird of Paradise*, and David sought to make a film of it in authentic surroundings. Searching for a director, he asked his father-in-law, Louis B. Mayer, to lend him King Vidor. The director was dispatched to RKO, and David gave him the play script of *Bird of Paradise*.

"I just can't do it," Vidor declared. "It's simply not my cup of tea."

"Please," David entreated. "Just give me three of your love scenes and do whatever else you want with the story. Oh, just one other thing: the girl has to jump in the volcano at the end."

Vidor couldn't resist such terms, and he departed for Hawaii with a full crew and no script. The film company encountered the worst Hawaiian storms in twenty years, but Vidor continued filming. *Bird of Paradise,* starring Dolores Del Rio and Joel McCrea, proved to be a creditable film, adding luster to David Selznick's growing reputation as a studio production boss.

David's most astute decision during the RKO period was to encourage Merian Cooper and Ernest Schoedsack in a film based on an Edgar Wallace story, *The Beast.* It concerned a prehistoric monster who survived to modern times and went on a rampage when introduced to New York as a freak attraction. The film involved enormously expensive miniatures, but David had faith in the project and approved the cost. To prevent imitations and possible lawsuits for plagiarism, he ordered the purchase of a faintly similar tale, *The Lost World,* by Arthur Conan Doyle. David supplied the title for the immensely popular film—*King Kong.*

The year 1932 was eventful for David O. Selznick. In August, Irene gave birth to their first child, Jeffrey. David continued to make a dazzling record at RKO, and his plans for future productions held portents of greatness. He signed the Broadway dancing star Fred Astaire to appear in film musicals, despite claims that Astaire was too long-faced and thin to offer box-office appeal. He prepared a version of *Little Women* to star Katharine Hepburn.

Despite his achievements, David's relationship with his New York superiors was proving unsatisfactory. He resented the growing insistence that he had to clear his command decisions with the RCA hierarchy, radio men who knew nothing of the intricacies of movie showmanship. He demanded more freedom to act on his own taste and instincts. RCA was intent on maintaining control. The arguments became acrimonious, and Myron stepped in to represent his brother and add heat to the dispute. On December 17, 1932, David O. Selznick announced he was

Clark Gable and Mickey Rooney, Manhattan Melodrama

leaving his post as head of production at RKO.

Louis B. Mayer, ever the Machiavellian, made his move. Mayer had become embroiled in a bitter and bewildering dispute with his onetime protege, Irving Thalberg. The youthful production genius had deeply offended Mayer with his demands for more money and independence at M-G-M, and the pair engaged in furious, name-hurling arguments. Always in frail health, Thalberg fell seriously ill, and Mayer was concerned about the future of M-G-M production. Thalberg's adherents also claimed that Mayer sought to rid himself of the man who had been accorded the lion's share of credit for building M-G-M into the most prestigious studio in the industry. Mayer entertained hopes of establishing a dynasty by bringing David Selznick back to M-G-M as a producer. Nicholas Schenck, president of M-G-M's parent company, Loew's, agreed to the hiring of Selznick, since Thalberg's delicate health made it essential to seek other suppliers of films.

David Selznick was reluctant to rejoin M-G-M. He disliked being placed in the position of Irving Thalberg's rival. Although Thalberg had once fired him and they had later competed as studio heads, the two men had developed a mutual respect that was blossoming into warm friendship. David did not want to be a party to Mayer's undermining of Thalberg's authority at M-G-M. Nor did David enjoy the stigma of going to work for his father-in-law.

But the temptation was great. Mayer offered David his pick of M-G-M's vast stable of stars, his choice of story properties, and the use of the superb technical staff of the studio. All this, plus a two-year contract starting at $4000 a week.

In the midst of negotiations came the shattering news that L. J. Selznick had died.

In his latter years, Lewis J. Selznick had enjoyed the life of an elderly Jewish gentleman. He delighted in the success of his two sons, and he helped organize Myron's office, where secretaries came to know him as a bottom-pincher. The old man visited his friends, played poker in occasional all-night sessions, and took walks around Beverly Hills. He displayed none of the drive that

Robert Montgomery, Helen Hayes, VANESSA, HER LOVE STORY

had made him the gadfly of the movie business. He even became friends with his old enemy, Louis B. Mayer, and the two found amusement in being grandfathers of the same baby boy. After he had passed the age of sixty-two, L.J.'s health failed. He died on January 25, 1933.

Both David and Myron, who rushed home from a European business trip, were devastated by their father's death. They observed with bitterness how the funeral was attended by many top figures of the film industry, men who might have saved their father from bankruptcy.

On the day of the funeral, Florence Selznick related to David one of L.J.'s last remarks: "Tell Davey to stick with his own people; they're the only ones you can trust." David took the advice to mean that he should do business with his father-in-law. On February 6, 1933, Mayer happily announced that M-G-M had signed a contract with David 0. Selznick to head his own production unit at the studio.

Mayer ordered a sprawling studio bungalow lavishly decorated for the coming of his son-in-law, and he placed the studio's entire facilities at Selznick's disposal. David took full
advantage. His first film at M-G-M was as star-filled as Thalberg's
Grand Hotel of the previous year. He chose the hit play by
George S. Kaufman and Edna Ferber, *Dinner at Eight,* and peo-
pled it with Marie Dressler, the Barrymore brothers, Wallace
Beery, Jean Harlow, Lee Tracy, Edmund Lowe, Billie Burke,
Madge Evans, Jean Hersholt, Karen Morley, Louise Closser Hale,
Phillips Holmes, May Robson, and Grant Mitchell. David
brought George Cukor to M-G-M to direct the film and, despite
the large and potentially explosive cast, shooting was complet-
ed in twenty-seven days.

Dinner at Eight propelled David Selznick to a fast start at
M-G-M, and he followed with other top-notch attractions. He
cast the Barrymores, Clark Gable, Helen Hayes, Robert
Montgomery, Myrna Loy, and William Gargan in *Night Flight,*

Irene, David and Florence Selznick

Irene and David Selznick, Norma Shearer, and producer David Lewis at a Hollywood Premier

an Antoine de Saint-Exupery story directed by Clarence Brown. It had moments of excitement in the scenes of flying over the Andes, but the characters were thinly drawn, and the film was not totally successful. Next came *Dancing Lady,* an entertaining musical — curiously, the only musical Selznick ever produced. It starred Gable and Joan Crawford and introduced to the screen both Fred Astaire, borrowed from RKO, and Nelson Eddy.

Viva Villa proved to be a problem picture. Selznick had cast Wallace Beery as the Mexican revolutionist and Lee Tracy as a newspaperman who covered his campaigns. The combination proved highly effective on the screen, but Tracy's drinking made production difficult. When the company went to Mexico City for locations, Tracy indulged in too much tequila. One morning as he was trying to sleep off a hangover at his hotel, he was disturbed by crowd noises in the street below.

Some said that he mistook the balcony for the bathroom.

Marion Davies (foreground) and David Selznick entertain a famous visitor to M-G-M, George Bernard Shaw

Others claim he expressed in a graphic manner his opinion of those who were disturbing his sleep. Since the Mexicans were parading in honor of their independence, this gesture was taken as a national insult. To placate the outraged government, Louis B. Mayer removed Tracy from the picture, and he was hurried out of Mexico amid threats of bodily harm. He was replaced by Stuart Erwin. Despite the upset, *Viva Villa* proved to be a stirring adventure film, highlighted by one of Wally Beery's most effective portrayals.

Manhattan Melodrama came next. To co-star with Clark Gable, Selznick chose William Powell and Myrna Loy, thus initiating the screen combination that flourished in *The Thin Man* and other sophisticated films. For the role of Gable as a child, Selznick picked a sprightly lad he had observed in a table tennis tournament at the Ambassador Hotel. The young man had starred in a series of comedy shorts as Mickey McGuire, later billing himself as Mickey Rooney. *Manhattan Melodrama* proved to be one of M-G-M's big money-makers

W.C. Fields
DAVID COPPERFIELD

of 1934.[2]

Less successful was *Vanessa, Her Love Story,* in which Helen Hayes starred, much against her will. David had become enamored with the dusty old Hugh Walpole novel which concerned a woman who lived with another man after her husband had been committed to a mental institution. Such a situation risked a script turndown from the moral guardians of the Production Code Administration, which censored all films. Selznick ordered the script changed so that Miss Hayes would cohabit with her lover, to be played by Robert Montgomery, but their relationship would stop short of the bedroom.

"But that makes her a dreadful tease!" Miss Hayes protested. "How could I ever make a woman like that believable?"

David was insistent. So was Miss Hayes; she refused to appear in *Vanessa, Her Love Story.* David's father-in-law, Louis Mayer, intervened to remind the actress that she had a contract with M-G-M. If she did not make the picture, the studio would sue her for $90,000, the amount that had been expended in pre-production costs. The prospect of a lawsuit terrified Miss Hayes, and she acquiesced.

But then Joseph Breen, the tough Irish Catholic who administered the Code, decreed that David's plot solution did not remove the basic immorality of the script.

"You've got to save the picture, Helen," David pleaded. "You're a good Catholic; you can convince Joe Breen. Go talk to him."

With great reluctance, she agreed to argue David's cause. She told the industry censor: "Mr. Breen, I wouldn't be at all surprised if you rejected this script on esthetic grounds. But I honestly don't see any reason in the world to turn it down for moral reasons."

Breen acquiesced to her logic, and *Vanessa, Her Love Story*

---

[2] *Manhattan Melodrama* attracted millions of customers, including a famous young man in Chicago. After viewing the picture with a female companion, desperado John Dillinger walked out of the theater and was slain by FBI agents.

W.C. Fields, Freddie Bartholomew
DAVID COPPERFIELD

Temporary director W.S. Van Dyke, Ronald Colman, Edna May Oliver, Claude Gilingwater (in mirror)
A TALE OF TWO CITIES

received the Code seal. As Miss Hayes had anticipated, the film proved to be mawkish and unbelievable. It marked the end of her career as a leading lady in films.

As David Selznick's position in the film community continued to rise, so did his manner of living. Following the gospel according to Lewis J. Selznick, David seemed determined to maintain his spending and gambling on a par with his income.

Gambling became a compulsion. He spent night after night at the roulette table of the Clover Club, a gambling place that operated on the Sunset Strip without interference from local authorities. Often at the end of a studio day, David telephoned the proprietor of the club and asked him to bring in a croupier for some early gambling. David took a few of his co-workers and arrived as the croupier was setting up the wheel. David liked to play with large stacks of chips, which he placed on combinations of two and five. He remained at the table, drinking Scotch and smoking continuously, until Irene telephoned to say it was

Freddie Bartholomew, Fredric March, Greta Garbo
ANNA KARENINA. *Director Clarence Brown (with cap)*

time for dinner.

Because of his erratic bets, David almost invariably lost, sometimes $15,000 in an evening. During one disastrous losing streak, David suspected foul play. "I think it's the booze," he confided to his production associate, William Wright. Before his next visit to the club, David asked a studio prop man for a flask. After ordering a drink that night, David stepped away from the roulette table and poured the liquid into the flask. He sent it to a laboratory, but the analysis failed to support his suspicion that he was being drugged. The drink contained only Scotch.

David became almost a pitifully easy mark for Hollywood's

gamblers. Once Joe Schenck won $100,000 from David in one gambling encounter and said to him: "David, I'm not going to play with you any more. You don't know what you're doing." To many of his fellow gamblers, it appeared that he didn't. When playing for big stakes at gin rummy, David insisted on holding onto his face cards, even when unmatched; the normally cautious player would discard them to avoid being caught with a high penalty.

Throughout much of his career, David had an outstanding bill with the bookies, but he always paid off his gambling debts; he never was a sore loser. He became so well known as a pigeon that the town's gamblers kept each other informed of his whereabouts. If he were dining at the Brown Derby, the word was spread, and two or three players would encounter him there, not entirely by chance. A game was suggested, and David inevitably joined it, with the usual results.

One night David was engaged in a poker game with Joe Schenck, Jack Warner, directors Jack Conway and Mervyn Leroy, and producer Lawrence Weingarten. Irving Berlin arrived at two in the morning and he sat behind David to observe the game. Berlin was astounded to see David's maladroitness with the cards. With one hand David lost $10,000 by calling when he obviously had no chance of winning. Recalling Lewis J. Selznick's reputation as a loser, Berlin remarked, "David, if your father was alive, he would have been proud of you!"

Gambling was a game to David, as was almost everything else in his life. Love was a game too. He fell in love with each of his leading ladies, to one degree or another. Sometimes it was an idolatrous love of beauty and talent, expressed in idealistic terms; sometimes it was purely physical. David could be overwhelming in his affection, and many an actress allowed herself to be overwhelmed, out of sheer attraction or hope of furthering her career.

He was lavish with affection, niggardly with love. The affectionate display—warm embraces to male and female alike, gifts for any occasion, cries of "darling" and "sweetheart"—was common currency in the film world, and David knew how to express himself in such terms. But he knew that love was an uncommon commodity among movie people; he had seen how quickly L.J. had been abandoned. Therefore David was sparing with his love.

He was devoted to his mother. Florence Selznick was consulted in all important business matters, and she gave of her wisdom, gained partly from observing her husband's mistakes. She was included in all of David's social affairs, even the poker games. One night at David's house, a group that included Joe Schenck, Darryl Zanuck, and Myron Selznick sat down to the regular poker game. Schenck lightly asked if Florence would like to join them, and she said she would.

"I don't know about that, Joe," complained Zanuck. "I've never played poker with a woman before."

"That's all right, Darryl," Florence replied calmly. "Neither have I."

Despite their sometimes pugnacious behavior toward each other, there was a deep bond between David and Myron. As producer and agent, they were in a sense antagonists, and Myron could enforce as tough a deal with his brother as he would with any other producer. Yet David confided in Myron as he did with no one else. He never made a major decision without first conferring with Myron. David found his brother's counsel unfailingly wise, even when Myron was drinking heavily. That was happening with greater frequency, and David often urged Myron to temper his drinking, to no avail.

For Irene, David felt deep affection, and he often expressed his feelings in lavishly sentimental poems. More than once Irene had provided the key to a troublesome decision. Yet she was careful not to impose her will on David; she realized that David's particular genius could not flourish if fettered.

Once the wife of screen writer Herman Mankiewicz commented on the difficulty of managing a household for a husband with the erratic habits of David Selznick.

"What is more important in my life than to please David?" Irene replied unblinkingly.

Irene's management of the Selznick home was impeccable.

First at Santa Monica and then in the Beverly Hills home that David had built, Irene conducted a household that was a model for other Hollywood wives. Two shifts of cooks remained on duty because David might have demanded a meal at any hour of the day or night. If David arrived home long after the dinner hour, Irene ordered the meal discarded and another one prepared for him. Irene was prepared to feed any number of guests, from one to thirty. The staff included a maid, personal maid, nurse and relief nurse for the two boys—a second son, Daniel, was born in 1936—chauffeur, and two full-time gardeners to maintain the well-manicured lawns and hedges of the three-acre estate.

The Beverly Hills house was decorated in elegant but unostentatious style. The two main rooms were paneled in blond, hand-carved wood and filled with overstuffed chintz-covered furniture and rare English antiques. The playroom-projection room was furnished in Early American with white wooden walls. The dining room was manorial, with white marble floor and an antique English dining table that seated thirty. Upstairs were separate bedroom suites for David and Irene and a wing for the children; the two boys dwelt apart from their parents much of the time, eating in their own dining room.

The Selznicks lavished the same taste and planning on their parties as David did on his films. Their dinners were splendidly appointed, and David often hand-wrote the place cards with a graceful personal message for each guest. Dinner was usually followed by the showing of a new movie, as was the Beverly Hills ritual. Then came the games. David was an insatiable games player, excelling at charades, word games, etc. He could play for hours, and he urged his guests to remain until early in the morning. He never liked to see a party end.

Sunday afternoon at the Selznicks' became an institution. The important figures of Hollywood, as well as visiting celebrities, gathered every Sunday to play tennis, to swim, to talk movies, to eat Irene's elegant food and to drink. Guests had to qualify on the basis of reputation or achievement; not just anyone was invited.

Once Herman Mankiewicz sought to bring a couple who were close friends. "No, they can't come," David replied. "They don't spell 'Sunday.'"

In truth, David was a bit of a snob. Despite his father's downfall, he believed that the Selznicks were among the elite of film society, and he aimed to impress his contemporaries with that notion. He lived and acted accordingly. He chose his close acquaintances with care, and he nourished friendships with the rich and influential. He abhorred the common stereotype of the movie producer as an uncouth Jew, and he sought to divorce himself from such a view. More and more of his intimates were rich gentiles, and he declined to identify[3] himself with the Jewish community of Hollywood.

For a variation of the entertaining routine, David sometimes rented yachts for weekend parties. The guest list was even more selective than for Sunday parties, and each person received an elaborate invitation in the form of sailing orders. The yacht left San Pedro at midnight on Friday night, and the voyagers sailed to Catalina Island for a weekend of water sports, excellent food and spirits, and bright conversation.

David traveled in the most luxurious style. On trips to New York, he had the best accommodations on the *Chief* and the *Twentieth Century Limited.* Once he decided to travel to New York by boat "so I can get a rest." He took along Irene, script writer Donald Ogden Stewart, actor Donald Crisp and his scenarist wife Jane Murfin, Marcella Bennett and two other secretaries. The script of *A Tale of Two Cities* was completed during the voyage.

He was both lavish and thoughtful in his gifts to Irene. Once

[3] During World War II, Ben Hecht sought David Selznick's support for a drive to aid the Jewish cause in Palestine, David replied: "I don't want anything to do with your cause, for the simple reason that it's a Jewish political cause. And I am not interested in Jewish political problems. I'm an American and not a Jew ... It would be silly of me to pretend suddenly that I'm a Jew, with some sort of full-blown Jewish psychology." Undaunted, Hecht said, "If I can prove you are a Jew, David, will you sign the telegram as co-sponsor with me?" Selznick agreed, and Hecht telephoned Nunnally Johnson, Leland Hayward, and trade magazine editor Martin Quigley with the question: "Would you call David 0. Selznick an American or a Jew?" All three replied, "A Jew." Selznick lent his name to the cause.

he commissioned a Mexican artist, whom he had hired to create the Viva Villa titles, to make a profile drawing of son Jeffrey. A florist re-created the drawing with flowers, and David presented the portrait to Irene. On another occasion he ordered an ermine throw-blanket for Irene's bed, together with matching ermine slippers.

Irene greatly enjoyed the life they were leading. She seemed content to follow the same pattern that Florence Selznick had known.

Once Frances Goldwyn was studying the front of the Selznick house, which had been designed in the same style as the Goldwyns'. "I wonder what our houses will look like in twenty years," Mrs. Goldwyn mused.

"Good Lord, David and I won't be here in twenty years," Irene Selznick replied. "We'll have had the auction before then."

"Myron, you'd better come over here," David Selznick said to his brother over the telephone. "I'm going to fight Charlie MacArthur."

Myron Selznick rushed to his car and sped from Beverly Hills toward Culver City. He could not resist a good fight, even when his brother was battling one of the Myron Selznick clients.

Leland Hayward, whose New York talent agency was associated with Myron's company, had brought Charles MacArthur and Ben Hecht to Hollywood for a script assignment with Samuel Goldwyn. The two playwrights had met Goldwyn in a New York hotel elevator; before they emerged, Hecht and MacArthur had outlined a story for a movie, and Goldwyn had bought it. Later Hecht and MacArthur couldn't recall what the story had been, but they went to Hollywood anyway, taking along a young short-story writer named John Lee Mahin. Their plan was to enlist young writers for a script factory, and they rented a huge old rancho in the hills above Culver City as base of operations.

The Spanish-style mansion was ablaze with lights when Myron Selznick raced up the hill. He leaped from his car and rushed into the house, which was filled with stars, starlets, writers, and directors talking noisily and dancing to a jazz band.

"Where's David?" Myron shouted above the din.

"Upstairs," answered Lewis Milestone.

Myron rushed up the stairs and found his brother and MacArthur in the hallway hurling insults at each other while Ben Hecht watched with quiet amusement. Myron didn't pause to inquire into the nature of the dispute; he joined David in castigating MacArthur.

"All right, both of you come in the bedroom," MacArthur snarled. "I'll take you both on."

"No, you don't," Myron replied. "We'll beat the hell out of you one at a time."

"Damn right!" David added. "Let's go."

The two Selznicks and MacArthur stalked into the bedroom, followed by the grinning Hecht. As Hecht locked the door, MacArthur swung widely and knocked David over one of the twin beds.

"So you won't fight fair!" Myron growled, leaping onto MacArthur's back. Both men fell over the bed and onto David. All three began writhing, kicking, and slugging in the tight quarters between the two beds. Perceiving his disadvantage as the two brothers grappled with him, MacArthur sank his teeth in David's leg.

David howled in pain, crying, "He bit me!"

Myron was outraged. "Dracula!" he screamed at MacArthur. All were on their feet, and Myron and MacArthur continued exchanging blows while David examined the bite on his leg.

The commotion could be heard downstairs, and many of the actors, alarmed about becoming involved in a party scandal, rushed to their cars and sped down the hill to safety. News of the battle reached Irene Selznick and she hurried upstairs and pounded on the bedroom door. Hearing the sounds of fighting inside, she cried, "Let me in! They're killing my husband!"

"Oh, he's doing all right," Ben Hecht reported on the other side of the door. MacArthur had successfully retired Myron from the fight, but now David had re-entered the action and had MacArthur pinned to the floor.

Irene's pounding became insistent, and Hecht unlocked the

door. Irene rushed in the bedroom and found MacArthur atop David. She pulled off her shoe and began beating MacArthur over the head with the heel. Leland Hayward arrived to rescue MacArthur and hustle him off to bed in a tower apartment in the mansion.

The combatants assessed the damage the following day. As MacArthur was commenting on what a fine fight it had been, a tooth fell onto his breakfast plate. David's bite wound required cauterizing. In the sober light of day neither David nor MacArthur nor any of the witnesses could recall what the fight had been about.

Nor could anyone explain the reasons for the continuing antagonism between David Selznick and Charles MacArthur. Some theorized that it may have stemmed from David's fondness for MacArthur's partner, Ben Hecht, who was David's favorite screen writer. Whatever the reason, David and Charles almost invariably ended in fisticuffs whenever they met. When MacArthur and his wife, Helen Hayes, were invited to large Hollywood parties, she began making a practice of inquiring, "Is David Selznick coming?" If the answer was affirmative, she politely declined, explaining that she couldn't risk another battle.

After successfully avoiding a confrontation, Miss Hayes relented, and she accepted an invitation to a party where David was to be among the guests. In the early part of the evening, she was seated with a lady friend who remarked, "Well, isn't that nice?"

"Isn't what nice?" Miss Hayes inquired.

"Over there. Charlie and David. See how well they're getting along."

Miss Hayes turned her head and glanced toward the bar. To her delight, she saw her husband and David Selznick engaged in a lively, smiling conversation.

"I'm so pleased," she remarked, returning to her companion.

A few minutes later, she heard a commotion behind her. She turned her head and saw Charlie and David rolling on the floor, muttering threats and striking blows at each other.

David Selznick once expounded to his writers the tenets of adapting a popular novel to the screen: "The millions of people who have read the book and who worship it would very properly attack us violently for the desecrations which are indicated by this treatment. But quite apart from the feelings of these few millions, I have never been able to understand why motion picture people insist on throwing away something of proven appeal to substitute things of their own creation. It is a form of ego which has drawn upon Hollywood the wrath of the world for years."

David applied his theory to his next film achievement, *David Copperfield.*

It had been Lewis J. Selznick's favorite book. As a Russian lad newly arrived in England, he had helped himself to learn English with *David Copperfield.* Every scene, every character remained vivid in his mind throughout his lifetime, and he induced each of his sons to read the book at an early age. David was seven when he began poring over the adventures of young Copperfield, dictionary close at hand.

David plunged ahead with the film version of *David Copperfield* despite the opposition of Louis Mayer, who claimed that such classics were poison at the box office. Unable to dissuade his son-in-law from undertaking the project, Mayer then urged the casting of M-G-M's popular child actor, Jackie Cooper, in the title role. David argued that it would be foolish to cast an American boy in the English classic, and he sent his director, George Cukor, to England in search of a youth to play the title role. Cukor returned with a winning young man, Freddie Bartholomew.

David assembled an impressive cast: Lionel Barrymore as Peggotty, Edna May Oliver as Aunt Betsy, Charles Laughton as Micawber, Lewis Stone as Mr. Wickfield, Basil Rathbone as Mr. Murdstone, Roland Young as Uriah Heep, Herbert Mundin as Barkis, Jessie Ralph as Nurse Peggotty, and Elsa Lanchester as Clickett.

After the filming of *David Copperfield* had begun, Laughton became uneasy with his role as the debt-plagued Micawber. He asked to withdraw from the picture, and David Selznick reluctantly agreed. Searching for a replacement, David hit upon an inspiration: W. C. Fields.

It was a long chance. Fields had never appeared in a dramatic picture, and there were fears that he might play his own comedic self instead of a Dickens character. Fields himself was dubious about the assignment, and he attempted to inject one of his standard routines, the juggling act. Reminded that Dickens made no mention of Micawber's juggling, the comedian replied, "He probably forgot it."

David vetoed the juggling act, as well as the pool-table routine Fields tried to include. But David gave in when Fields refused to adopt an English accent.

"My father was an Englishman, and I got this accent from him," Fields remarked in his nasal drawl. "Are you trying to go against nature?"

He spoke the lines in his unique manner, though at a slightly slower pace. Fields had always mumbled his way through movies, often inventing his own dialogue. Selznick and Cukor insisted that he adhere to the Dickensian prose. Unable to remember the lengthy dialogue, Fields resorted to reading his lines from cue cards off-camera. His readings became less polished as the filming day continued, since he was consuming two fifths of whisky daily.

When David assembled *David Copperfield*, the picture ran two and a half hours, an hour longer than the average film. The preview was held in Bakersfield, and the reaction was poor. An important prizefight was being held in the town on the same night, and the theater was two thirds empty. The patrons were apathetic to the struggles of a boy in Victorian England.

Mayer urged his son-in-law to cut *David Copperfield,* and David felt inclined to do so because of the Bakersfield reaction. He wrestled with the problem and decided there was only one solution: to eliminate the Lionel Barrymore role. Two of the original twelve reels were snipped from the picture.

A preview in Santa Ana drew an excellent reaction, but David was dissatisfied. He noticed four women in the lobby talking animatedly, and he approached them to ask what they thought of the picture. They were schoolteachers.

"We loved the picture," said one of them, "except for one thing: how could you possibly film *David Copperfield* and not include Peggotty? "

David smiled. "Next time you see the picture, he'll be back in it."

Lionel Barrymore was restored to the film, and David completed it at the length of two hours and thirteen minutes. Expectably, the M-G-M sales force protested.

"How long can it be?" demanded the company president, Nick Schenck.

"How long is good?" David replied.

Critics and audiences alike pronounced *David Copperfield* good, and David Selznick proved to himself two important lessons: don't tamper with a classic; don't worry about a picture's length, as long as it is good.

David was encouraged to attempt other classics. He cast Greta Garbo in *Anna Karenina,* which she had made as a silent film, *Love*, opposite John Gilbert in 1927. For the 1935 version she appeared with Fredric March, and Freddie Bartholomew portrayed her son. It proved to be an excellent adaptation.

So was *A Tale of Two Cities,* with Ronald Colman playing the Dickens hero, Sydney Carton. By this time David Selznick had decided that an independent company was a far, far better place to produce pictures than in the film factory dominated by his father-in-law. David announced his intention to leave M-G-M.

"You'll fail! You'll fail!" shouted Louis Mayer.

"I'm thirty-two," David replied. "I can afford to fail."

III

●●●●●●●●●●●●●●●●●●●●
INDEPENDENCE
●●●●●●●●●●●●●●●●●●●●

In a Tradition of
Quality

John Hay Whitney, Chairman of the board, and David O. Selznick, president of Selznick International Pictures.

WHEN DAVID SELZNICK WAS THIRTY-THREE,
he telephoned his wife, Irene,
and told her, "Drop everything you're doing
and come to the studio—at once!"
Mystified, Irene Selznick left her home
and drove swiftly to Culver City.
She turned off Washington Boulevard
and motored up the curving driveway before the studio,
and she leaped out of the car and asked him,
"What is it, David?"
He grinned and gazed up at a painter on a scaffolding
above the gleaming white colonnade.
The painter was completing the sign that read:

SELZNICK INTERNATIONAL STUDIO

David and Irene embraced each other and cried.

David Selznick had sworn to his dead father that the name of Selznick would once more emblazon the world's movie screens. The man who helped him accomplish this was Merian C. Cooper, his former associate on *Four Feathers* and *King Kong*. A restless innovator, Cooper had allied himself with Dr. Herbert T. Kalmus, a college professor who had developed a three-color film process, Technicolor. Cooper enlisted his good friend, John Hay (Jock) Whitney, to invest in the new company.

Whitney and Cooper formed Pioneer Pictures with the announced promise "to color the world." Their aim was to demonstrate to the film companies how practical and exciting Technicolor could be.

Pioneer invested $80,000 in a short subject called *La Cucaracha*, which offered excitement in its swirls of scarlets and greens amid the fiesta atmosphere of Old Mexico. But the studios weren't convinced. Their pictures were prospering in black and white. Why add to their costs by paying tribute for the use of Technicolor, which required extra lighting, longer production schedules, and great expense for prints?

Pioneer plunged on. Cooper assigned Lowell Sherman to direct and Miriam Hopkins to star in *Becky Sharp*, based on Thackeray's *Vanity Fair*. Sherman died in mid-shooting and was replaced by Rouben Mamoulian, who scrapped most of the footage and began anew. *Becky Sharp* was not a success.[1]

Next, Cooper decided to make a film in which color itself was the star. It was a musical, *Dancing Pirate*, which featured great splashes of color. Pioneer launched the film with a record outlay for publicity and advertising at the premiere in Detroit. The first week's receipts provided another record: the lowest total in the history of the theater.

Jock Whitney was beginning to despair over his venture into the movie business. Then Merian Cooper proposed a new plan.

---

[1] *Becky Sharp* offers a historical footnote: One of the extra players in the film was Patricia Ryan, who later became Mrs. Richard M. Nixon.

He knew of David Selznick's restlessness at M-G-M. Why not join with Selznick in a new company to exploit the uses of Technicolor? Whitney agreed to the idea, and negotiations with David began.

Mayer beseeched his son-in-law to remain at M-G-M. He vowed that David would some day be head of production at the studio and could rule without interference. Irving Thalberg also urged David to stay. Thalberg's own independent company was progressing well at M-G-M, and he did not consider David a competitor. As one of M-G-M's major stockholders, Thalberg saw the value of retaining a film maker with a devotion to quality. He and Mayer even offered David a share of their profits. David remained firm. In September of 1933, he announced the formation of Selznick International Pictures with himself as president and John Hay Whitney as chairman of the board. The directors were Dr. A.H. Giannini of the Bank of America, Wall Street financier Robert Lehman, Cornelius Vanderbilt Whitney, Myron Selznick, and attorney Loyd Wright. All were investors in the company, as were John Hertz and Jock Whitney's cousin, Joan Whitney Payson. The capitalization was $3,200,000, to which David Selznick contributed nothing.

Another partner remained silent: Irving Thalberg. He invested $100,000 in the new company; to avoid complications at M-G-M, he made the investment in the name of his wife, Norma Shearer.

With customary thoroughness, David Selznick searched long and hard for a trademark to symbolize the new company. He wanted something with a classical connotation, and he sent a camera crew to the Louvre to photograph the Winged Victory, Venus de Milo, and other works of art. None satisfied him. One day he gazed at the white colonial facade of the studio and made a decision.

He delegated his film editor, Hal Kern, to photograph the front of the studio. The result pleased David, and he decided it would be the trademark to precede Selznick International films. The company motto hinted a tribute to Lewis J. Selznick: "In a Tradition of Quality."

For his first film David selected another favorite story of his father's, *Little Lord Fauntleroy*. Louis Mayer grudgingly agreed to lend Freddie Bartholomew for the title role. Although Selznick International had been formed to help further Technicolor, the company's initial movie was photographed in black and white.

Little Lord Fauntleroy proved to be an auspicious if unexciting start for Selznick International. It was a handsome film that exhibited the tradition of quality, and while it was no great hit, the picture contributed a modest profit. But it demonstrated to David and his New York backers that independent production was not inexpensive. *Little Lord Fauntleroy* cost $750,000 to produce. Two years earlier, David had made the all-star *Dinner at Eight* at M-G-M for $420,000.

David Selznick blundered on his next movie.

He decided to film an Edwardian novel, *The Garden of Allah* by Robert Hichens. His aides, including Willis Goldbeck who had written a silent version, argued that the tale of desert passions was hopelessly dated. David remained firm. He assigned playwright Lynn Riggs to modernize the script and Richard Boleslawski, formerly an actor with the Moscow Art Theatre, to direct. Although Marlene Dietrich's career was in a slump after her departure from Paramount, David hired her for $200,000, an immense sum for a star in 1936.

Among the production staff for *The Garden of Allah* was Joshua Logan, whom David had hired from the Broadway theater to be dialogue director. Logan arrived at the studio after a long plane ride and was immediately plunged into a conference with Selznick, Riggs, Goldbeck, and others.

Midway in the conference Selznick turned to Logan and snapped, "I didn't pay for you to come all the way to Hollywood and just sit there, Logan. Say something!" Logan attempted some suggestions, not admitting that he hadn't been able to read completely through the book.

A secretary entered and whispered a message to Selznick. "My God, Dietrich's here," he exclaimed. "Logan, you go out and talk to her. Now listen, she doesn't like the script. Tell her it's

Marlene Dietrich and David O. Selznick

great. Boley would do the same if he were here, but he isn't. Boley is the general, and you're his lieutenant. Go do the job. And *don't let her knock the script!*"

Logan went to the anteroom and came face to face with the star he had worshiped on the screen. She wore jodhpurs with a white silk open-necked shirt, her hair perfectly coiffed. Logan stuttered an introduction.

Speaking in her low-voiced lisp, she replied, "It's so nice to meet someone from the New York stage, someone who is intel-

David Selznick, Marlene Dietrich, and Charles Boyer on location for
THE GARDEN OF ALLAH.

ligent. This script—you know it is twash."

"Not really, Miss Dietrich, it's—"

"Garbo wouldn't do this script; she has that innate intelligence that peasants have. And you, an intelligent man from New York City, you know that this is strictly twash. Don't you?"

Logan was melted by her wide, staring eyes. "Well, maybe it's a little trash, but it can be fixed," he gulped.

The Garden of Allah was to be one of the first outdoor pictures in Technicolor, and Selznick insisted that the desert scenery be authentic. For the location scenes he chose a section of Arizona desert so primitive that the roads were made of wooden planks. A tent city was raised in the wilderness with living facilities for a couple hundred film workers. Palm trees were trucked from Los Angeles to decorate the barren sand, and a desert pool was created with black cement.

All the auguries boded ill for *The Garden of Allah*. When the wind didn't blow sand through the tent community, the sun bore down at 110 degrees. Sickness plagued the company. The use of Technicolor in the outdoors brought a myriad of problems. Charles Boyer, the leading man, photographed red in his ordinary makeup; he had to be painted gray for flesh tones.

Then there were the accents.

"This script is desert poetry," Selznick had rhapsodized to the dialogue director, Joshua Logan. "I want to hear every syllable on the sound track. Every consonant, every vowel. Everything!"

Logan found himself the only participant in the shooting who could speak clear English. Director Boleslawski talked in the heavy tones of his native Poland, Dietrich in her Teutonic lisp, Boyer in a French accent. Logan tried to coach Boyer, but to little avail. The actor complained: "I can say 'wiz the' or I can say 'with ze.' But 'with the' is impossible!"

When he arrived on the set for the first day of shooting, Logan found Boleslawski planning action scenes. "What do you want me to do?" Logan asked.

"Direct the scenes; I'm busy," said the director.

Logan was faced with directing a scene with Dietrich and

Boyer at the Black Pool Inn. The shooting went well until she came to the lines "Listen—that song again. The slaves sang it when they were set free."

There seemed to be no way to escape the banality. Logan finally suggested, "Miss Dietrich, could you try saying it as though the song were getting under your skin?"

Logan next came to scenes with Joseph Schildkraut, who was playing an effeminate poet in dragoman's coat and fez, with hibiscus over one ear. To Logan's astonishment, Schildkraut insisted on playing the role with a heavy Russian-Jewish accent.

Alarmed by the introduction of yet another accent, Logan withdrew a small truck from the motor pool and drove miles over the planked highway to a railroad stop. There he found a telephone, and he called David Selznick at the studio in Culver City.

"Yes, what do you want?" Selznick said with annoyance.

"Did you know that Schildkraut is playing the role with a thick Russian-Jewish accent?"

"Logan," said Selznick testily, "Mr. Schildkraut is one of America's most famous actors. I'm sure that whatever devices he employs will be in the best possible taste and in keeping with the character."

"Yes, sir. I just wanted to make sure you knew, sir."

After the first three days of rushes had reached Culver City, Selznick made a hurried trip to the location. His first order was for Boleslawski to re-shoot Schildkraut's scenes without the accent.

One by one, each major figure in the production was called to Selznick's Yuma hotel room to explain what was going wrong. Logan's turn came at 3 A.M.

"What's the idea of telling Dietrich to read that line as if she were annoyed?" Selznick demanded.

"I simply suggested that the song might be getting under her skin," Logan replied. "It was the only way I could get some tone into the scene."

"Did you or did you not ask her to seem annoyed?" Selznick insisted.

David and Myron Selznick at the Grauman's Chinese premiere of THE PRISONER OF ZENDA.

Logan's patience snapped. "Mr. Selznick," he said, "let me get off this picture. I'm poor as a turkey and I need the money, but I don't want to see you or this picture as long as—"

"Oh, no, you don't!" Selznick replied. "You can't get off that easily. You're going to stick it out, just like the rest of us."

Selznick fired a few members of the company, shuffled others, and tried to inspire everyone to get *The Garden of Allah* running smoothly. His improvements were temporary. The heat rose to 120 degrees, and most of the film workers became ill. Selznick ordered the company back to Culver City, bringing with it truckloads of sand. A huge dune was created on a sound stage, and the film was completed there.

The Garden of Allah failed to thrill audiences with its desert poetry. Critics, either. One of them commented: "The dialogue was obviously written by Alf Landon."

Myron Selznick continued his one-man war against the producers, including his brother's father-in-law. During a heated negotiation at M-G-M, Myron bawled at Louis B. Mayer, "Don't think that you're going to put one over on me just because David married that silly daughter of yours!"

"Liar!" Myron yelled at Adolph Zukor during a conference at Paramount.

His pugnacious tactics made him the scourge of the producers and brought clients flocking to his agency. Here at last was an agent a star or director could trust. Most other agents kowtowed to the bosses, currying favor with gifts, trading one client to the disadvantage of others. Not Myron. His manner with the producers was fearless and unrelenting. And he achieved results.

When Pat O'Brien was making his film debut in *The Front Page*, Myron appeared on the set and inquired, "Who's your agent?"

"I haven't any," O'Brien admitted.

"You have one now, sweetheart," Myron said. "But I won't take a dime until I improve your present deal."

The actor agreed to the proposition, and soon Myron landed him a contract at Warner Brothers. O'Brien gazed at his first paycheck and asked, "Do they pay by the month out here?"

"No, you stupid Irish bastard," Myron replied. "That's your weekly salary."

Myron's fellow agents recognized his power. When Loretta Young became discontented with her contract at 20th Century-Fox, she asked her agent to negotiate a release. "I'm not powerful enough, Loretta," the agent admitted. "You'd better hire Myron Selznick."

"That drunk? No!" she replied. A friend, director Edward Sutherland, agreed that Myron was the only agent who could deal with the studio boss, Darryl Zanuck. She decided to seek Myron's help.

Loretta rebelled when she was assigned a secondary role in *Lloyds Of London,* which was designed to build up the studio's new star, Tyrone Power. She refused to report for the picture and went off to Hawaii. When she returned, she was greeted with a telegram from the studio lawyers threatening a costly lawsuit unless she reported to the studio. She sent for Myron.

He came to her house and placed a call to Zanuck's office. Zanuck was not available. "Just tell him he can reach me at Loretta's house," Myron told the secretary.

Two minutes later, Zanuck telephoned Myron. A conference was arranged, and Zanuck insisted he would make peace only if Loretta agreed to a new seven-year contract to replace that one that had two years to go. She refused, reasoning that Zanuck was a man's producer and had no concern for the careers of actresses. She refused to sign for more than the remaining two years of her contract.

Zanuck was furious when she refused to renew her contract at the end of the two years. He barred Myron from the studio. For nine months, Loretta's career languished; none of the studios made offers. "I think I'm being blacklisted," she told Myron. He investigated, and her suspicion seemed to be correct.

Myron calculated there was one way to beat the blacklist: offer Loretta Young at half her usual salary. There was one studio boss who couldn't resist such a bargain—Harry Cohn at Columbia. Myron made a three-picture deal with Cohn. The blacklist was broken, and Loretta's salary soared far beyond what Zanuck had offered to pay her.

"Stars should get the money while they can," Myron philosophized. "Their careers don't last very long."

When stars didn't come voluntarily to his agency, he went after them. Myron bought the contract of Fredric March from another agent to whom he promised future commissions. By controlling March, Myron could merchandise package deals, in which he would sell March, another star, a story property, director, and screen writer to a studio. This kind of ready-made picture deal was an innovation in the film industry.

Myron introduced other practices which were later put to use by other high-powered agencies that followed him in Hollywood. He formed production companies for his clients, who could thus earn and keep more money than on a straight salary. Myron also provided financial services for his clients, investing their earnings, caring for their income taxes, overseeing their personal and household expenses. This was the beginning of the business-agent industry in Hollywood.

He trusted no one. All clients were signed to five-year, unbreakable contracts. He put no faith in verbal contracts. Every stipulation of agreements between clients and studios had to be rendered in writing. He accepted the word of no studio boss.

In March of 1935, the quiet, capable Frank Joyce died, and Myron Selznick assumed complete control of the agency, vowing never again to have a partner. At that time he was top man in the

ACTRESSES

Adrienne Allen	Betty Lawford
Rosemary Ames	Evelyn Laye
Mary Astor	Carole Lombard
Binnie Barnes	Myrna Loy
Elisabeth Bergner	Ida Lupino
Edna Best	Jean Muir
Mary Boland	Merle Oberon
Billie Burke	Maureen O'Sullivan
Mrs. Patrick Campbell	Princess Natalie Paley
Ruth Chatterton	Pat Paterson
Constance Collier	ZaSu Pitts
Peggy Conklin	Lily Pons
Frances Dee	Barbara Robbins
Ann Dvorak	Ginger Rogers
Sally Eilers	Dorothy Stickney
Kay Francis	Margaret Sullavan
Helen Hayes	Verree Teasdale
Katharine Hepburn	Genevieve Tobin
Miriam Hopkins	Lupe Velez
Benita Hume	Helen Vinson
Josephine Hutchinson	Fay Wray
Elsa Lanchester	

ACTORS

Walter Abel	Charles Lawton
Richard Arlen	Victor McLaglen
Fred Astaire	Fredric March
Leslie Banks	Herbert Marshall
Richard Barthelmess	Raymond Massey
Ben Bernie	Thomas Meighan
Charles Bickford	Adolphe Menjou
Clive Brook	Thomas Mitchell
Tulio Carminati	Owen Moore
Walter Connelly	Pat O'Brien
Gary Cooper	Laurence Olivier
Jackie Cooper	Eugene Pallette
Ernest Cossart	William Powell
Dudley Digges	George Raft
Henry Fonda	Stanley Ridges
Pierre Fresnay	Guy Standing
Cedric Hardwicke	Lee Tracy
0. P. Heggie	Hugh Williams
Ian Hunter	Robert Woolsey
Boris Karloff	Roland Young
Roscoe Karns	

agency field in Hollywood. His acting clients, in conjunction with his New York liaison, Leland Hayward, were:

In his representation of these performers, Myron adhered to one principle: producers were the enemy. This generality also extended to his brother. He instructed the agents in his employ: "When you talk to David, he's a producer, not my brother."

He proved his point in a negotiation for Fredric March.

David had signed March to a contract for a picture at the salary established by Myron—$15,000 a week. As the starting date for the picture approached, David telephoned Myron to ask for a week's extension because the script wasn't ready. Myron grudgingly agreed. A week later, David called to ask for another week of grace. Myron hung up on his brother.

"You report for work tomorrow," Myron instructed March. "Report every day for a week, and then go in for your check. If it isn't there, we'll sue the hell out of David."

A week passed, and the script was still not in shape. David called his brother to plead for more time. "Give me thirty-five thousand dollars, and we'll give you a further extension," Myron declared. David grudgingly agreed. The film was never made, and March kept the $35,000—less the ten percent that Myron exacted from every transaction for his clients.

Myron Selznick had become the most important agent in Hollywood, a man who wielded more power than some heads of studios, yet he was an intensely unhappy man. He adored his wife Marjorie and their daughter Joan, but he spent an increasing amount of time away from home. And when he did return to his wife, he was usually drunk.

Inviting Myron to a party became more of a social hazard. He usually showed up drunk and exchanged insults or fisticuffs

Fredric March and Janet Gaynor on the set of A STAR IS BORN.

with one or more of the guests. Once he appeared at a party given by the Edgar Selwyns, arriving at 1 A.M. in a state of alcoholic bravado. An alarmed butler inquired, "Sir, were you invited?"

"I was not only invited," Myron replied grandly. "I declined."

Film producers had long shunned movies about Hollywood. Few such films had been successful, the unreal atmosphere of the movie world being difficult to convey on the screen. And producers shrank from film subjects that might denigrate the industry.

David Selznick felt such reservations, even though he had made the entertaining *What Price Hollywood?* at RKO. His attitude was changed after the arrival at his studio of his old friend from Paramount days, William Wellman. The bellicose director had been fighting with Louis B. Mayer ar M-G-M and had asked for release from his contract. Mayer allowed him to go—to Selznick International.

Wellman took with him a young writer, Robert Carson, and a screenplay they had been preparing. It had been drawn from Wellman's own experiences in Hollywood, as well as the saga of John Bowers, an actor whose career had been ruined by talkies. After telling a friend he would commit suicide by "sailing into the sunset," Bowers rented a sailboat on November 15, 1936. Two days later his body washed ashore at Malibu.

David was not immediately enthused about *A Star Is Born*. But Irene Selznick liked it, and after a vacation in Hawaii, he announced he was going ahead with the project. Wellman and Carson were assigned to prepare the script. They were not alone.

Rowland Brown, who had written *What Price Hollywood?* with Adela Rogers St. Johns and Gene Fowler, was hired to rewrite *A Star Is Born*. "But David, the script is fine as it is," said Brown. He was discharged. David was convinced that no first draft of a script could be satisfactory.

David engaged Dorothy Parker and Alan Campbell to work on a completely new version of *A Star Is Born*. When they submitted their script, David summoned Robert Carson to his office.

"I've got somebody's script of *A Star Is Born,*" Selznick said in a confidential tone. "I'd like you to look it over and make whatever changes are necessary."

"Whose script is it?" Carson asked.

"Dotty Parker and Alan Campbell's."

"But I can't rewrite their script!" Carson protested.

"Don't worry—they won't know."

One day over lunch Miss Parker was fretting, "I don't understand. Our script is constantly being changed. I must talk to David about it."

"You don't have to; I'm rewriting your script," Carson confessed.

"Why, that son of a bitch!" Miss Parker exploded.

She confronted Selznick with his deviousness. He was unconcerned. Next he summoned his junior writers, Budd Schulberg and Ring Lardner, Jr., and put them to work on a rewrite of the Parker-Campbell-Carson rewrite of the Wellman-Carson original. "But don't tell anyone what you're doing," David cautioned.

Schulberg and Lardner conducted their work in secrecy, but one day their pages were mistakenly routed to the office of Miss Parker and Campbell.

Wellman was furious with the script changes and restored much of his original. His contract with David had been negotiated by Myron Selznick, and it was as tough and restrictive as any Myron had imposed on the major studios. One clause limited the number of visits David could make to a Wellman set.

For the role of the movie actress David took a chance on Janet Gaynor. Her career had flourished at Fox in the late-silent and early-talkie period, but by 1936 her innocent sweetness seemed passé. As the fated Norman Maine, David chose Fredric March. He had to pay dearly for the actor, whose agent was Myron Selznick.

The filming proceeded smoothly, despite a degree of tenseness between Miss Gaynor and Wellman, who had clashed with her on *Small Town Girl* at M-G-M. Wellman suffered an attack of influenza toward the end of shooting and asked his friend Victor

Fleming to direct the sequence of March's funeral. After viewing the footage, Wellman told David, "I want to shoot it over."

"Why, for God's sake?" David replied. "Vic did a good job."

"I know he did. But the scene needs something. I want the audience to get a real shock. When the crowd moves in on her, I want her to scream."

David agreed to the retake, and the cast was reassembled. Wellman asked Miss Gaynor, "Can you scream?"

"I don't know; I never tried," she answered.

"Goddammit, you'd better scream!" he said. She did, providing an electric moment at the climax of the picture.

The first preview was in Pomona, and the Selznick International hierarchy, headed by David and Jock Whitney, traveled in limousines to the orange-country town. Wellman was nervous about the preview, and he and Robert Carson stopped at bars en route to bolster their courage. Wellman's fears seemed to be confirmed at the beginning of the film; the screen was gloomy and indistinct.

"My God, I shot it too dark," exclaimed the director, who had tried to mute the garish hues of Technicolor during the filming. Now he feared he had gone too far. He sent Carson to tell the projectionist to brighten the picture.

The adjustment did little good, and Carson was dispatched again. On his third trip to the booth, Carson was told by the projectionist: "What do you want me to do—burn up the film? I can't turn the light up any higher. The trouble is the smudge."

"The smudge?" Carson asked.

"Yes, they're smudging in the orange groves tonight because of the freeze. The smoke is coming through the ventilating system."

The explanation did little to raise Wellman's spirits. He was devastated when half the audience evacuated after the first half hour.

"Jesus, they hate it!" he muttered.

Carson rushed to the lobby and interviewed the walkouts. They were enjoying the picture and hated to leave, they said, but it was time to refuel the smudge pots.

Carole Lombard, NOTHING SACRED

The Selznick delegation gathered on the sidewalk in front of the theater after the preview. David was worried. Jock Whitney was crying. He had been profoundly moved by the funeral finale.

"What we've got here," David analyzed, "is a picture that is half comedy and half tragedy. We've got to reshoot it and make it all comedy or all tragedy."

Wellman was incensed by the proposal and challenged David to a fistfight on the spot. The sidewalk conference ended amid shouts and threats, and the caravan returned to Los Angeles.

Jock Whitney and Joan Payson Whitney opted for all comedy. They had been impressed by *My Man Godfrey,* the comedy hit of 1936. David was undecided, and he asked John Lee Mahin to work on possible solutions. The writer viewed *A Star Is Born* and reported, "David, the picture is damn near perfect. You can't make it a comedy. The handwriting is on the wall when March first sees the girl at Hollywood Bowl. It has to be a tragedy."

Mahin offered one additional scene in which March prepared sandwiches for his wife's return from the studio, then she came home too tired to make love. The scene helped motivate the husband's suicide. Selznick ordered the beach house rebuilt, and the additional scene was filmed.

A second preview in Huntington Park was enthusiastically received. Afterward Jock Whitney was once again crying. David Selznick beamed.

A Star Is Born proved to be the first big success of Selznick International, winning Academy nominations for the picture, Miss Gaynor, March, Wellman for direction and original story (with Robert Carson[2]), and Campbell, Miss Parker, and Carson for screenplay. David Selznick pondered what film project to undertake next. Unable to decide, he made one of his periodic ventures to New York—in style, as always.

A private railroad car was hired and attached to the Santa Fe

---

[2] Only Wellman and Carson won Oscars, for their original story. W. Howard Greene was given a special award for his color photography of *A Star Is Born.*

Tommy Kelly

The Cave Scene, THE ADVENTURES OF TOM SAWYER

Chief. At each end of the car were drawing rooms occupied by Mr. and Mrs. David 0. Selznick and Mr. and Mrs. John Hay Whitney. Quarters were provided for the maids of Mrs. Selznick and Mrs. Whitney and the manservants of Mr. Selznick and Mr. Whitney. So he could discuss film projects en route, David also brought along William Wellman, Ben Hecht, Robert Carson, and the new member of Hecht's writing factory, Charles Samuels. They occupied bedrooms in the middle of the car, a matter which rankled both Wellman and Hecht. They were further irritated when the Selznicks and the Whitneys remained in their drawing rooms to eat their specially prepared meals and drink from the large supply of vintage Moët champagne which the Whitneys had brought along.

At Chicago, the private car had to be moved from the LaSalle Street Station to the Dearborn Street Station, where it would be joined to the *Twentieth Century Limited.* Much to the annoyance of the stationmaster, the transfer was delayed because Selznick did not emerge from his drawing room. Newsmen were waiting to interview him, and they recorded an exchange between the stationmaster and Selznick's manservant.

"I've got to move this car off the tracks!" the stationmaster insisted.

"Mr. Selznick," the valet sniffed, "does not yet have his trousers on."

David finally pulled on his trousers and emerged for the press conference. The railroad car was moved to the other station, where the journey was continued without the Selznicks and Whitneys, who flew on to Louisville for the Kentucky Derby.

"Let's have a party!" said Hecht as the *Twentieth Century* began rattling through the Chicago suburbs.

"Damn right!" Wellman agreed. "What about booze?"

"The Whitneys' champagne, of course," said Hecht.

The proposal was too delicious to resist, especially after the slights of the eastward journey. Samuels and Carson were dispatched to the other cars with instructions to invite the most attractive women on board to share the Whitneys' champagne. The pretty passengers were unbelieving at first, but a few ven-

David Selznick at his desk.

tured to the private car. Word of the party spread through the
train, and others joined the riotous festivities.

The party continued through the night and did not cease
until the *Twentieth Century* had pulled into Grand Central
Station. All were reeling from their indulgence, and Hecht
announced that he had turned stone blind. He recovered his
sight after stepping onto the platform. He and his fellow revelers
had managed to consume every bottle of the large supply that
the Whitneys had transported east. Mr. Whitney was displeased.
David Selznick was mildly amused.

The social order resumed in New York. David and Irene
Selznick were quartered in the Waldorf Towers; his employees
occupied rooms in the lower part of the hotel. One evening

Selznick summoned Robert Carson to his suite.

Carson found Selznick in one of the bedrooms, lying naked on a table as he was being rubbed by a masseur. David was uttering loud cries of pain.

"My God, what's the matter?" Carson asked.

"Gas," replied David. "I have a terrific pain in my lower abdomen. Owww!"

"But it might be appendicitis. You shouldn't massage it."

"Gas," David insisted. "Been eating too much."

"I still think you should call a doctor."

"No, it's just gas. Oooh!"

Selznick instructed Carson to sit down, and as the rubbing continued, he said, "I've got to make a decision about my next picture. It's between that comedy Bill wants to do, *Nothing Sacred*, and the story you like, *Dark Victory*. Now I want you to tell me the story again. Oh, God, it hurts!"

"David, I don't really think you're in any shape to listen to a story."

David waved his hand. "That's all right—go ahead. I can listen. Ohhh!"

Carson dutifully began his recital of the tale of a headstrong woman who goes blind. His narrative was punctuated by groans, shouts of pain, and emissions of gas from Selznick. All three had subsided by the time Carson reached the end of his tale.

"It's a good story," Selznick commented. "And I feel much better. I'll let you know what I decide."

A day later David announced that his next picture would be *Nothing Sacred*.[3]

Nothing Sacred, David Selznick's only excursion into farce, was the product of an inspired collaboration. Ben Hecht's script provided a fine cynical view of small-town narrow-mindedness and big-city exploitation. Dorothy Parker supplied witty lines, and

[3] Selznick sold *Dark Victory* to Warner Brothers, where it became a successful vehicle for Bette Davis.

Bill Wellman added brilliant slapstick. Selznick edited the script with taste and made humorous contributions of his own. Their imaginations ran wild. Seeking a way to illustrate the small town's antagonism toward the city slicker, Wellman devised an outrageously funny scene: as Fredric March strode down a dusty street, a small child rushed out to bite him on the leg.

March was capital as the smooth-talking promoter, and Carole Lombard gave one of her superb characterizations as the country girl doomed by radium poisoning. Hecht had written a brilliant script, but he didn't finish it. He and David had one of their occasional imbroglios, and Hecht stalked off.

David was desperate for a finish. Hecht had written up to the point where the girl's ailment was discovered to be spurious, after a nation-wide campaign to exploit it. If he knew what was to happen next, Hecht had left no hint. David canvassed his writers for a solution, offering young Budd Schulberg and Ring Lardner, Jr., their own picture to write if they could provide an ending. Theirs was admittedly a weak one—March and Lombard sneaked off to Europe together. But it was the only one David could find, and he ended the film that way. The reward for Schulberg and Lardner never eventuated.

David's passion for Victorian novels again asserted itself with *The Prisoner Of Zenda*. The Anthony Hope adventure was given a sumptuous production, with romantic portrayals by Ronald Colman, Madeleine Carroll, and Douglas Fairbanks, Jr., and it proved to be a popular attraction.

The Young in Heart was less successful. It was a wry, sentimental tale of an amiable family of crooks, but it lacked enough excitement to capture a wide audience. For the matriarch of the family David had sought the services of the famed Broadway star Maude Adams, who was then teaching dramatics at Stephens College. David persuaded her to come to Hollywood for a screen test, but she left the following day, convinced that she should not attempt a comeback. David cast a lesser star of the American theater, Minnie Dupree, along with Janet Gaynor, Douglas Fairbanks, Jr., Paulette Goddard, Billie Burke, and Roland Young. The film was notable for marking Miss Gaynor's retirement from the screen.

Next came another classic, *The Adventures of Tom Sawyer.*

David launched a nation-wide campaign for an unknown boy to play the title role, and he selected an East Bronx fireman's son named Tommy Kelly. H. C. Potter began directing the film, but after ten days he rebelled against David's interference and walked off the picture. Norman Taurog replaced him. *The Adventures of Tom Sawyer* was authentic Americana, but it did only fair business. Tommy Kelly failed to develop the appeal of a previous Selznick discovery, Freddie Bartholomew, and after a middling career as a juvenile actor he retired and later became a schoolteacher.

Made for Each Other was a disappointment. David considered it good showmanship to cast Carole Lombard in a tragedy at a time when she was highly successful in screwball comedies. For her leading man he borrowed the engaging young James Stewart from M-G-M. The completed film, which concerned the vicissitudes of a young married couple, seemed ineffective to David.

Myron Selznick suddenly fell ill. He had been drinking at his usual pace, paying scant heed to his health, and a slight cold turned into lobar pneumonia. His condition worsened, and his chances of survival were said to be critical. David was frantic. He sought advice from doctor friends and was told that Myron's life might be saved by a new serum being developed in New York.

David quickly made arrangements. For five thousand dollars he chartered a TWA plane to transport the serum from New York to Los Angeles. The flight arrived in sixteen hours and nine minutes, two hours faster than normal. The serum was rushed to Santa Monica Hospital, where Myron lay in a coma. A day later he was reported out of danger.

"This is too good to waste on Myron," David announced to his staff. "Let's put it in the picture."

Made for Each Other went back into production for a sequence in which the child of Stewart and Lombard was saved by a serum flown across the country. The device was more successful in the case of Myron. The picture died.

David Selznick entertains D.W. Griffith on a movie set.

The memos.

After David Selznick had become an independent producer, the flood became a Niagara. The memo became as endemic to Selznick as the Goldwynism ("Anybody who sees a psychiatrist should have his head examined") was to Sam Goldwyn. Unlike Goldwyn, who first fostered, then repudiated his reputation for the Goldwynism, David Selznick clung to the memo to the end of his life. Ignoring cavil and satirical jibes, he maintained the memo as his own peculiar mode of communication.

The memo fitted his temperament and his way of functioning. He realized that talk was cheap inside a studio and the logorrhea of production conferences was wasteful and often futile. The written word had more permanence and value, he believed.

He also was concerned about the fleeting nature of ideas, particularly his own. Since he frequently conceived his ideas during the dark hours of the morning, he could not always expect his studio aides to be present. The memos were distributed the following day.

Long-time Selznick employees became skilled in determining the nature of the boss's message by the opening phrase of the memo. There were two main categories:

1. The Retrospective Memo, which began: "It is a great pity that . . ." This was followed by a criticism of functions neglected or mishandled.

2. The Anticipatory Memo, starting: "I am worried lest . . ." Then came a warning against mistakes in future operations.

David was also addicted to the thinking-out-loud memo which sometimes ended with the curious message, "Disregard the above." Occasionally a memo contained a cryptic sign-off such as: "Report to me immediately at your earliest convenience." Most of the memos carried the phrase "Dictated but not read." David hated to read memos, particularly his own.

The Selznick memos grew more verbose with the years. The company's sales chief, Neil Agnew, once sent David a telegram urging that a new film be cut in length. David was furious, and he answered with his reasons why the film should be released intact. The message measured twelve feet in length. Agnew wired Selznick: "Never mind the picture—cut the telegrams."

Taking dictation from David Selznick was punishing work for a stenographer. He insisted that his every word be recorded, and he even supplied his own punctuation. Two secretaries were available for dictation, as well as Marcella Rabwin, who had married a noted surgeon but remained as executive secretary. A file clerk was employed full-time to cross-file the memos.

Some of the memos were nonsense, many were repetitive. When he put his mind to it, David could produce some creditable writing. This was especially true when he was working under a deadline, rather than when he had leisure to compose his words. "I work best under pressure," he admitted. His weak point was dialogue. Screen writers despaired of David's attempts to write scenes; the language was stilted and sentimental. Commenting on his style and on his choice of Victorian novels as screen material, Ben Hecht remarked, "Unfortunately, David, you did all your reading before you were seventeen."

David was a tireless executive. Through the memos and through personal conferences, he directed every phase of production. He was not intuitive. David needed to think his way through problems, and he did that best while alone, soliloquizing to a stenographer. He found the memo had another advantage: it discouraged back-talk. He meant his instructions by memo to be carried out, without further questioning.

He usually arrived at the studio in late morning and continued working until long past midnight. He expected office staff to conform to his own erratic schedule. Once he finished dictating to a secretary at seven-thirty in the evening and told her: "That will be all for now; I'll call you later."

"But Mr. Selznick, I have a dinner engagement at eight," she said.

"Nobody in this office has a dinner engagement," he replied coldly.

He thought nothing of calling his aides at three and four in the morning to deliver instructions which could not be acted upon until the following day. One Saturday afternoon, his publicity director, Joseph Steele, was paged three times from golf fairways to answer the telephone; each time Selznick was on the wire with a new suggestion about a publicity campaign.

Selznick's disregard for normal working hours prompted John Lee Mahin's own interpretation of the initials D.O.S.: Death On Sleep.

Waiting for an appointment with the boss could be a nervewracking ordeal. The employee was told by Marcella Rabwin, "Stand by; Mr. Selznick wants to see you." Many writers and directors did their standing by at the bar across Washington Boulevard from the studio, and some later blamed Selznick for their alcoholism.

An appointment for a conference at Selznick's home offered

no assurance of punctuality. The conferees could wait in the Selznick living room for hours while David conducted business on the telephone upstairs. He extended no hospitality to his employees. If they had been waiting through midday, the butler appeared and announced: "Mr. Selznick is not available now. Would you please go and have lunch and come back?"

Such treatment infuriated director William Wellman. When he and his writer, Robert Carson, were turned away one day, Wellman insisted that they drink their lunch. Selznick recognized their condition when he finally joined them. "I think you'd better go home and come back tomorrow," he said with unamused indulgence. "You're not making much sense."

With his insatiable zest for work, David pushed himself to the utmost. He took Benzedrine pills to keep himself alert through the long studio hours, then gulped down barbiturates so he could sleep. He worked punishing hours while editing a picture. He sat beside his chief cutter, Hal Kern, while scene after scene unreeled on the projection room screen. When Selznick failed to respond to a question, Kern walked him through the darkened studio streets. They returned refreshed to the projection room and continued their work. Kern repeated the ritual three times, until it was impossible for David to maintain his attention.

David's search for perfection was inexhaustible. During one cutting session he personally took a pair of scissors and removed one frame of film from a scene he considered minutely overlength.

A scene in *The Prisoner of Zenda* called for the villain, Raymond Massey, to strike a spy over the head with an iron bar. Because the actual blow had to be played off-screen, David wanted the sound effect to resemble the crushing of a skull. Hal Kern recorded a crowbar pounding a leather pillow. "That doesn't sound like it," David said. Kern returned to the recording studio and struck blows on a watermelon, coconut, pumpkin, etc. "No, you don't have it," David insisted. Kern finally went to a local slaughterhouse and purchased a calf's head. He smashed it with a crowbar and played the sound for David.

"That's it!" David declared.

As independent producer, David was obviously enjoying himself tremendously. He was doing exactly what he wanted to do: to make pictures. And to make them without interference, in a tradition of quality, and in doing so honoring his father's memory. He was so convinced of the rightness of his course that he couldn't understand why Budd Schulberg didn't want to do the same thing.

After leaving Dartmouth University, Budd had been hired as a junior writer by Selznick. He began first as a reader of story material at fifty dollars a week, then became a writer at seventy-five dollars a week, rising to a hundred after six months. David, who had firm notions of dynasty, enjoyed the notion of hiring the son of B.P. Schulberg, who had given David his first important job in Hollywood. David cherished the dream that Budd, like himself a second-generation film maker, might play an important role in the Selznick organization. He assigned Budd to work with another son of a famous man, Ring Lardner, Jr.

Budd became discontented with his service at the studio. He realized that the Selznick operation, concentrating solely on big-budget productions, was not geared for the junior writer. His work rarely appeared on the screen. Once Budd declared himself on strike and went off to Malibu to write short stories. After sixty days he felt remorse and returned to the studio. Before Budd could apologize, David remarked: "I'm sorry I haven't been able to see you; I've been terribly busy." Budd's frustration was compounded; he hadn't even been missed.

Finally he confronted David and said: "I want out. I'm disappointed working here."

David was astonished. "Why?" he asked.

"Because I have written four scripts for you and nothing has happened to them. You always go for Maxwell Anderson or some other big name. Not until I become a big-name writer will you use anything of mine."

"I'm disappointed in you, too, Budd," Selznick replied.

"Why?—I've written my ass off."

"I know you've been conscientious as a writer. But when I

was working for B.P., I peppered him with memos—about buying book properties, about picking up stars' options, about everything. You've been here eighteen months and you've never written a memo."

"David, the difference is that when you were sending those memos to my father, you were preparing yourself for what you're doing now. I don't want to be a producer. I want to write."

"I know," David said resignedly. "But I was just hoping that some day your producers' blood would assert itself." He agreed to let Budd leave the studio.

"Please tell me about yourself."

"Mr. Selznick, you sent for me. Please tell me about yourself."

David Selznick leaned back in his desk chair and roared with laughter. "This is the first time I've been put on the defensive by a man I'm considering for a job," he said. "I like your psychology."

They formed an immediate bond, David and the slim, self-assured Texan with a mustache that looked penciled on. In the early stages of Selznick International, Russell Birdwell had been summoned to the Selznick office from the Los Angeles *Examiner,* for which he had been covering the Weyerhauser kidnaping in Tacoma. He had been reporting crime for the Hearst newspapers for seventeen years, and his colorful succinct dispatches had attracted David's attention.

David rose from his chair and began pacing the room as he talked of plans for his new company. The movies would be made and sold with the vigor shown by his father, David said with a glance toward the oil painting of L.J. Selznick. He told of his father's rich imagination for showmanly stunts; for example, his payment of a thousand dollars daily to Alla Nazimova. David himself had worked in the Selznick publicity department as a lad, and he believed he might have turned to public relations work if he hadn't become a film producer.

"I don't want any press-agentry," David declared. "I want imagination, but it must be accurate and true and possess a quality that will fully match the product we hopefully will produce. You may be daring, but never sensational for the sake of sensationalism."

Those instructions, though not always heeded, provided the basis for Hollywood's most successful marriage of showman and exploiteer. In an industry that respected ballyhoo almost as an art form, the Selznick-Birdwell association was unparalleled in outrageous invention.

Birdwell resigned from the Hearst organization and moved into the studio bungalow Joseph P. Kennedy had built for Gloria Swanson when he was sponsoring her career. Birdwell acquired two secretaries, blonde and brunette, whom he dubbed Miss Lightning and Miss Thunder, and he hired the largest publicity staff of any independent film company. Then he began startling the industry wih his flash and noise.

For *Little Lord Fauntleroy*, Birdwell hired dozens of painters and assigned them to create the world's largest sign. In the middle of the night they daubed a three-mile section of Washington Boulevard, from the Los Angeles City limits to the entrance of M-G-M studio, with the message in ten-foot letters: DAVID 0. SELZNICK'S PRODUCTION OF THE IMMORTAL LITTLE LORD FAUNTLEROY WILL HAVE ITS WORLD PREMIERE AT . . . The sign continued with the date and place of the premiere and other salient facts about the production, inscribed in shining white paint on the black pavement.

Birdwell sat back and awaited the reaction. It began shortly after dawn as aircraft workers on their way to the Douglas Aircraft plant stuck their heads out windows and zigzagged their cars while they tried to read the sign. Calls poured into the Culver City police station and city hall from perplexed citizens. Irate city officials consulted the statutes and could find none that covered the Birdwell stunt. Their indignation melted as reporters and photographers flocked to Culver City to cover the event, spreading the city's name throughout the world.

Birdwell next mused on why Culver City, which produced as many movies as Hollywood, should not be entitled to the name of Hollywood, especially since the Culver City product included the quality films of Selznick International. The civic leaders of the incorporated Culver City happily agreed with Birdwell's rea-

Russell Birdwell and Carole Lombard planning a publicity campaign.

soning and plumped for use of the name Hollywood, since Hollywood itself was merely a neighborhood within the city of Los Angeles.

Civic and business leaders of Hollywood were inflamed by the proposal, and threats and resolutions were hurled back and forth by the two suburbs. Birdwell stepped in as peacemaker. He invited both factions to the premiere of *Little Lord Fauntleroy* at Grauman's Chinese Theatre, where they buried a symbolic hatchet in the forecourt cement.

Edward VIII abdicated the English throne as *The Garden of Allah* was being released, and Birdwell searched for a way to connect the two events. He learned that the author of the book, Robert Hichens, was still alive and living in a villa called The

Garden of Allah in Egypt. After considerable difficulty, Birdwell reached Hichens by telephone.

"Would you please invite the Duke and Duchess of Windsor to spend their honeymoon at The Garden of Allah?" Birdwell implored.

Hichens evidenced no interest in the suggestion. After a forty-five minute conversation, Birdwell concluded that his mission had failed. But a few days later, dispatches from Europe carried the news that the Windsors had been invited to visit novelist Hichens at The Garden of Allah in Egypt.

The Duke's successor, George VI, also figured in a Birdwell stunt. On the day of the new king's coronation, Birdwell assembled the British members of the cast of *The Prisoner of Zenda* for a solemn, well-reported ceremony in honor of the new monarch.

Birdwell assembled his staff to consider plans for the premiere of *The Prisoner Of Zenda*. An assistant provided the information that a town in Ontario had been named Zenda after the Anthony Hope novel. Total population: thirteen.

Publicity man Jackson Parks spoke up:"Why don't we fly the whole town to New York for the premiere at the Radio City Music Hall?"

"Brilliant!" exclaimed Birdwell, and he dispatched an agent to the Ontario hamlet to make arrangements. But the inhabitants were busy with the haying and cheese-making season and had no interest in the crazy proposal by a city slicker. Birdwell flew to Ontario and found to his consternation that the Zenda inhabitants were indifferent to his stunt. All except one. A farmer boy expressed interest in Birdwell's tales of the dazzling females to be found in New York. The boy converted his family, and they convinced the rest of the town to make the trip.

Twelve of the thirteen Zenda residents were flown to New York, where press coverage of their visit was immense. The Zendan left at home was an ancient lady deemed unsafe for travel. Canadian news services visited her and splashed the country with stories and photographs of "The Prisoner of Zenda."

A chance remark about a onetime star prompted a Birdwell

stunt for *The Young in Heart*. He convinced the casting department to hire nine former stars as extras for the picture. Then he persuaded them to sign a petition to the Governor of California pleading for Career Insurance, or the Mandatory Film Savings Law.

For another Selznick production, Birdwell hired a Lady Godiva to ride a horse through Los Angeles streets wearing only a long wig and a sign with the words NOTHING SACRED.

Birdwell sought a pregnant woman to give birth in the theater on premiere night, but could find none who could guarantee such accurate timing. Instead, he hired a double for the picture's star, Carole Lombard. The look-alike arrived early for the premiere and posed for photographs as Carole Lombard. Later the real Carole arrived, confounding the press.

Lombard proved an ideal accomplice for Birdwell's schemes. She had a sprightly imagination of her own, and she delighted in stunts that startled Hollywood and the world. One day she was expounding to Birdwell about a foreign director who had been complaining about paying his taxes. The actress excoriated the foreigner and declared she felt privileged to pay her taxes in a free country. Birdwell quickly sent for a wire service reporter, and Lombard's remarks drew headlines and a personal call from President Roosevelt. Birdwell received a personal commendation from David Selznick: "As a guy who thinks he's a pretty good publicity man himself, I congratulate and salute you on this one."

Selznick was not always in favor of the Lombard-Birdwell stunts. One day he summoned the actress and the publicist to his office for a lecture about their excess of zeal. As "Honorary Mayor of Culver City," Miss Lombard had declared a public holiday as her first act in office. The Selznick employees took her action literally and failed to appear for work.

"That little stunt cost the studio fifty thousand dollars," David declared. "Now tell me what stunt is worth fifty thousand dollars."

He was unconvinced by Birdwell's arguments that the holiday had garnered more than fifty thousand dollars' worth of publicity for *Made for Each Other*.

The Lombard-Birdwell collaboration continued. She spotted

a pretty young stenographer at Paramount named Margaret Tallichet and convinced David to give her a small role in *A Star Is Born*. For a full day Miss Lombard acted as makeup girl and hairdresser for the budding actress, who was given a term contract at Selznick International. Birdwell attracted further attention by insuring Miss Tallichet's Southern accent with Lloyds of London for a million dollars—the term of the policy having been twenty-four hours.

The climax of the Lombard-Birdwell association came when she took over his position as publicity director of Selznick International for a day. With ex-newspaperman Gene Fowler as her legman, she devised a variety of outrageous stunts.

Nothing was sacred to Russell Birdwell, including the Presidency. In 1937, Janet Gaynor was among the film personalities invited to the White House to help President Roosevelt launch the March of Dimes campaign for infantile paralysis. After the photographs had been taken, Birdwell lingered to speak to the President.

"Mr. President, did I overhear you say that Janet Gaynor is 'cute as a button'?" asked the publicist.

Mr. Roosevelt smiled. "That would make a good box in the AP, wouldn't it?" he said.

"Yes, sir," said Birdwell.

"In that case, you overheard me correctly," said the President. Birdwell handed out the item to the press, and it was printed widely, aiding Miss Gaynor's comeback in *A Star Is Born.*

Occasionally the Birdwell flamboyance came in conflict with David Selznick's growing reputation as a film industry leader. One day he summoned the publicity chief to his office for a reprimand over a stunt in which a former FBI man had been hired to guard the Selznick International story department.

"But you said yourself that an idea is worth a million dollars," Birdwell replied. "What could be more logical than to assign a brainguard—not a bodyguard—to watch over your story properties?"

"It's cheap," David said. "I'm embarrassed and shocked. My friends have called up this morning after seeing the story in the papers. You've made me the laughingstock of Hollywood."

Birdwell's face reddened. He glanced up at the oil painting of Lewis J. Selznick and said sharply, "I guess I've been working for the wrong Selznick."

He turned and stalked toward the door.

"Wait!" David said. David rushed across the room and took the publicity man by the arm.

"Bird, you're absolutely right," David remarked. "That's just the kind of stunt my father would have loved. I should have listened to Myron. He told me not pay any attention to the swells who thought your stunt was undignified. To hell with them!"

Russell Birdwell's greatest challenge lay ahead, as did David Selznick's. It was signaled by a message on the company teletype from the New York story editor, Kay Brown. She reported that she was sending David by air mail the galley proofs and a synopsis of a new novel. She added this message:

"I beg, urge, coax and plead with you to read this at once. I know that after you read the book you will drop everything and buy it."

IV

PINNACLE

*The Greatest Picture
Ever Made*

David Selznick and Vivien Leigh on Oscar Night, February 29, 1940

WHEN DAVID SELZNICK WAS THIRTY-SEVEN,
he had reached the height of his career.
The film world acclaimed his genius
in transferring Gone With the Wind *to the screen.*
Two Hollywood wives discussed the Selznick achievement.
"You must be very proud of David,"
remarked Frances Goldwyn.
"Indeed I am,"
replied Irene Mayer Selznick.
"How simply wonderful for him,"
said Mrs. Goldwyn.
"Yes, it has been wonderful,"
said Mrs. Selznick, adding reflectively,
"but I don't think it will be worth it."

David Selznick did not respond immediately to the entreaty of Kay Brown.

The book arrived, along with a twenty-five-page synopsis. At 1037 pages, *Gone With the Wind* was far too lengthy for a movie producer to read, even one as literate as David Selznick. He consumed the synopsis and was impressed, but not overly so. Like all producers, he had a built-in prejudice against Civil War movies. According to local legend, Civil War pictures never made money. Oh, there was *Birth of a Nation*, but that was long ago— a freak.

David stalled. Kay Brown's persuasion failed to move him, and she explained her plight to the board chairman of Selznick International, Jock Whitney.

"Keep at him," instructed Whitney. "If he doesn't buy the book, I will."

"The hell he will!" said David when he heard the news. On July 8, 1936, he directed Kay Brown to buy *Gone With the Wind* for fifty thousand dollars. Then he went off to Hawaii for a vacation with Irene, taking along a copy of Margaret Mitchell's novel.

He was astounded by the task that lay before him. Somehow he had to compress a half million words of labyrinthine plot into the stringent requirements of a movie script. It seemed impossible, but David plunged ahead in his usual, methodical manner. He made elaborate notes in the margin of his book, indicating what scenes and characters might be cut and what should be retained.

When he returned from Hawaii, he realized the wisdom of his purchase. *Gone With the Wind* was becoming a publishing phenomenon. Although some of the highbrow critics sniffed at the book's ponderousness and sentimentality, the reviews were generally good. At three dollars a copy—$2.75 pre-publication— *Gone With the Wind* began selling at an astounding rate. Within three weeks 176,000 copies had been bought. In six months sales totaled a million; in a year, 1,690,000.

David Selznick's gamble was looking better all the time. Yet *Gone With the Wind* was fraught with dangers. Obviously the film would require an immense outlay. His partners in Selznick

International were beginning to grow restive over his spending. Although he had produced prestigious films and some had been money-makers, the company was losing money at an alarming rate. In his constant search for quality, he had assembled a studio staff comparable to the best of the major studios. But the major studios used their staffs to pour forth fifty pictures a year while David produced a meticulously crafted two or three.

His problems with *Gone With the Wind* were not merely financial. Although he had proved himself adept at translating famous novels to the screen, he had never been faced with a book so recently established in readers' minds. He could make minor alterations of Dickens and not upset moviegoers who had not read *David Copperfield* since childhood. But millions of Americans were reading *Gone With the Wind* and envisioning its characters and scenes. A film producer who deviated too far from the Margaret Mitchell original could find himself pilloried by irate readers.

David was in no hurry to make the movie. He reasoned it would be wiser to let the novel's popularity run its course and to allow readers' memories to grow mellow and less distinct.

There was another reason for the delay in filming. Selznick International was obliged to deliver a number of productions for release by United Artists. Compelling reasons developed so that David did not want *Gone With the Wind* to be one of them. He continued making other films for United Artists while preparing *Gone With the Wind.*

David had learned enough about exploitation from his father to know that he could not allow an attraction to lie fallow for two or three years. He had to find means to keep alive the public's interest in *Gone With the Wind.*

The author was no help. From the beginning Margaret Mitchell made it plain that she would not go along with the Hollywood hoopla. The frail-looking but iron-willed Atlanta lady refused to consider traveling to California to assist on the script. She reasoned that if the picture turned out badly, she would then be blamed for it by Southerners. She also refused to participate in the national pastime of casting the picture. She made only one suggestion. A devout follower of the Marx Brothers, she proposed Groucho for the role of Rhett Butler.

A few weeks after he purchased *Gone With the Wind,* David summoned his publicity director, Russell Birdwell.

"I'm on trial with this book," said David. "If the picture fails, I'll lose everything. That's just what L.B. wants. He'd like me to fall on my ass so I'd have to crawl back to him at Metro. I don't plan to oblige him."

David outlined his need to keep *Gone With the Wind* in the public consciousness for the more than two years before he would be able to make the picture.

"Why don't we put on a nation-wide search for a girl to play Scarlett?" David suggested. "We did that stunt with Tom Sawyer, and we convinced both the press and public that the search was legitimate. We can do it again."

That was all Birdwell needed. He immediately put his staff to work on a campaign to seek an unknown to play Scarlett O'Hara. Three top-flight talent executives were dispatched throughout the country to interview hopefuls: Oscar Serlin to the North and East, Maxwell Arnow to the South, and Charles Morrison to the West. George Cukor, whom David had chosen to direct *Gone With the Wind,* was also sent to the South, and he barely escaped bodily harm in the melees that ensued.

Mail poured into the Selznick studio from hopeful Scarletts who offered their physical specifications; the letters were sometimes accompanied by photographs of the applicants wearing Southern-belle gowns, or, in some instances, nothing at all. On Christmas morning, David Selznick went to his front door to find a seven-foot replica of the book of *Gone With the Wind.* Out of it popped a hoopskirt-gowned girl who announced, "I am your Scarlett O'Hara!"

In time Selznick hired extra guards to prevent applicants for Scarlett from crashing the studio. Birdwell duly reported this fact to the press.

David hinted to columnists that he might consider an established actress if his Search for Scarlett should fail. The first name he mentioned was Norma Shearer, whose husband, Irving

Thalberg, had recently died. The Shearer fans erupted with indignation at the notion that the lady Norma might play the hellcat Scarlett. Miss Shearer announced that she would not consider the role.

Katharine Hepburn was not so reluctant. She insisted to her former boss at RKO: "The part was practically written for me. I am Scarlett O'Hara!"

David was blunt in his reply: "I can't imagine Rhett Butler chasing you for ten years." Still, he didn't rule her out as a possibility, and he instructed George Cukor to make a test of Miss Hepburn as Scarlett. She bluntly refused. "If you don't know whether I can act by now, you never will," she told David.

Many prominent actresses tested for the role of Scarlett, as did hundreds of unknown ones. Among the latter was a New York model named Edythe Marrener, who had been discovered by Irene Mayer Selznick in a millinery showing. After failing the test, the girl changed her name to Susan Hayward. Two other candidates who received serious consideration were Frances Dee, wife of Joel McCrea, and Margaret Tallichet, Carole Lombard's discovery.

Birdwell's publicity mill issued the figures: $92,000 had been spent in the Search of Scarlett; 1400 young women had been interviewed before cameras; 149,000 feet of black-and-white and 13,000 feet of Technicolor film had been used for the interviews; $10,000 had been spent to test 59 candidates at the studio.

At last David decided on his Scarlett. She was to be the vivacious Paulette Goddard, protégée of Charlie Chaplin.

Only one detail remained. In granting such a boon to an actress, David needed to be sure his choice was free from possibility of scandal. And although Miss Goddard was generally acknowledged to be the third Mrs. Chaplin, the circumstances of their wedding remained clouded.

"You can be Scarlett if you will show me the marriage license," said David.

"But we were married at sea!" she replied.

"Okay, but show me the license."

Miss Goddard failed to do so and was removed from consideration. The Search for Scarlett went on. By this time almost every female star in Hollywood had been mentioned for the role, and David was quite naturally delighted with the attention he was getting, both in the press and from the actresses themselves. Myron Selznick was also enjoying the Search. As an important investor in Selznick International, he had a big stake in his brother's gamble, and gambling was something the Selznicks greatly enjoyed. Myron helped the campaign by placing his own clients in the race for Scarlett; he also was able to lure new names to his agency with the promise that they would be seriously considered for the most-sought film role of the decade.

With boyish enthusiasm, David and Myron began planning a party. It was to be held at Myron's lavish mountain home near Lake Arrowhead, and all the famous candidates for Scarlett O'Hara would be invited. None of the weekenders would be privy to the scheme except David and Myron, who could watch with vast amusement the competition of the Scarletts.

Myron assigned one of his assistants, Collier Young, to make the arrangements. Everything was executed in the elegant Selznick style. The guests assembled at David's house, where they boarded a bus stocked with fine wines and superb food. A small orchestra provided entertainment for the drive through the orange groves and into the San Bernardino Mountains.

All of the Scarletts appeared for dinner in their loveliest gowns, and the gay laughter resounded among the towering pines. But then the laughter turned hollow when one or two of the famous actresses studied the amused faces of David and Myron. A glance around the gathering revealed the nature of the brothers' jest. The word quickly spread, and the frivolity turned into rancorous indignation.

And that amused David and Myron even more.

As part of the Search for Scarlett, David Selznick invited other studios to submit their contract actresses for auditions. One day the RKO casting chief, Ben Piazza, summoned eight of the studio's stock girls to his office.

"Look, girls, the boss wants you to try out for Scarlett

O'Hara," he told them. "Here are some script pages with three scenes from *Gone With the Wind*. I want you to study them and be ready in three weeks for an audition at Selznick. Oh, yes. If you need any help with the Southern accent, there's a guy out there who will coach you."

The stock girls filed out of the casting office. Some were giddy with excitement. A few were merely perplexed, and one of these was Lucille Ball, a lanky redhead who had previously been dropped as a Goldwyn Girl and fired from Columbia after appearing in a Three Stooges short.

"This is ridiculous!" she exclaimed. "Me play Scarlett O'Hara? Impossible!"

"Better do as you're told," advised another one of the stock girls. "The boss won't like it if you don't."

Not wishing to risk the loss of another contract, Lucille went home and began studying the *Gone With the Wind* scenes. She concentrated her efforts on the early scene in which Scarlett tried to work her wiles on Ashley Wilkes.

"I do declare, Ashley Wilkes, I don't for the life of me understand what you see in that skinny little Melanie . . ."

Lucille tried it over and over again in front of a mirror. Somehow she could never make it sound like Scarlett O'Hara. Coming from upstate New York, she hadn't the slightest notion of how to reproduce a Southern accent.

She drove to the Selznick studio in Culver City for an appointment with Will Price, a young Southern scholar who had been brought to the studio as an adviser. He coached her in how to soften the consonants and draw out the vowels in the Georgian manner. Lucille returned for more coaching, and she became acquainted with David O. Selznick's executive secretary, Marcella Rabwin, who offered help and sympathy to the scared young actress.

Lucille became terrified as the day for her audition approached. A cloudburst struck Los Angeles that day, and she could hardly coax her ancient Studebaker to make the journey to Culver City. Finally she parked the car at the studio and ran through the rain to the executive building.

She was soaked and bedraggled when she arrived at Marcella Rabwin's office.

"Oh, hello, Lucille," said Marcella. "We've been expecting you."

"I really can't stay," Lucille panted. "I just dropped by to say I can't make the audition today."

"But you're here, aren't you?" Marcella said warmly. "You might as well stay. Mr. Selznick is looking forward to meeting you."

"Mr. Selznick!" Lucille was terrified. "You mean I'm supposed to see him today? But I can't!"

"Surely you can. You'll feel better after I get you an aspirin."

"But I don't need an aspirin."

"Then I'll pour you some brandy."

"I don't drink brandy."

"Then I'll make you some nice hot tea."

Marcella ushered the protesting actress into Selznick's office and helped her take off the wet boots. Marcella brought some tea and suggested that Lucille practice her lines before Mr. Selznick returned from lunch.

Lucille plopped down on a couch and spread the script pages on the table before her. She sipped the tea and studied the lines, falling to her knees on the floor.

"Ah do declah, Ashley Wilkes, Ah don' foh the lahf of me understand what yo see in that skinny little Melanie," she recited.

"That was a very good reading, Miss Ball."

Lucille started at the sound of a voice behind her. Her eyes widened as she turned and saw the bulky figure of David 0. Selznick.

"I — I was just practicing," she said.

"Yes, and it was very good indeed," he said, taking a seat behind his desk. "Please go on."

"Go on? "

"Yes, I'd like to hear you do all three scenes."

Lucille plunged forward, reciting the lines with all the fervor she could manage. The final scene came at the end of the story, with Scarlett musing: "I'll think about it tomorrow, at Tara.

Tomorrow, I'll think of some way to get him back. After all, tomorrow is another day."

Tears rolled down her cheeks as she finished, and Selznick seemed moved. "Very good, Miss Ball," he said.

"Did you really think so?" she asked brightly.

"Indeed. We'll let you know our decision. Meanwhile, thanks for coming."

"Then I can go now."

"Yes. Here — let me help you."

He hurried around the desk to assist her to her feet. Only then did she realize that she had played all three scenes on her knees.

David Selznick searched for a writer to fashion the script of *Gone With the Wind*. Obviously no ordinary scenarist would do. The task required an expert constructionist, a demon worker, an author with a name prestigious enough to match the importance of the project. David selected Sidney Howard.

It was a brilliant choice. Howard was one of the leading playwrights of the American theater, having written such plays as *They Knew What They Wanted* (Pulitzer Prize, 1925), *The Silver Cord, Yellow Jack,* and *Dodsworth.* He also knew how to write under pressure for the screen, having been under contract to Samuel Goldwyn for such films as *Arrowsmith, Bulldog Drummond,* and *Raffles.*

Howard came to Hollywood in the spring of 1937 and was handed the copy of *Gone With the Wind* which bore David's handwritten comments in the margins. Howard wrote at a furious pace, eager to finish the chore and return to the East. For six weeks, he worked sixteen hours a day to compress months of narrative into single scenes, eliminating a host of minor characters. George Cukor collaborated with Howard to provide visual aspects from the director's angle.

Howard's labors brought forth a mountainous script that would have required five and a half hours to unreel on the screen. David liked what the playwright had produced, but the first draft of a screenplay was to David but an opening exercise.

Howard did a rewrite, then hurried back to Broadway.[1]

The script of *Gone With the Wind* underwent many metamorphoses after the departure of Sidney Howard. First David Selznick himself tried his hand at compressing the script to a more manageable length. Then he put Jo Swerling to work on it. In the two years before production began, David also assigned Charles MacArthur, John Van Druten, Oliver H. P. Garrett, Winston Miller, John Balderston, Michael Foster, Edwin Justus Mayer, and other writers to produce individual scenes or whole scripts.

The most famous of the contributors was F. Scott Fitzgerald. He grumbled about the novel in a letter to his daughter: "I read it—I mean really read it—it is a good novel—not very original, in fact leaning heavily on *The Old Wives' Tale, Vanity Fair,* and all that has been written on the Civil War. There are no new characters, new technique, new observations—none of the elements that make literature—especially no new examination into human emotions. But on the other hand it is interesting, surprisingly honest, consistent and workmanlike throughout, and I felt no contempt for it but only a certain pity for those who consider it the supreme achievement of the human mind."

One of Fitzgerald's chores was a rewrite of the staircase scene, and he struggled for a new approach to it. He enlisted Sheilah Graham in his search for the motivations of the two main characters. The columnist posed at the top of the winding staircase of their Encino house while Fitzgerald enacted both Rhett Butler and the director down below.

"Now, slowly—keep your eye on me," he instructed as Miss Graham descended the stairs holding to the hem of a make-believe gown.

"Miss O'Hara—" he murmured with a cocky smile.

"Captain Butler, I believe—" she replied with a coy wave of her fan.

The charade did little to aid Fitzgerald's writing, and he was

[1] Sidney Howard never saw *Gone With the Wind* on the screen. Before the film had been completed, he was run over by a tractor and killed on his farm at Tyringham, Massachusetts.

fired after two weeks' work. He complained to Maxwell Perkins: "I was absolutely forbidden to use any words except those of Margaret Mitchell; that is, when new phrases had to be invented one had to thumb through as if it were Scripture and check out phrases of hers which would cover the situation!"[2]

Clark Gable was Rhett Butler, and Rhett Butler was Clark Gable.

Millions of readers of *Gone With the Wind* knew it. David 0. Selznick knew it. To his great satisfaction, Louis B. Mayer knew it. Since he controlled the professional destiny of Gable, Mayer was in a position of power, which was where he most liked to be.

David was desperate to avoid capitulating to his father-in-law. He realized that Mayer would exact a difficult bargain for the services of Gable and would try to lure David back to M-G-M. David was determined to retain his independence.

He sought to defy the public's insistence on Gable by casting Gary Cooper as Rhett Butler. But his friend Sam Goldwyn had Cooper under exclusive contract, and friendship did not extend to lending such a valuable property as Gary Cooper for another producer's profit.

David next decided that Errol Flynn possessed the proper dash and suavity to portray Margaret Mitchell's anti-hero. Warner Brothers offered a package deal involving Flynn as Rhett and Bette Davis as Scarlett. But although Miss Davis coveted the role, she balked at playing opposite Flynn.

With heavy heart, David concluded he would have to deal with Mayer. Expectably, Mayer made an impassioned plea for David to return to M-G-M. David flatly refused. The rebuffed father-in-law decided David would have to pay dearly for the services of the indispensable Gable.

David did not want to negotiate with Mayer, and the contract talks were carried on with an M-G-M executive, Al Lichtman. David howled in pain when he heard the terms: M-G-M would lend Gable and supply half of the estimated production cost of

---

[2] Fitzgerald's firing from *Gone With the Wind* helped to destroy his confidence. He went on a drinking spree during his next assignment, *Winter Carnival*.

The Burning of Atlanta.

$2,500,000 in return for the releasing rights to *Gone With the Wind* plus half of the profits.

Clark Gable wasn't consulted. He was leery of the role, as he remarked later: "I was scared when I discovered that I had been cast by the public. I felt that every reader would have a different idea as to how Rhett should be played on the screen, and I didn't see how I could please everybody."

He was determined to refuse the role, but love—and the need

for money—changed his mind. Gable had become enamored of the madcap star Carole Lombard. He wanted to marry her, but he was still married to his second wife, Rhea Langham Gable. Mrs. Gable realized she could no longer hold her famous husband, who was seventeen years younger. But she wasn't going to part with him without an adequate settlement. This brought anguish to Clark Gable, who disliked giving up his newly acquired wealth. The divorce from Rhea was going to cost him $286,000, plus income tax on the money. Gable needed the $100,000 bonus he was offered for *Gone With the Wind.* He agreed to do the film and on August 25, 1938, he flashed his dimpled smile while David Selznick and Louis Mayer signed the contract before news photographers.

David Selznick never gave serious consideration to any other actor but Leslie Howard for the role of Ashley Wilkes. To David's consternation, Howard wasn't interested.

"I haven't the slightest intention of playing another weak, watery character such as Ashley Wilkes," announced the British star. "I've played enough ineffectual characters already."

David had dealt with enough actors to realize that each possessed an area of temptation. Unlike Gable, Howard's was not money. Howard was a college man with literary pretensions. He had little respect for the acting life and much preferred to spend his time turning out magazine articles and short stories. David offered him the opportunity to partake of a creative experience. If Howard agreed to portray Ashley Wilkes, he would be allowed to function as associate producer on another Selznick film, *Intermezzo.* Howard agreed.

The search for Melanie was less publicized than the one for Scarlett. Many actresses had been tested in that part, including Andrea Leeds, Elizabeth Allan, and Anne Shirley. Scores of others were interviewed and auditioned. One day George Cukor sent for Joan Fontaine and asked if she would read for Melanie.

"Certainly not," Miss Fontaine replied. "Melanie doesn't interest me. If you want someone to play Melanie, I suggest you call my sister."

It seemed like a good idea, and Cukor arranged for an interview with Olivia de Havilland. She read from the script, and Cukor was enthused. "I must have you perform for David," he said.

On a Sunday afternoon, Cukor escorted Miss De Havilland to the hilltop home of David Selznick. Cukor had chosen a scene between Melanie and Scarlett, and for lack of anyone else to play the role, he assumed the guise of Scarlett. The stout, curly-haired director flounced about the Selznick living room as Scarlett while Miss De Havilland mouthed the homilies of the benign Melanie. The performance impressed Selznick.

"You are *the* Melanie!" declared David. He ran the tests of other prospective Melanies in his projection room and became even more convinced. He decided on Olivia de Havilland without a test.

But she remained under contract to the feudal-minded Jack L. Warner. She pleaded for permission to do the role, but Warner replied: "Oh, you don't want to be in *Gone With the Wind;* it's going to be the biggest bust of all time."

Indeed, after two years of publicity campaigning, boredom and ill will had been aroused in the Hollywood community, and many were predicting that *Gone With the Wind* would be David Selznick's white elephant. But Olivia de Havilland would not be dissuaded.

She telephoned Warner's wife and arranged to have tea at the Beverly Hills Brown Derby. Olivia poured out her plight. Mrs. Warner, who had once been an actress, was sympathetic. "I will try to help you," she said.

Shortly afterward, a deal was arranged whereby David Selznick, who had a loan-out commitment for James Stewart from M-G-M, lent Stewart to Warner Brothers in return for the services of Olivia de Havilland as Melanie.

David continued to assemble a distinguished cast: Thomas Mitchell as Gerald O'Hara, Hattie McDaniel as Mammy, Ona Munson as Belle Watling, Harry Davenport as Dr. Meade, Laura Hope Crews as Aunt Pittypat, Barbara O'Neil as Ellen O'Hara. All the major roles had been cast—except Scarlett.

The search had gone on so long that David could not make up his mind. Among the actresses who had been considered were Miriam Hopkins, Tallulah Bankhead, Claudette Colbert, Joan Crawford, Margaret Sullavan, Carole Lombard, Jean Arthur, Joan Bennett, Ann Sheridan. None seemed perfect for the mercurial Scarlett.

Time was getting short. Under terms of the contract with M-G-M, David was required to put Gable to work no later than February 15, 1939, and could retain his services only for a reasonable period of time. By December of 1938, David had still arrived at no decision on Scarlett, but preproduction had to begin. He planned to build Tara on the Forty Acres backlot of Pathé studio. Before he could do so, an immense amount of old movie sets had to be removed.

Assistant director Eric Stacy made the suggestion: why not assemble all the sets in a replica of 1864 Atlanta and send the whole thing up in flames?

Work crews shifted the sets, among them the gates to the kingdom of *King Kong.* Carpenters pounded up new facades to represent Atlanta storefronts. Plumbers ran pipes throughout the sets to supply coal oil to build the flames, water to extinguish them. Production manager Ray Klune rounded up seven Technicolor cameras to film the fire from every possible angle; there could be no retakes on this particular scene.

For two weeks camera crews ran through procedures. The firing was rehearsed as the Culver City fire department stood by. Three sets of doubles were hired to pose as Rhett Butler and Scarlett O'Hara as they rode a wagon past the holocaust. Klune calculated that the entire filming would have to be accomplished in one hour.

The date was set for the Burning of Atlanta: December 11, 1938. And still there was no Scarlett.

On the night of the fire, David had assembled his close friends and associates on a special platform. A place of honor was reserved for Florence Selznick, who wrapped herself in a blanket for protection against the December cold. As the final preparations were being made, David glanced nervously at his watch.

"Where the hell is Myron?" he complained. Aides had been delegated to telephone Myron's favorite drinking places, but no trace of him could be found. The setting of the fire was delayed an hour.

"Goddammit, he's got to be here to see this!" David said. Ray Klune argued that the twelve fire companies from Los Angeles could not remain much longer. David reluctantly gave the signal for the fire to begin.

Oil flowed through the pipes, and jets of flame began to leap from various parts of the set. The dry wood of the ancient sets quickly blazed, sending showers of sparks into the sky. George Cukor signaled the action, and the first set of doubles began the wagon ride past the burning buildings.

Myron arrived. He came with a group of dinner guests, including his client Laurence Olivier, who escorted a young British actress. Myron, a trifle unsteady, led his party up the stairs to the grandstand and tugged at David's sleeve.

"So there you are!" David said angrily. "Where the hell have you been?"

Myron merely grinned.

"Dave," he said woozily, taking Vivien Leigh by the arm, "I want you to meet Scarlett O'Hara."

Vivien Leigh was in love, as were the other stars of *Gone With the Wind.*

Clark Gable was involved with Carole Lombard. Olivia de Havilland was being romanced by Howard Hughes. Leslie Howard, whose pursuit of offscreen amour belied his gentle image in films, was having an affair with an attractive young woman.

Vivien Leigh's love was Laurence Olivier, the brilliant young British actor. She had first seen him on the London stage when he was appearing in *The Royal Family.* She was so impressed that she turned to a girl companion and said, "That's the man I'm going to marry."

"Ridiculous!" her friend replied. "You're both married already."

"That doesn't matter," Vivien said. "I will still marry him one day."

She met Olivier when a friend introduced them in the Savoy Grill, and he asked her for a weekend in the country—with her husband along. Later her husband, a lawyer named Leigh Holman, no longer accompanied her, and Olivier saw less of his wife, the actress Jill Esmond. Now Vivien Leigh had also become a star with her appearance in *Mask of Virtue,* and her attachment to Olivier was becoming a London scandal. He left for

The Confederate wounded at the Atlanta railroad station.

Hollywood, where he had an offer to star for Samuel Goldwyn in *Wuthering Heights*. Vivien followed along.

She had hoped to play Cathy opposite Olivier, but Goldwyn cast Merle Oberon instead. Then Vivien set her mind on getting the role of Scarlett O'Hara in *Gone With the Wind*. Olivier's friends in Hollywood's British colony sought to discourage her.

"David would never cast an English girl in the part," they told her. "The South would lynch him if he did."

Vivien would not be dissuaded. Larry's agent was Myron Selznick and she figured he could help her acquire the role. She figured correctly. To placate his drunken brother at the Atlanta fire, David had promised to test the young English actress.

George Cukor directed her in a scene with Leslie Howard. David was so impressed that he ordered two more tests of Miss Leigh to determine if she could manage a Southern accent. She could. She was the picture of Scarlett O'Hara except for one distracting thing: her eyes were blue, and every reader of *Gone With the Wind* knew that Scarlett's eyes were a pale green. The cameraman, Ernest Haller, resolved the problem with a yellow spotlight that gave the actress's eyes a greenish cast.

"Well, I guess we're stuck with you," George Cukor said casually to Vivien at a Hollywood party. It was her first inkling that she had been awarded the role.

There was surprisingly little uproar over the selection of an English girl to play the South's most famous heroine. The Ocala, Florida, chapter of the United Daughters of the Confederacy threatened a boycott of the picture, but other areas of the South remained silent. There seemed to be general relief that Selznick had not chosen a Yankee.

Vivien Leigh signed the contract—on Friday the thirteenth of January, 1939—without informing Larry Olivier. She feared that he would be upset because she committed herself to Selznick for seven years. She was right about Larry's reaction. He stormed into David's office and announced that he would not allow Vivien to fulfill the contract. They intended to get married, Larry said, and he did not want to risk separation.

"Larry," David said calmly, "do you remember when I was head of RKO and I wanted Jill Esmond in *A Bill of Divorcement?*"

"Yes," the actor replied.

"And you insisted that your wife give up the part and go back to England with you?"

"Yes."

"Larry, don't be a shit twice."

Laurence Olivier relented and allowed Vivien to fulfill her contract with Selznick.

"Everyone is talking of war, war, war," Scarlett complained . . .

The filming of *Gone With the Wind* began on January 26, 1939; the initial scene was the first one in the script, in which the Tarleton twins vied for the opportunity to escort Scarlett to the barbecue. It was typical of David Selznick's thoroughness that the scene was reshot three times before filming was concluded—because of a change in directors, because David didn't like the costumes, and because the twins' dialogue was indistinct.

David's passion for meticulous planning came into full flower with *Gone With the Wind.* He insisted that every element of the picture be completely authentic. Will Price checked the Southern dialects. Susan Myrick, a noted expert on Southern social customs, advised on manners and morals. Artist-historian Wilbur G. Kurtz was consulted on historical matters.

Walter Plunkett designed the costumes with complete authenticity. David insisted that the petticoats for the Southern ladies be made of costly Val lace.

"Why?" asked Ann Rutherford, who was playing Carreen O'Hara. "Nobody will know it's there."

"But *you'll* know it's there," David replied.

Horseman Jock Whitney thought he detected an error when he viewed early scenes of the picture. The chairman of the board of Selznick International Pictures sent off a letter to the president of the company expressing shock that Ashley Wilkes's horse appeared with a cropped tail. Chagrined, Selznick summoned his technical advisers. They returned with thirty-five books proving that Southern gentlemen did ride horses with

In happier moments — David Selznick, Vivien Leigh, Victor Fleming, Carole Lombard and Clark Gable.

cropped tails. "I give up," replied Whitney.[3]

William Cameron Menzies occupied the unique position of production designer, overseeing all the visual aspects of *Gone With the Wind,* including the color. Pioneering the field of production design, he drew three thousand sketches of the scenes, including every camera angle. His visualizations were carried out by Lyle Wheeler, the art director, who amassed thousands of drawings, photographs, and descriptions of the Southern locales which figured in the story.

David Selznick was not satisfied with the early footage that Cukor had directed. Cukor produced excellent results in the scenes with Scarlett and Melanie, but David felt the scope of

---

[3] No serious question was raised about the authenticity of *Gone With the Wind.* The use of an oral thermometer was criticized by nurses who cited a textbook indicating the oral thermometer was introduced in 1866. Selznick researchers proved the book wrong; oral thermometers had been used as early as 1861.

One anachronism went unnoticed. To avoid expense, the studio used 1875 railroad cars in the Atlanta station scenes.

The tension tells — Vivien Leigh, Clark Gable, and Victor Fleming on location.

the picture was being neglected. Also, Clark Gable was grumbling that his role was being overlooked while Cukor concentrated on the female stars. Gable lacked confidence in his acting, and he always felt more comfortable under the guidance of a tough-willed director. Although good personal friends, Selznick and Cukor began arguing over elements of production. David did not like to have his will questioned.

He decided to fire George Cukor. Since he had a distaste for such unpleasant duties, he sent the studio's general manager, Henry Ginsberg, to break the news to Cukor.

Only three weeks of filming had been completed, and David realized he had to move swiftly. If he faltered now, Louis Mayer would be certain to swoop down and take over the production. That would be a humiliation David could not endure.

David realized he needed Clark Gable's support. He told Gable that Cukor had been relieved of his duties. The actor made no effort to mask his delight at the news. David handed him a list of proposed replacements: Robert Z. Leonard, Jack Conway, King

Victor Fleming under pressure. At left, David Selznick.

Vidor, Victor Fleming.

Gable unhesitatingly chose Fleming. The tall, tough part-Indian was Gable's kind of director, and had guided the star through such films as *Red Dust* and *Test Pilot.* He had also displayed his sensitivity with *The Wizard of Oz, Treasure Island,* and *Captains Courageous.* Fleming was hired from M-G-M.

When Vivien Leigh and Olivia de Havilland heard the news of Cukor's firing, they were horrified. Costumed in their widow's weeds for the Atlanta bazaar, they rushed to David Selznick's office and poured forth tears and arguments for the continuance of George Cukor as director. David was impressed by their performances, but not their arguments. Cukor remained fired.

Vic Fleming read the script of *Gone With the Wind* and was

unimpressed. He convinced David that a rewrite was necessary. Speed was an obvious necessity, since the production was standing idle at a cost of $50,000 per day. There was only one man who could manage an emergency rewrite with the necessary skill: Ben Hecht.

Selznick and Fleming arrived at Hecht's house on a Sunday shortly before dawn. They outlined their predicament, and Hecht sleepily agreed to help. Driving to the studio at sunrise, they decided on the fee for Hecht's service—$15,000 for a week's work.

David was dismayed to learn that Hecht had never read *Gone With the Wind.* David proceeded to outline the entire story. After the hour's recital, Hecht explained, "My God, that's the most involved plot I've ever heard! Can't you just throw it away and write a new one?"

Impossible, David said testily, since millions of the book's readers would be outraged. Hecht then suggested that sometime during the two years of script-writing at least one of the scenarists must have produced a cohesive plot line. David remembered Sidney Howard's original treatment. After an hour's search it was found, and David read the Howard version to Fleming and Hecht. The first, forgotten script provided a skillful, authentic retelling of Margaret Mitchell's novel.

The three men set to work. Each of Howard's scenes was analyzed and acted out by Selznick, who portrayed Scarlett and her father, and Fleming, who took the roles of Rhett Butler and Ashley Wilkes. Hecht made notes and suggestions, then sat down to a typewriter and wrote the scenes. The process continued eighteen hours a day. On the seventh day more than two thirds of the script had been created, and they rested.

After a two-week lull, production resumed under Fleming's firm control. "I'm going to make this picture a melodrama," he announced, reasoning that only by a flamboyant approach could he bring credulity to the panoramic happenings of *Gone With the Wind.* He resolved to keep his camera on the people and depict their reactions to the cataclysmic events, rather than let those events overwhelm the characters.

Gable was delighted with the turn of events. Leslie Howard was indifferent; he wanted only to finish the picture so he could go on to *Intermezzo*. Vivien Leigh and Olivia de Havilland remained distraught.

Both actresses felt they had been betrayed by David Selznick. Miss Leigh strove to preserve Cukor's softer approach to Scarlett while Fleming hammered at her to toughen the role. She often fled the stage in tears after a stormy encounter with the volatile Fleming.

Olivia de Havilland avoided any confrontations with Fleming. But privately she fretted over the loss of George Cukor. One evening at dinner she poured out her feelings to Howard Hughes. He listened carefully, then counseled her: "Don't worry. Everything is going to be all right. George and Victor have the same talent. But Victor's is strained through a coarser sieve."

The comment heartened Olivia, but she still required reassurance. She telephoned George Cukor and asked if she could talk to him about Melanie's scenes. He graciously agreed, and they met at his house and in out-of-the-way restaurants throughout the filming to discuss ways to make the overwhelming goodness of Melanie seem credible. Unbeknown to Olivia, Vivien Leigh was also making clandestine visits to Cukor, exploring how to make Scarlett's bitchery more appealing. Thus George Cukor ended up directing Scarlett and Melanie after all.

As the filming progressed, David Selznick realized that the $2,500,000 cost estimate for *Gone With the Wind* was unrealistic. His visions continually outdistanced the budget; always he ordered more elaborate sets, additional actors, more retakes to perfect each scene.

He decreed that the scene of the wounded in the Atlanta railroad station would be the most impressive in film history. He wanted 2500 extras to portray the wounded and dying Confederate soldiers awaiting treatment in the railroad yards. His production aides asked if he wouldn't settle for 1250 extras and 1250 dummies.

"Absolutely not!" he replied. His aides argued that no screen could accommodate 2500 moving figures, and David finally agreed to permit 1600 extras and 500 dummies. The Extras Guild heard of the plan and demanded actors for all the wounded. The studio agreed, but the Guild could muster only 1300 members. Dummies filled in for the rest.

To capture the full scope of the scene, David wanted the camera to pull back to skyscraper height. William Cameron Menzies sketched the scene, then David handed it to his technicians to work out the details. They calculated the camera would need to be 95 feet off the ground at the end of the shot—and the tallest camera boom in Hollywood was only 25 feet. Production manager Ray Klune called in construction engineers to study the problem. Their company owned a 90-foot crane with extension that would provide 125 feet in height. The crane was tested and found to be too jerky at the start; the camera had to move with utter smoothness as it focused on the red-dressed Scarlett, then rose to take in the entire panorama.

More consultations. Why not build a concrete ramp down which the crane could roll by gravity? It seemed like a good plan, and crews laid cement of extra thickness to support the 120-ton crane. The studio rented the rig for ten days while camera crews tested the plan. Over and over again the multiwheeled truck rolled down the ramp as the camera platform lifted into the sky.

The day for the sequence arrived. Extras and dummies were outfitted in Confederate gray, splashed with fake blood, wrapped in bandages, and spread prone throughout the vast set. The huge crane rolled smoothly down the ramp and the scene was captured in the first take.

Such extravagances required an additional transfusion of cash to complete *Gone With the Wind* in accordance with David's standards. He was reluctant to approach M-G-M for more money, and he sent Henry Ginsberg to do the asking. The answer was no. David turned to the Whitneys, but C. V. Whitney responded coldly, "You've spent your last Whitney dollar."

The rival camps arrive for the Atlanta premiere: Olivia de Havilland, David Selznick, Vivien Leigh, Irene Selznick. Overlooked by photographers was Miss Leigh's escort, Laurence Olivier, seen over Selznick's shoulder.

A.P. Giannini of the Bank of America was invited out to the studio to view the footage that had been filmed thus far. He was impressed by what he saw. But the wily Italian would advance the finishing money only if the Whitneys provided half. The Whitneys resignedly agreed, and David was given $1,500,000 to finish *Gone With the Wind.*[4]

Production continued on an even grander scale, and the strain of responsibility was beginning to show on Victor Fleming. He was a curious combination of tough guy and esthete, and the two sides of his nature seemed at war with each other. He was an adventurer who had flown in World War I, hunted tigers in India, and raced automobiles before becoming a cameraman, then director. Many of his co-workers believed that

---

[4] The final production cost was calculated at $3,200,000. With the addition of overhead, cost of prints, and other expenses, the total came to $3,957,000.

the screen characterization of Clark Gable was created in Vic Fleming's image.

Fleming's nerves became more frayed because of the constant bickering with Vivien Leigh, who was herself overworked and unsure in her role. One of the low points in filming was reached on a bonechilling predawn location on a mesa in the San Fernando Valley. The scene was an important one: the conclusion of the first half when Scarlett pulls a radish from the earth and vows that she will never be hungry again. Ray Klune had scheduled the location call for 4 A.M. with filming to begin at dawn. It had rained the previous night, but the weather bureau predicted clearing skies by dawn.

The company assembled on the wet, chill mesa in moods that matched the weather. Vivien Leigh directed her scorn at Klune for calling such a location. Fleming was even more outspoken.

"Why the hell did you bring us out here on this goddam mis-

The Gable contingent: Carole Lombard and Clark Gable in center, Kay Kyser at her right.

Margaret Mitchell leaves the microphones. Right, David Selznick.

At the Hollywood premiere: Jack Whitney, Irene Selznick, Olivia de Havilland, David Selznick, Vivien Leigh, Laurence Olivier.

erable morning?" he demanded of Klune.

"Because you might get one of the most sensitive shots of all time," the production manager replied.

Fleming grumblingly assembled the crew in the half darkness and placed Miss Leigh on the red-dyed Tara earth to await the sunrise. Slowly the sun ascended over the California hills, casting golden rays through a Tintoretto sky. All agreed that the misery was worth what had been captured on film, and Ray Klune breathed with relief.

Vic Fleming displayed moments of elation, then lapsed into periods of despair. His worst times came when the scenes required emotional conflict; he seemed to suffer along with the characters. When *Gone With the Wind* was three quarters finished, he came to the sequences in which Scarlett and Rhert tore at each other unmercifully. He and the two stars grew more edgy and irritable. One day they reached the climactic scene of Scarlett's final rejection of her husband.

"I can't do it!" Vivien Leigh cried. "I simply can't do this scene. This woman is a terrible bitch!"

"While we're at it," Gable added, "I might as well tell you, Vic, that I can't do that 'don't give a damn' scene tomorrow."

Fleming exploded, directing his fury at Vivien as the cause of his troubles. He rolled up his script and said to her, "Miss Leigh, you can insert this script up your royal British ass!" He threw the script at her feet and stomped off the set.

Fleming did not return. Nor did he appear the second day. He remained in his Malibu home and refused to answer the telephone. On the third day, David Selznick, Vivien Leigh, and Clark Gable appeared at his home bearing a cage of lovebirds.

Fleming grinned and said, "Let's have a drink." They drank together, and he agreed to return to *Gone With the Wind.*

But the attrition of the filming had depleted his emotional resources, and he became more erratic and unreasonable. Driving home one night, he contemplated heading his car over the edge of a cliff. He was hospitalized with a nervous breakdown.

David Selznick realized he could not allow *Gone With the Wind* to falter. A delay would be costly, and he could not be assured that the Bank of America and the Whitneys would advance any more money. Moreover, a lull in filming would destroy the rhythm that he considered important to the making of every picture. Good pictures developed an *esprit*—a sense of devotion to the common purpose.

Sam Wood was hired to take over for Vic Fleming. A versatile craftsman, he stepped in and began directing without delay. Sidney Franklin and William Wellman directed other dramatic scenes. Reeves (Breezy) Eason, an expert in action scenes, staged the battles. Jack Cosgrove directed the special effects, and William Cameron Menzies oversaw some of the scenes involving designs he had created. Fleming returned after four weeks, but David retained Sam Wood. Stars found themselves being directed by Fleming in the morning and Wood in the afternoon.

Clark Gable had his own personal troubles during the film-ing of *Gone With the Wind.* He grumbled that he had only a day's honeymoon after his elopement with Carole Lombard. He did not get along well with Vivien Leigh. She seemed foreign, distant, and temperamental to him, and he had no tolerance for tem-peramental costars. He always reported promptly to the set, and it rankled him when she didn't.

The role of Rhett Butler troubled him. It was the longest and most complex he had ever attempted. Despite everyone's claims that he was the personification of Rhett, many of the character's actions and motivations were foreign to him. One scene in the script terrified him: his breakdown following Scarlett's miscar-riage.

"I can't do it!" he ranted to Olivia de Havilland, who shared the scene with him. "I won't do it! I'm going to leave acting and go off to my tractor in Encino. I'll quit pictures—starting with this one!"

When the day arrived for the scene, Gable was in an agitat-ed state. He seemed utterly unable to portray the anguish of Rhett Butler in his darkest hour. Fleming reasoned with him. Olivia offered feminine encouragement. Gable paused for a silent moment before the final rehearsal. Then out of his inner feelings he seemed to reach the resource to enact Rhett's grief. The take was eloquent and immensely human, the single most moving scene of Gable's career.

The immense strain of portraying Scarlett O'Hara began to show on Vivien Leigh. She continued driving herself sixteen hours a day, six days a week. She asked for no time off, because the sooner she finished the picture, the sooner she could rejoin Laurence Olivier. He now was appearing on Broadway in *No Time for Comedy,* and the separation was agony for both of them. Once he took an airplane after the Saturday night per-formance and flew sixteen hours to California. He spent part of Sunday with Vivien, then flew back to New York—missing the Monday night curtain. Such trips were banned by the play man-agement, and Vivien had to be content with his letters, which she avidly consumed.

David Selznick receives the Thalberg Award from Ernest M. Hopkins, president of Dartmouth University.

The last scene to be filmed was the first. Selznick the perfectionist decreed that Scarlett's scene with the Tarleton twins should be filmed one more time. Once again Scarlett was to fret, "Everyone is talking about war, war, war."

But David saw the emaciated, hollow-eyed Vivien in the rushes and decided she was unable to play a girl of sixteen. He gave her a two-week vacation, and the exuberant actress went off for a holiday on the Riviera with Larry Olivier, who had been released from his play.

However, in her absence, Selznick decided to use an earlier take for the first scene, so when Vivien returned to Hollywood, the filming of *Gone With the Wind* had been completed.

The last scene of *Gone With the Wind* was photographed on July 1, 1939.

During five months of production, a half million feet of film had been exposed. Unlike usual productions in which one or two takes were printed, David authorized as many as ten prints for scenes in *Gone With the Wind*. Now he was faced with a mountain of celluloid.

David plunged into the task. Day after day and far into the night he labored with his cutter, Hal Kern, and with his executive assistant, Barbara Keon. One session in his office lasted a nonstop fifty hours. Secretaries wilted, and Miss Keon was carried out unconscious after forty-seven hours. David continued on.

He was determined to pare the film to four hours; even that would be a prodigious length for a movie, but David feared he could not do justice to the story in less time.

Scoring was an enormous project. David assigned Max Steiner to create three hours of background music—and to do it on a deadline. Steiner, a volatile Viennese who had scored *The Informer, King Kong,* and *Jezebel*, broke the assignment down into 282 passages. He developed themes for each of the main characters, for the loves of Melanie and Ashley, and Scarlett and Ashley, and for Tara itself. Into the fabric he wove a host of Civil War songs, from *Dixie* to *Battle Hymn of the Republic*.

David pressed Steiner to finish the score. The composer replied that it was madness to expect him to compose the equivalent of four symphonies within three months. David inquired if Herbert Stothart could be borrowed from M-G-M to augment Steiner's work. Stothart was available. Upon hearing of this, Steiner accelerated his efforts and finished on schedule.

The next hurdle was the showing of *Gone With the Wind* to Louis B. Mayer and other M-G-M executives. Mayer had lent his wary support throughout the filming, but he was concerned about the running time. "My God," he exclaimed, "they'd even stone Christ if he came back and preached for four hours!"

Mayer and his underlings trooped to Pathé studio and sat down in a projection room to watch the four-and-a-half-hour *Gone With the Wind*. Mayer interrupted the picture several times while he went to the men's room. Despite the interruptions, he was profoundly moved by the film. So were the other executives. They returned to M-G-M in a state of euphoria. Because of the indispensable nature of Clark Gable, the company had acquired the greatest bargain in film history: a half interest in a huge money-maker for $1,250,000.[5]

After they had departed, David Selznick earnestly inquired of his cutter, Hal Kern, "Do you think they were kidding us when they said they liked the picture?"

"They've got to sell it, and they're up in the clouds," Kern replied. "They're not kidding us."

For the first time, David Selznick was confident that *Gone With the Wind* would be a winner.

Next came the ultimate test: exposure before an audience.

David decided on Riverside as the testing ground, and the Selznick staff traveled there in utmost secrecy. The theater manager was not told the name of the picture, and no patrons were admitted after the running began. David ordered the telephones cut off lest word of the showing leak out.

Despite the four hours and twenty-five minutes running

[5] For the remainder of his lifetime Clark Gable was bitterly resentful that he had not been given a percentage of the profits.

time, the audience was enthralled. The applause was thunderous at the end, and Selznick and his executives congratulated each other on the realization of a dream. Jock Whitney cried.

More previews followed, and David continued trimming the footage until the running time was three hours and forty-two minutes[6]. Sales executives favored no intermission, since the saved time might allow theaters to squeeze in an extra showing per day. David insisted that an intermission was necessary. He proved his point by tabulating the number of patrons who visited the rest rooms during a showing.

David vacillated in his feelings about *Gone With the Wind.* "At noon I think it's divine, at midnight I think it's lousy," he admitted. His spirits plunged when trade paper reviews proved only lukewarm. He called a staff meeting to ponder the import of the critiques. Russell Birdwell argued that it had been a mistake to show the film to a press-only audience, traditionally a cold house. Birdwell predicted the reception would be far different before a regular audience.

As *Gone With the Wind* approached its release, David came to grips with the issue of Rhett Butler's final line.

Realizing that the industry's self-censorship code prohibited profanity, Sidney Howard had changed the line to "Frankly, my dear, I don't care." The scene had been filmed and previewed that way, but David decided the "damn" was essential. Censor Joseph Breen refused to approve the word. David appealed to film czar Will Hays, arguing that the censorship system would be held up to ridicule if the famous line had to be bowdlerized. Hays permitted Rhett to say, "Frankly, my dear, I don't give a damn." But, because the use of profanity on the screen was still a punishable offense, David was required to pay a $5000 fine to the Producers Association. He figured it was worth it.

---

[6] One famous viewer complained that *Gone With the Wind* was too lengthy. Mrs. Eleanor Roosevelt once told the author that her husband had slept through a White House showing of *Gone With the Wind.* When the picture had finished and he was awakened, President Roosevelt commented, "No movie has a right to be that long!"

David continued to supervise every detail for the picture's release. Memos poured forth in staggering volume; nothing escaped his scrutiny. He fired off a telegram to Howard Dietz, head of publicity and advertising for Loew's, expressing his fear that the theater program might be printed on paper that would make a crackling sound. Such interference with the sound track of *Gone With the Wind* could not be tolerated, said David. The telegram was delivered to Dietz at 3 A.M. He wired back that the program paper was indeed soundproof, but perhaps he had erred in arranging for a peanut brittle manufacturer to hand out *Gone With the Wind* candy to all customers.

The Atlanta premiere was scheduled for December 15, 1939, and M-G-M exploitation men invaded Georgia weeks in advance to organize the most elaborate film opening in history. The governor proclaimed a statewide holiday; Atlanta's mayor declared a three-day festival and urged citizens to wear Civil War costumes. The Grand Theatre was fronted with fake columns to resemble Twelve Oaks in the Margaret Mitchell novel. All was in readiness for the arrival of the star contingent from Hollywood.

The contingent was rife with dissension. On the day the *Gone With the Wind* special plane was to leave for Atlanta, Victor Fleming showed up drunk at John Lee Mahin's Encino home.

"You were right: he's a son of a bitch," muttered Fleming.

"Who's a son of a bitch?" Mahin asked.

"Selznick," Fleming replied. He explained that he had come across a press release which declared, "There were three directors on *Gone With the Wind*, all supervised by David O. Selznick." No amount of persuasion by Mahin could convince Fleming to make the flight to Atlanta.

Clark Gable heard of the incident and sided with Fleming. Gable refused to join the special plane, which included Selznick, Vivien Leigh, her bridegroom Laurence Olivier, Olivia de Havilland and other notables. Instead he accepted the offer of a DC-3 from C.R. Smith, who was anxious to garner publicity for his fledgling American Airlines. He was accompanied by his bride, Carole Lombard, the M-G-M publicity chief, Howard Strickling, and a studio publicity man, Otto Winkler.

Before leaving, Carole Lombard announced to Russell Birdwell her plan for the journey: "I'll make that fat-assed Dutchman the biggest man in America. I'm not going as a movie star, but as Mrs. Clark Gable. From the moment the plane lands, I'm going to cling to his arm and do nothing but gaze into his eyes. He'll end up being an absolute hero!" She remained true to her vow, subordinating her own effervescent personality for her husband's moment of glory.

The Selznick plane almost didn't make it. During the descent to Atlanta, the plane made a sudden swerve, knocking famous passengers into the aisles. The pilot later explained the plane had almost collided with Stone Mountain.

The Gable entrance was carefully managed. All the other celebrities had been assembled for the big parade before 300,000 Atlantans. The parade's start was delayed while Gable's plane circled the field and made a leisurely landing. Throughout the three-day celebration, Gable remained aloof from the rest of the Hollywood party; he was still nursing his grudge over the slight to Vic Fleming.

The reticent Margaret Mitchell also declined to take part in most of the festivities. But she made an appearance at the premiere, and she offered her homage to David Selznick: "He's the man that every one of you cracked that joke about—'Oh, well, we'll wait till Shirley Temple grows up and she'll play Scarlett.' I want to commend Mr. Selznick's courage and his obstinacy and his determination in just keeping his mouth shut until he got exactly the right cast he wanted, in spite of everything everybody said."

She thanked the audience "for me and my poor Scarlett," and added, "It's not up to me to speak of the grand things these actors have done, for they've spoken so much more eloquently than I could ever do."

David Selznick beamed with pride. It was the moment he had long dreamed of, when the name of Selznick would be proclaimed to all the world as the ultimate in film quality. Lewis J. would have been proud.

But the Atlanta accolades were not enough; David needed

more. The climax was reached on February 29, 1940, when the twelfth annual awards of the Academy of Motion Picture Arts and Sciences were presented at the Cocoanut Grove of the Ambassador Hotel in Los Angeles.

"What a wonderful thing, this benefit for David Selznick," cracked Bob Hope as one Oscar after another was awarded to *Gone With the Wind.* There were eight in all, plus a Thalberg Award for David.

Still David was not satisfied. As he drove with Russell Birdwell to the celebration party, David was strangely silent. Then he blurted, "I don't know why we didn't get the best-actor award for Gable. Somewhere you failed. You didn't put on the proper campaign; otherwise Clark would have been sure to get it."

Birdwell couldn't believe that David was serious. *Gone With the Wind* had won more Oscars than any other film in history; David himself had won two top prizes. Yet he was carping over the loss of one of the nominations.

The publicity man didn't report to work for two days. Then David called to him to apologize: "I was a pig. I worked so hard and waited so long, I got piggish and wanted everything."

David regained his sense of proportion and realized the extent of his triumph. Not only had he won honors and riches with *Gone With the Wind,* not only had he achieved supreme vindication of the family name; he also had justified all his long-held beliefs about the nature of quality film making.

Nearly all of the Hollywood films were the product of the big studio factory-like system. While many of the pictures were excellent entertainment—1939 also brought forth *Ninotchka, Stagecoach, The Wizard of Oz, Wuthering Heights, Of Mice and Men, Mr. Smith Goes to Washington, Young Mr. Lincoln*—the majority had the look of manufactured entertainment. David Selznick still believed what he had told his Paramount bosses eight years before, that a motion picture was like a painting that had to be painted and signed by a single artist.

He was convinced that the artist must necessarily be the producer, and he felt that he had proved his theory with *Gone*

With the Wind. It was the culmination of many talents and personalities—Margaret Mitchell, Sidney Howard, Victor Fleming, William Cameron Menzies, the stars and featured players, etc. But one person had seen *Gone With the Wind* through from beginning to end, despite changes of directors, alterations of scripts, casting problems, etc. That person had been David Selznick.

To most people in Hollywood it appeared that he had everything. He was at the peak of his career, enjoying critical and commercial success, as well as the approbation of his peers. He was blessed with a dynastic marriage to an understanding, helpful wife who had given him two fine sons. David Selznick was at the top, but he faced a fearful question: Where could he go from here?

V

●●●●●●●●●●●●●●●●●●●●

POSTLUDE

●●●●●●●●●●●●●●●●●●●●

*What Can You Do
For An Encore?*

David Selznick before a portrait of Vivien Leigh as Scarlett O'Hara

WHEN DAVID SELZNICK WAS FORTY-SIX,
he remained haunted by his greatest hit.
Gregory Peck stopped by the Selznick office for a drink
after a day's work on The Paradine Case.
He found David immersed in new plans
to make the picture bigger and broader.
"My God, David, aren't you going overboard
on the grandeur of this little drama in Old Bailey?" Peck
asked.
"The picture must have scope," David said.
"But why?" the actor asked.

"Why?" said David. "I'll tell you why.
Because I've got to do better than Gone With the Wind.
I may never make it.
But I've got to try."

Dear Sir:

I note in the latest issue of *National Cyclopedia of American Biography* the name of David O. Selznick is not included. It occurs to me that this might be an omission since . . .

Dear Sir:

It is with sincere regret I note that *Who's Who in Filmland* does not include in its gallery of prominent people biographical data concerning Mr. David O. Selznick. Since Mr. Selznick is listed in a score of similarly important publications . . .

With *Gone With the Wind* an acknowledged triumph, David O. Selznick decided that his achievements should be given official recognition. He directed his publicity staff to canvass biographical publications of the world to determine which included him. A shocking number did not; among them: *Who's Who in Transportation and Communication, The Universal Jewish Encyclopedia, Who's Who on the Pacific Coast, The Book of Knowledge,* and *The Columbia Encyclopedia.* Many reference volumes printed biographies of David O. Selznick that were not up to date. The publicity staff was directed by David to supply all the publications with current biographies, including the official list of his pictures—the failures were eliminated—and all of his honors, including the Thalberg Award, the International Exposition Cup, and the League of Nations medal.

In view of his achievements, he mused, would it not be fitting for a university to bestow upon him an honorary degree?

The publicity staff voiced hearty assent, and discreet inquiries were made. After months of negotiations, only one possibility could be found: the University of North Carolina.

"Not good enough," David replied. "If the degree isn't from an Ivy League college, I don't want it."

Failing in the Ivy League, he set about to become Selznick the Statesman. He enmeshed himself in Republican politics—but not of the rock-ribbed kind of his father-in-law. "I am a free-enterprise liberal," he proclaimed, "a passionate believer in FDR's social reforms and at the same time a Roosevelt hater." He put his money and support behind the liberal-minded new California governor, Earl Warren, and got himself elected a delegate to the 1940 Republican National Convention. There he became intrigued with the candidate of his good friend Henry Luce[1] — Wendell L. Willkie—and he offered his advice throughout the campaign to prevent the Third Term.

Willkie's defeat did not end David's ambitions of statesmanship. With the war raging in Europe, he wanted to serve the nation, and he composed extensive memos on war mobilization for the entire film industry. He fired off the document to Presidential aide Harry Hopkins. The plan was turned down as being premature.

David would not be discouraged. He spent forty hours dictating a memo to Secretary of War Harry Woodring concerning procurement of Air Corps officers. Nothing happened. Next he suggested a national newsreel digest for all branches of the government. Again, no response.

Republican Selznick concluded: "It was made very clear to me they didn't want experts, they wanted politicians."

When he completed *Gone With the Wind,* David O. Selznick was thirty-seven and at the height of his power and prestige. He remained boyish in appearance, with round face, lively eyes

---

[1] The friendship of David Selznick and Henry Luce was warm, even though Luce had once tricked Selznick out of the services of a screen writer. In 1935, David had signed Clare Boothe to a writing contract with Selznick International. In the same year, she became the wife of Henry Luce. They had planned a Hawaiian honeymoon before she was to report to the Selznick studio, and on the trip they became engaged in a series of backgammon games for money. Although Mrs. Luce had recently written a book on backgammon and her husband had little interest in games, he defeated her soundly. On their return to the mainland, Luce calculated that she owed him $35,000. "And you are going to pay me, too," he said. "I will buy you from David Selznick for thirty-five thousand dollars." The transaction was made, and Clare Boothe Luce never went to work for David Selznick.

behind thick lenses, and a profusion of dark-brown curly hair that prompted Gene Fowler to dub him Chinchilla Head. He was a gangly, lumbering six feet one, and he plodded slue-footed down studio hallways, often bumping into doors and other protuberances. He was powerfully built, but fleshy, weighing about two hundred pounds. He was a gourmand, scarcely caring whether he dined at Romanoff's or at a hot dog stand. Meals were important only to stoke his enormous energies, and he gobbled his food in a farmhand manner. He smoked incessantly, never removing the cigarette from his mouth until it burned down. Unlike his brother Myron, he had no addiction to liquor. David could throw down six highballs before dinner, more out of distraction than desire to get drunk. At parties he sometimes did get drunk, and then he was inclined to extremes of sentiment or pugnacity.

In sentimental moods he sometimes composed poems describing fellow party guests whom he admired. At a holiday occasion he scrawled a word-portrait of his dinner partner, Barbara Stanwyck:

BARBARA
A Quick Impression on a Drunken Christmas Night
By David 0. Selznick

> Without guile . . .
> 0. Henry style . . .
> Evening prayers at home . . .
> Corned beef at the Court of Rome
> Minsky learns emotion . . .
> Devotion . . .
> Grant Wood on 48th Street
> Salome's Vine Street Beat . . .
> Guff . . .
> Helen Hayes gets tough . . .
> Situation found . . .
> Talent on a merry-go-round . . .
> Rhapsody in Blue . . .
> Spangles for Sunbonnet Sue . . .
> The Manhattan Nation . . .
> Appreciation . . .

David enjoyed a fight, even if it was someone else's.

During one Selznick party, John Huston and Errol Flynn became embroiled in a dispute. Flynn had made a disparaging remark about a lady friend of Huston's. "That's not true!" Huston replied hotly. "And even if it were true, you are not a gentleman to say it!"

"Do you want to make something of it?" Flynn challenged.

"You're goddam right I do!" Huston replied.

The two men, both attired in tuxedos, retired to the garden of the Selznick estate, and began a slugging match more brutal than any in Flynn's film adventures. No one was aware of the encounter until the headlights of departing guests' cars shone on the combatants in the garden. David Selznick hurried to see what was going on. When he learned the nature of the dispute, he shouted at Flynn, "Put up your fists, you son of a bitch, and fight like a man!" Huston and other guests had to restrain David from continuing the attack on Flynn.

Working for Selznick could be a punishing ordeal. Several of his secretaries were driven to nervous breakdowns by his erratic hours and stringent demands. Other Selznick employees required hospitalization for overwork; in all cases David paid all the medical bills and kept the workers on salary. He was astonished when one secretary announced she could no longer stand the strain of working for him. David offered to send her to the Menninger Clinic for psychiatric observation.

Spurning a writing contract with Selznick, Nunnally Johnson replied: "I should certainly like to work for you, although my understanding of it is that an assignment from you consists of three months of work and three months of recuperation."

The Selznick way of life was described in a *Saturday Evening Post* article: "For a time he was, with medical permission, on a daily ration of Benzedrine pills and six or eight grains of thyroid extract—enough to send many a man to heaven. Rather than yield to fatigue, he occasionally left his office at 2 or 3 A.M. and went to a gambling house. This was an expensive cure for drowsiness, but after a few hours of roulette he would return to his office refreshed and wide awake, with all the fatigue toxins cleared out of his brain."[2]

Even when he went home at night, David avoided sleep. He ran movies in his den until early hours, prompting Charlie Chaplin and other neighbors to sign a petition protesting the noise. David soundproofed the screening room.

David was casual about social engagements. The Fredric Marches delayed a dinner one night because David had not arrived. When it finally appeared that the meal would be ruined, the ravenous guests were invited to dine without him. David arrived during the second course. "I won't have any dinner; I had a drink and a sandwich at the studio, he said offhandedly. Later in the evening he announced he was hungry, and Mrs. March ordered a food tray for him in the living room.

Extravagance became almost a mania with David, both in his personal life and with his company. He lavished gifts on his wife Irene and at Christmas time showered all his personal friends and close business associates with expensive presents. When someone performed a special service, he invariably responded with a gift. Daniel O'Shea one day maneuvered a contract that was especially favorable for the company. At ten that night, a messenger appeared at the O'Shea home with an envelope containing a bonus check of $75,000.

Selznick representatives always traveled with the best accommodations. David decreed: "There are only two kinds of classes—first class and no class." The Selznick tradition was obviously first class.

David's extravagances continued unchecked. He had been heartened by the enormous success of *Gone With the Wind,* not realizing the toll it had exacted from his creative energies. He had no reason to believe that his good fortune would not continue.

During the time he was producing and releasing *Gone With*

---

[2] The *Post* article caused David to worry that the public might consider him a dope addict and compulsive gambler. He ordered a special Gallup Poll of public opinion and was relieved to learn that those questioned held no such opinion of him.

the Wind, David Selznick made two other important pictures. One was *Intermezzo,* the first American film of Ingrid Bergman.

Selznick's New York scout, Kay Brown, knew an importer of Swedish movies, and he showed her a new film, *Intermezzo.* The story, about a married violinist who fell in love with his pretty accompanist, seemed to offer possibilities for an American remake, and Miss Brown sent a print of the film to Selznick. He agreed with her suggestion and dispatched her to Stockholm to secure the rights to the story.

She made the trip and returned to New York with the rights to the film. Ten days after her return, David had an afterthought: he also wanted her to sign the Swedish actress who appeared in the picture. Miss Brown made the return flight to Sweden, to negotiate with Ingrid Bergman and her husband, Dr. Peter Lindstrom, a dentist and medical student.

Miss Brown arrived at the Grand Hotel in Stockholm and telephoned the Lindstroms, offering to visit them. Lindstrom said no, they would visit her. He and his tall blond wife appeared, Ingrid bearing a bouquet of flowers. The meeting was stiff and formal, and the Lindstroms left early, explaining that they had to attend a family party.

On the following day, Miss Brown went to the Lindstroms' apartment. Lindstrom admitted that there had been no family party the night before; he and his wife merely wanted to see what kind of person she was. Since becoming a star in Sweden, Ingrid had received many Hollywood offers, usually from brash, fast-talking representatives she distrusted. But, she told Miss Brown, "You are so sweet and human that anyone you work for couldn't be nearly as crazy as I expected."

The actress admitted she was wary of going to Hollywood. She had seen too many European actresses who went there and had their names, personalities, and appearances changed. Later they vanished and reappeared in their native countries devoid of the attributes that had made them stars originally.

"Yes, I would be very careful, if I were you," said Miss Brown. "You have a very successful career here in Sweden. You have a husband and baby. You should be entirely certain in your own

Ingrid Bergman and David Selznick.

mind that going to Hollywood is what you want to do."

Ingrid admitted that she was curious to see Hollywood, but she would make a picture there only if Mr. Selznick provided a good script, director, and leading man. Since he promised her *Intermezzo*, William Wyler to direct and Leslie Howard to play opposite her, she could not refuse. But she insisted she would go to Hollywood for only one picture. If she stayed on, it would be her own decision.

Kay Brown cabled Miss Bergman's acceptance to David Selznick. She added the cautionary information: that the actress measured five feet, eight and one half inches in height. He cabled back: "Go ahead and sign her. And bring a ladder for

Leslie Howard."

Ingrid Bergman arrived in New York aboard the *Queen Mary* on May 6, 1939. She spent two weeks in New York, viewing the World's Fair and other sights and trying to improve her faltering English. When her train arrived in Los Angeles, she expected David O. Selznick to greet her on the platform with a bouquet of roses. Instead, she was met by a brisk press agent, George Glass, who relayed Mr. Selznick's instructions on publicity: "Soft-pedal the angle about having a husband and baby in Sweden." Miss Bergman received the instructions in stony silence.

After she had been taken to her hotel, Miss Bergman asked if she could go to the studio and meet Mr. Selznick.

"No, he's busy," she was told. "The studio will call you."

She waited all afternoon and no messages came. She telephoned the Selznick house and was told that Mr. Selznick would not be coming home for dinner. "Does he know that I have arrived?" she asked plaintively. Yes, Mr. Selznick was aware of her arrival.

Irene Selznick came to the hotel and took the actress to a Polynesian dinner at Don the Beachcomber's, where she stared at the movie stars. She saw more stars later at Miriam Hopkins' house, where a movie was being shown. During the showing, a butler tapped Miss Bergman on the shoulder and said, "Mr. Selznick would like to see you. He is eating dinner in the kitchen."

She was led into the kitchen, where she saw a chunky, bespectacled man leaning over a plate of food. He looked up at her and said, "Take off your shoes."

"I'm sorry, Mr. Selznick," she replied. "I am this tall."

"Oh my God!" he muttered, stuffing another bite into his mouth.

"You know your name is impossible," he said.

"It is?"

"Yes. Ingrid is too hard to pronounce. And Bergman—it sounds too German."

"No," she said firmly.

"What do you mean—no," he said with surprise.

"No, I am not going back to Sweden with a new name."

"We'll discuss that later," he replied with a wave, returning to his meal.

On her first visit to the Selznick studio, Miss Bergman was taken by David to the makeup department. He and the makeup artists studied her and discussed the changes that were needed: hair dyed, teeth capped, eyebrows plucked, etc.

"I am sorry, but I am going home," the actress announced.

David gazed at her in astonishment. "What are you talking about?" he asked.

"I am not going to stay here and have you change me into something I am not," she said. "I thought you liked *Intermezzo.*"

"I did. What's that got to do with it?"

"You must have liked me to have brought me all the way over here. And I did not have plucked eyebrows or dyed hair in *Intermezzo.*"

"Wait a minute—let me think," David said. He paused and then continued with enthusiasm: "That's it! A great publicity plan! We'll present you as a natural kind of beauty, without the usual kind of glamour treatment."

Miss Bergman was equally adamant about the customary publicity buildup. She refused to don a bathing suit and assume coy poses on the Santa Monica sands, and she shunned interviews. "If you build up the American public to expect something great from me, they are bound to be disappointed," she argued with David. "Why don't you let them discover me for themselves? Then they might be happily surprised."

David reluctantly agreed, and Miss Bergman saw no reporters, except for the ritual interview with the reigning press queen, Louella O. Parsons.

Intermezzo received little attention from David Selznick, who was involved in the completion and release of *Gone With the Wind.* William Wyler had left the picture after a dispute with David, and he was replaced as director by Gregory Ratoff, whose Russian-accented English added little to Miss Bergman's understanding of the language. Leslie Howard assumed some of the production duties, but he was impatient to return to England, then at war with Germany.[3] Miss Bergman went back to Sweden as soon as the film was completed.

The film proved a disappointment, but critics and audiences were impressed by the natural beauty and emotional depth of Ingrid Bergman. David Selznick was convinced that he had created a new star, and he was pleased when she decided to leave Sweden and continue her Hollywood career.

Out of England came puckish Alfred Hitchcock, an extraordinary innovator in the art of suspense and a valuable addition to the Selznick collection of talent.

The Englishman's first connection with the Selznick world had been with Myron. In 1924, Hitchcock had worked as scenario writer and art director on an English film, *The Passionate Adventure,* starring Clive Brook and Alice Joyce. The film was a co-production with the Lewis J. Selznick company, and Myron went to London to oversee the production, as well as visit his future wife, Marjorie Daw, a member of the cast. He struck up a friendship with the rotund Hitchcock. Years later, when Myron became an agent, he signed Alfred Hitchcock as a client.

During the filming of *The Lady Vanishes,* Hitchcock received a cable from David Selznick asking him to come to Hollywood to discuss a film about the sinking of the *Titanic.* In August of 1937, Hitchcock made his first trip to America and conferred for ten days with David in Culver City. David talked excitedly of a grandiose scheme. The liner *Leviathan,* claimed as a prize of war after World War I, had been taken off the Atlantic run and was tied up at Hoboken awaiting disposal as scrap. David wanted to buy the *Leviathan,* tow it through the Panama Canal to California, overhaul its top deck to resemble the *Titanic,* shoot the picture on it, then sink the ship off Santa Monica.

The project stirred Hitchcock's whimsy, and he imagined a Selznick operative dropping into the Fifth Avenue offices of the

---

[3] *Intermezzo* was Howard's last Hollywood film. He was aboard an airliner that was shot down by German planes between Lisbon and London on June 1, 1943.

United States Lines and having this exchange with a ticket agent:

"Excuse me—"

"Yes, what can I do for you?"

"Could you tell me how much is the Leviathan?"

"Oh, I'm sorry, the Leviathan *isn't running any more. Now I can offer you the* Manhattan—"

"No, no. I want to buy the Leviathan."

As the discussion of the *Titanic* film continued, Hitchcock's imagination ranged further. He pictured the *Leviathan* lying off Santa Monica and David Selznick instructing him, "Now make the most of it." How to do so? Hitchcock devised a scene in which he would open with the closeup of a rivet, then dolly back five thousand feet to include the entire ship.

He also envisioned the final sinking of the *Leviathan*, with himself giving the command, "All right now, pull the seacocks!" Then he pictured the huge vessel sinking into the Pacific just as the cameraman declared, "I do believe the electrical system went wrong and we missed getting the shot." To which the speculation would have been: "Now who's going back to the studio to tell Mr. Selznick?"

Hitchcock related his visions to David, who was unamused.

The director returned to London and began researching the *Titanic* disaster. Meanwhile David Selznick instructed Kay Brown to purchase the *Leviathan*. She had performed many a chore for Selznick International, but the buying of an ocean liner was an entirely new problem. She went to Board Chairman Jock Whitney and asked, "How do I buy the *Leviathan*?"

Whitney referred her to a friend in marine insurance, a Mr. Green. She called him and said, "Mr. Green, this is Miss Brown and this is no joke. This is also not a joke: I want to buy the *Leviathan*."

"You're too late," Mr. Green replied. "It has just been sold for scrap for two million dollars."

"But that's impossible!" she protested. "I must buy it for David 0. Selznick so he can tow it to California and sink it."

"Miss Brown, it would cost two million dollars just to tow it to California. So I suggest you tell your Mr. Selznick to forget about it."

Regretfully, David abandoned the *Titanic* project. He had acquired a best-selling novel by Daphne du Maurier, *Rebecca*, and he decided to film it as Alfred Hitchcock's American debut.

Then he learned that Myron's underlings were negotiating contracts for Hitchcock at Paramount and RKO. David was furious, demanding that Myron reprimand the agents. Myron refused, declaring that David received no special favors from his agency. The pair battled furiously, and Myron snapped, "Oh, go back to your father-in-law!" David finally agreed to pay Hitchcock $75,000 per picture.

Robert E. Sherwood was assigned to write the script of *Rebecca* with the assistance of Joan Harrison, who had worked with Hitchcock on his British films.

"Manderley is as important as any member of the cast," David told his staff. "It must be real and it must be impressive. There are many houses in England, but we can't go there because of the war. Somewhere in this country there must be a house that looks like Manderley. Find it!"

William Cameron Menzies, Lyle Wheeler, and Ray Klune inspected mansions throughout the United States and Canada. A few possibilities were found in New England and in British Columbia, but their remoteness posed problems, as did the requirement to destroy Manderley at the end of the picture. The solution seemed to be in creating a miniature of Manderley at the Selznick studio. Production manager Ray Klune presented sketches to David.

"That's it! That's Manderley!" David exclaimed. "Where did you find it?"

"We didn't find it," said the production manager. "We're going to build it."

"But that would cost a fortune!" David protested.

"Not if we build a miniature."

"Oh, no you don't!" David replied. "No Selznick picture is going to have a phony miniature."

"Look, David," Klune reasoned, "this will be no ordinary miniature. This will be the most expensive ever made. We'll get you something you can be proud of."

David reluctantly agreed, and the studio craftsmen began building the immense miniature on the scale of one inch to one foot.

Laurence Olivier was signed to play the master of Manderley, and a distinguished supporting cast was assembled: Judith Anderson as Mrs. Danvers, plus George Sanders, Nigel Bruce, C. Aubrey Smith, Reginald Denny, Gladys Cooper, Leo G. Carroll, Lumsden Hare. Britishers all. Obviously the heroine—the second Mrs. De Winter—had to be British as well. David had almost as much trouble casting the role as he did with Scarlett O'Hara. Olivier was eager to have Vivien Leigh play opposite him, but that proved impractical. The filming of *Rebecca* would soon follow *Gone With the Wind,* and Vivien was too exhausted to undertake another role. In addition, David did not want to detract from her impact as Scarlett O'Hara.

One night at Charlie Chaplin's house, David found himself seated at dinner next to Olivia de Havilland's younger sister, Joan Fontaine, who had been playing ingenues at RKO. They began talking about novels and poetry, and David was impressed with her knowledge of literature.

"Have you read *Rebecca?*" she asked.

"Yes, I bought the film rights," David replied. "Would you like to test for it?"

Joan Fontaine tested several times for the role, then married Brian Aherne and went off on a fishing honeymoon at a mountain lake. One day she was called off the lake for a telephone call. It was her agent telling her she had won the role in *Rebecca.*

"But I don't want it," answered the new bride.

She went back to the boat and told Aherne about the message. "Oh, why don't you do it for hat money?" he suggested.

Laurence Olivier was incensed because Selznick did not give the role to Vivien Leigh. The actor directed his hostility toward his costar, dropping four-letter obscenities during rehearsals.

"Be careful, Larry," Hitchcock chided. "Joan is just a bride." Olivier arched an eyebrow. "Oh, really? Who did you marry?" he asked.

On the set of Rebecca: *Alfred Hitchcock, Gladys Cooper, Nigel Bruce, and Joan Fontaine.*

"Brian Aherne," Joan replied with a smile.

"Couldn't you have done better than that?" Olivier comment-ed. Other members of the cast sided with Olivier during the film-ing. On October 22, 1939, Joan Fontaine marked her twenty-sec-ond birthday on the set of *Rebecca*, and she spent most of the day alone in her small dressing room. Late in the afternoon she heard voices singing "Happy Birthday to You." She emerged to find mem-bers of the cast and crew bearing a cake and a few presents. A flustered Reginald Denny admitted to her in private that he had tried to enlist Olivier, Judith Anderson, and Gladys Cooper for the celebration "but they said they couldn't be bothered."

Joan found more sympathetic understanding from Hitchcock, who devoted careful attention to her role. In keeping with the Selznick philosophy of not tampering with widely-read books, the script adhered to the Du Maurier novel. But Hitchcock shot it in his own way, planning every scene in detail, photographing only the scenes he required. This was partly out of habit, partly as a defense against David Selznick. He knew of the producer's propensity of tampering with films after their

Scene from REBECCA.

completion.

"I can't figure out this goddam jigsaw puzzle of yours," David complained.

Hitchcock blithely continued shooting in his own economical style.

David peppered him with suggestions, including the idea of having smoke from the burning Manderley form a giant R in the sky. Hitchcock argued him out of it by suggesting a scene in Rebecca's bedroom showing a pillow with the monogram R being consumed in flames.

David was preparing for the *Gone With the Wind* premieres while Hal Kern edited *Rebecca*. David had calculated $250,000 worth of retakes would be needed, but after he previewed

Rebecca he decided only a day and a half of new scenes would be needed. Hitchcock objected, declaring he had filmed *Rebecca* correctly the first time. David insisted, and the director was forced to acquiesce. But he remained aloof, barring Selznick from the set. David stationed himself at the far end of the stage, and Hal Kern carried messages back and forth between director and producer.

Rebecca won critical applause for Alfred Hitchcock and Joan Fontaine, but it was not a big financial success on its first release. Upset because M-G-M had won the gold mine that was *Gone With the Wind,* United Artists made little effort to push *Rebecca,* selling it routinely along with the rest of the 1940 releases. Wider distribution was provided when *Rebecca* was chosen by the Academy as best picture—the second year in a row that a David O. Selznick film had been so chosen. Joan Fontaine's award was postponed until 1941, when she was chosen as best actress for another Hitchcock film, *Suspicion.*

David Selznick stopped making pictures.

He made no announcement of temporary retirement, and indeed he seemed to have no such notion in mind. He continued to issue announcements of ambitious projects and prepared them with his usual thoroughness. But no new films appeared under the prestigious Selznick banner. He seemed to have expended all his vitality on *Gone With the Win.* It was an achievement of a lifetime: the most honored, the biggest, the most successful film in Hollywood history.

David had no reason to hurry back into production. *Gone*

With the Wind had hastily paid off the five million dollars owed to the banks. Jock Whitney was planning to join the Navy, and he saw the opportunity to get out of the movie business. It had brought him excitement, but also many worries and little return for his investment. Now at last *Gone With the Wind* was providing a great deal of profit, but it was taxable income, which he little needed. It appeared wiser to sell out his interest in Selznick International for capital gains.

His confidence in David Selznick was eroding. The two men engaged in lengthy arguments over the extravagance of David's mode of operation. Selznick International had not known a profitable year until *Gone With the Wind;* conceivably, David's spending could wipe out the immense profits that were pouring in. He had grown more erratic in his daily operations. He was gambling more and more at roulette and poker. It was a good time for Jock Whitney to get out.

David sold his interest in Selznick International to Whitney for two million dollars, and Whitney in turn sold the rights to *Gone With the Wind* to M-G-M. Except for small interests retained by Myron Selznick and C.V. Whitney, M-G-M acquired full ownership of the picture,, which was to earn scores of millions in re-releases for decades to come.

In the sell-out to Whitney, David retained contracts with stars and directors. Lacking the incentive to make pictures, he plunged into the talent business. He developed a roster of players who commanded the same prestige and respect as had his films. But instead of employing those players, he loaned them to other studios, sometimes in conjunction with completed scripts. It was a quick and sure way to turn a profit, but in the end it seemed like poor business.

America was at war. Servicemen, factory workers, and war-weary citizens eagerly sought the escape of screen entertainment, and film company profits soared. Other studios welcomed the use of Selznick's appealing stars and his handcrafted scripts and were willing to pay dearly for them. The major companies thus reaped the returns which David Selznick could have had, if only he could have brought himself to produce again.

Olivia de Havilland was naturally suspicious of the late-evening telephone call from her agent, Myron Selznick.

"You are going to make a lot of money Olivia," he exclaimed. "One hundred and twenty-five thousand dollars! Isn't that wonderful?"

The actress, who had engaged in constant battle with her employer, Jack L. Warner, was incredulous. "You mean," she asked, "that Warners will pay me that much for a loan-out?"

"Oh, no!" Myron replied. "You're not going to get it. You'll just make it. David's going to get it."

David had maneuvered a contract arrangement so cleverly complex as to win the admiration of his own brother. It began with Warner Brothers' urgent necessity to engage Ingrid Bergman as co-star with Gary Cooper in *Saratoga Trunk*. Miss Bergman, of course, was the property of David O. Selznick. Selznick offered to lend Miss Bergman at the bargain rate of $125,000—$25,000 less than the usual figure—in return for a one-picture commitment with Olivia de Havilland.

Warner Brothers agreed to the proposal, and Selznick hurriedly sold his commitment for Miss De Havilland to RKO for $125,000.

She was starred against her will in *Government Girl* with Sonny Tufts.

After Joan Fontaine's emergence as a star in *Rebecca,* David anticipated earning high profits from her services. His hopes were realized, over the protests of the strong-willed and independent actress. The deterioration of their relations was evidenced by his Christmas gifts to her.

After the first year of her contract, David sent her a set of English bone china, plus a bonus check for $30,000.

The following year was marked by constant wrangles over her loan-outs. For Christmas, David sent her a potted geranium which bore the price tag of $5.

The steel-willed Miss Fontaine protested the poor quality of scripts for the loan-out films, as well as the inequitable arrangement for her salary. She claimed that David reversed the usual formula of Myron Selznick and other agents—"You take ninety percent and leave the actors ten percent," she cried.

David, who actually kept $120,000 of her $150,000 loan-out fee, argued that he had brought Joan's career into flower after she had been dropped by RKO. He added that he provided important services, pointing to his forty-page memo to Paramount concerning the treatment of Joan Fontaine on *Frenchman's Creek.* She was unimpressed, and the gulf between her and David widened. During her five years under contract to Selznick, she made ten movies. Only one—*Rebecca*—was a Selznick picture.

Ingrid Bergman was more content with her loan-outs; in fact, she pleaded with David to be loaned more often. One of her assignments was *Gaslight,* which brought her an Academy Award. Another was *Casablanca* with Humphrey Bogart. The role she wanted most was that of Maria in the Ernest Hemingway story, *For Whom the Bell Tolls.* David Selznick wanted her to do it, but he was unable to convince Paramount, which had purchased the novel. The studio tested several other actresses before deciding on Vera Zorina, a ballet dancer in Broadway musicals.

David refused to accept the Zorina casting as a *fait accompli.* Coincidentally, both Hemingway and Miss Bergman were clients of Myron's. A luncheon was arranged for the author and the actress in San Francisco before his departure for China.

"You are Maria!" Hemingway proclaimed, perhaps forgetting his description of Maria in his book: "Her teeth were white in her brown face and her skin and eyes were the same golden tawny brown. She had high cheekbones, merry eyes and a straight mouth with full lips. Her hair was the golden-brown of a grain field that has been burned dark in the sun . . ."

Paramount remained undissuaded, and filming began in the Sierras, which doubled for the mountains of Spain. David still did not give up hope. After two weeks of production, filming was suspended, and Miss Zorina was dropped from the cast. David rubbed his hands and waited for the Paramount emissaries to come and plead for Miss Bergman's services. He agreed to lend her for $120,000. Her previous loan-out price had been $90,000.

During the following year, David extracted $425,000 for renting the services of Ingrid Bergman to other producers. While the actress displayed little dissatisfaction over being so exploited, her husband became increasingly disturbed. Peter Lindstrom had come to the United States, and Selznick had been instrumental in gaining his entrance to medical school at the University of Rochester. Despite his medical studies, Lindstrom resumed his management of his wife's career, and he insisted that Ingrid should receive a greater share of the fees exacted for her services.

David was eager for more talent which he could deal to the other studios—and perhaps use himself when he felt like producing again. He had been impressed with Joseph Cotten, part of the Orson Welles troupe in *Citizen Kane*. David sent for Cotten, who was appearing in *Journey Into Fear* at the Pathé studio. "Read this book," said Selznick, handing Cotten a best-selling novel.

Cotten took the book home and read it. He hated it, but didn't know how to tell Selznick. He consulted his friend, author MacKinlay Kantor, and they composed a telegram which carried the name of the book's hero: "I think I would be the worst ------ you could choose."

Kantor had an afterthought: "That's a pretty strong wire; he's liable to sign you up." That is what happened. When Welles's Mercury Theatre was ousted from RKO, Cotten signed a contract with Selznick.

Cotten soon found himself working at a furious rate in the Selznick employ. At one point he was engaged in two films at once. One of them was *Gaslight* with Ingrid Bergman, who was also appearing in *Saratoga Trunk* at the same time. A tireless prankster, Cotten enlisted Miss Bergman in a joke on their employer. One Saturday night after their day-long labors on movie sets, the pair reported to the rear door of the Selznick mansion. They donned uniforms of maid and butler and served trays of hors d'oeuvres to guests of the large dinner party David and Irene were giving. The presence of the two stars went undetected for an hour. Finally Miss Bergman identified herself to David with the comment: "As long as Joe and I are your slaves,

Ray Corrigan, Phylis Isley, John Wayne, NEW FRONTIER.

we figured we might as well serve your guests."

Gregory Peck had received a flurry of interest from the studios after he appeared on the New York stage in *The Morning Star* in 1947. Among those recommending a screen test was Selznick's Kay Brown. The gaunt Californian was unimpressive in the test, and Selznick executives agreed that his ears were too prominent. He wasn't signed.

But then Casey Robinson brought Peck to Hollywood for *Days of Glory,* and other producers began to take interest. Among them was David Selznick, who had a property called *The Keys of the Kingdom* which was both difficult to cast and troublesome to clear with the Production Code because of theological matters. David decided to cast young Peck as the maverick priest and sell the problem package to 20th Century-Fox, which was looking for properties. David prudently retained commitments on Peck's services for future projects.

More packages. David was impressed with the Broadway performance of Dorothy McGuire in *Claudia.* He sent George

Cukor to New York for an extensive test of the young actress. Selznick signed her to a contract, acquired the rights to Claudia, and sold the play and half of Miss McGuire's contract to Twentieth Century-Fox.

David had another commitment with Vivien Leigh but could find no property he wanted to produce with her. Through a devious arrangement, David acquired *Waterloo Bridge* from Universal, solved its censorship problems with industry censor Joseph Breen, and sold star and story to M-G-M, which co-starred Miss Leigh with Robert Taylor.

Jane Eyre had long been a Selznick project. David had hired William Pereira, an architect who had designed films for Cecil B. De Mille, to plan the visual aspects of the production in the same manner that William Cameron Menzies had designed *Gone With the Wind.* Joan Fontaine was cast as Jane, with Robert Stevenson to direct a script by Aldous Huxley. David lost interest in the project and sold it to 20th Century-Fox, where Miss Fontaine appeared opposite Orson Welles.

Another actress who came into the Selznick realm was Phylis Isley.

She was a curious candidate for stardom. Although she had been born into the theater—her parents ran a touring stock company in Oklahoma, and later operated movie houses—she was excessively shy and withdrawn. But something propelled her toward amateur theatrics, in which she excelled, and she went on to study at Northwestern University and the American Academy of Dramatic Arts. A fellow student at the Academy was tall, equally shy Robert Walker, whom she married on January 2, 1939. Sons were born to them in 1940 and 1941.

They earned a precarious living from radio and Broadway plays; for one brief period they prospered when Phylis was called to Hollywood to appear in a John Wayne western and a Dick Tracy serial for Republic. Bob Walker earned twenty-five dollars a week reading scripts for an agent. Phylis's option at Republic was dropped, and they returned to Manhattan for another try at soap operas and neighborhood plays. An agent saw Phylis at Paul Gilmore's Little Theatre and brought her to the attention of David Selznick's New York representative, Kay Brown. When her boss next came to Manhattan, Miss Brown arranged a reading for the brunette from Tulsa.

Selznick was impressed. He ordered a test, and the results proved exceptionally good. One major hurdle remained. David had Phylis Isley replace Dorothy McGuire during one performance of *Claudia* on Broadway. The cast was hostile toward the newcomer who threatened Miss McGuire's chances of starring on the screen as Claudia. Phylis nevertheless performed well enough to win a contract.

David sent his new contract player to Santa Barbara, where John Houseman was operating a season at the Lobero Theatre for the development of Selznick performers and scripts. Miss Isley was cast opposite Harry Bratsburg (later Harry Morgan) in a new one-act play by William Saroyan, *Hello, Out There*. The play was well received, and Houseman invited the actress to join a party with the Los Angeles press on the Santa Barbara pier after the performance.

She did not appear, and Houseman telephoned to inquire about her. She explained that she had to call home to her husband and two sons in New York. In reality she was terrified lest Selznick's new female star be exposed by members of the press as the girl who had appeared in a Republic western.

David Selznick believed during the history-making years of the early 1940s that he was destined for more significant accomplishments than creating film entertainment. Thwarted by the Democratic Administration in his desire to serve inside the Government, he sought another area of public service.

The opportunity came when David was appointed Hollywood chairman of China War Relief. This was what he had been waiting for: a chance to make a contribution to the war effort, and, incidentally, to show himself as a pillar of the community. China Relief allowed him to work in solemn collaboration with prestigious members of the New York social community, since the cause was the special interest of the noted Chinophile, Henry R. Luce.

David Selznick, chairman of the Hollywood Committee for United China Relief, with Mrs. Chester La Roche, chairman of the dinner for Generalissimo and Madame Chiang Kai-shek at the Waldorf-Astoria, June 18, 1941.

Luce sent one of his top editors to California for a conference with the new Hollywood chairman of China War Relief. The easterner found David bristling with ideas.

"I've got a great plan," said David. "We get a bunch of Chinamen and dress them in blue cloth and rags, like peasants. We load them on buses and send them across the country. They go through a town, collecting money for China Relief in their rice bowls. Then we load them back on the buses and drive to the next town. We could make millions that way."

The Luce representative convinced David that ill will might be engendered by sending Chinese across the land like money-raising locusts. His fervor undimmed, David went on to other schemes.

David was impressed by the success of *The White Cliffs,* the narrative poem by Alice Duer Miller which had been published in *Life* and had become a best-selling book as well as the basis for a hit song and a motion picture. He suggested to his staff, "Let's write a *White Cliffs of Dover* about China."

The staff agreed, but who in Hollywood was capable of taking on such an assignment? Gene Fowler was a writer of verse, though usually of a bawdy nature. Selznick asked him to try his hand at a China poem. Fowler declined.

David assigned the chore to one of his writers, Peter Viertel, and to his story editor, Val Lewton. Both men grumbled over the assignment, but they retired and produced their verse. David asked John Houseman what he thought of the result.

Houseman found Lewton's poem in the Kipling tradition, rumbling with portent about the mysteries of the East. Viertel produced a freeverse conversation of an American taxi driver facing dangers on the Burma Road. Houseman thought both poems were awful, but he realized the importance Selznick attached to them.

"Perhaps—uh, you could combine the two into one poem," Houseman said tentatively.

"Good idea!" exclaimed David. The two poems were inter-mingled, and the result was printed in *Life,* without the equal success of *The White Cliffs.*

David urged his staff to contribute ideas for China Relief, his zeal matching anything he had displayed for one of his motion pictures. Endless memos poured forth from his office; meetings were held throughout the day and far into the night. At one meeting an underling suggested that since Madame Chiang Kai-shek was in Washington, why not invite her out as guest of honor at a fund-raising program in the Hollywood Bowl?

The idea was brilliant, David decided. He arranged the affair with the Chinese Embassy, then enlisted enough stars to assure a top-notch show. For weeks he supervised every detail. Besides the spectacle at the Hollywood Bowl, he scheduled an industry dinner at the Ambassador Hotel.

David consulted with the State Department on matters of protocol. The dinner, he decided, would be limited to only the most prestigious members of the film community—no outsiders or Johnny-come-latelies allowed. The guests would be admitted to a reception room, where Madame Chiang Kai-shek would receive them on a canopied platform resembling a throne.

When the time arrived for the reception, Irene Mayer Selznick arrived to check on final arrangements. She noticed a group standing by the doorway. "Who are those people?" she asked of a Selznick publicity man. He told her they were the press, and she replied that they must leave. The alarmed publicist appealed the edict to David, but he replied, "Don't bother me; take care of it." And so the reporters and photographers were asked to leave.

Since the event was for China, a reporter and a photographer for *Life* remained. Also present was a columnist whose longevity in the film community and intimacy with the movie powers gave her special status. She took a position in the receiving line second only to Hollywood's First Lady, Mary Pickford.

Regrettably, the columnist was overcome by the excitement of greeting one of the world's most famous women. The other guests gazed in rapt horror as an ever-widening pool began to form at the feet of the columnist.

David was also horrified. The State Department had offered no protocol to cover such a situation. He decided to ignore it and hope that no one had the bad taste to notice. But then he gazed over and saw the *Life* photographer aiming his camera directly at the puddled columnist. David accosted both the *Life* men and excoriated them, accusing them of trying to sabotage the entire affair. They pointed out that since their employer was Henry Luce they would scarcely attempt anything that would denigrate an affair in honor of Madame Chiang Kai-shek. David was not placated.

The exclusive dinner continued without further incident, and David was pleased and proud. He was less pleased the following day when he read accounts of the dinner in the Los Angeles newspapers. The reporters who had been ousted from the gathering neglected to include the name of David O. Selznick in their stories.

It was mid-morning, and Myron Selznick poured himself a tumbler of Johnny Walker Black Label Scotch. He was oblivious of the reproving stare of his brother David, a visitor to the modern, circular Myron Selznick Building on Wilshire Boulevard in Beverly Hills.

"Myron," David began, "you are going to ruin yourself drinking the way you do."

Myron fixed his gaze on his younger brother. "I'm going to ruin myself, huh?" he said.

"That's right," David said firmly.

"I see. Let me ask you something: what are you doing here?"

"You know damn well what I'm doing here," David replied indignantly.

"Tell me anyway."

"I am here," David said with embarrassment, "to borrow some money so I can pay my income tax."

Myron paused to allow the lesson to sink in. "You are borrowing money from me so you can pay your income tax. And I'm the one who is ruining himself! By God, I think I'll have another drink on that!"

No amount of argument from his brother, his clients, or his friends could dissuade Myron from his relentless consumption of whisky. His alcoholism became accepted as part of his pattern of life. Studio bosses maintained bars in their offices, primarily for the use of Myron Selznick. As soon as he entered to negotiate a contract, he went directly to the bar and poured himself a drink. There was no evidence that the negotiations were made easier by Myron's indulgence. But the executives feared that

Myron Selznick, his wife and daughter on a European trip.

Myron would be much tougher without a drink.

He refused to discuss his drinking with anyone, including his own brother. Rarely did he indicate the inner torment that caused him to drink. Once he disclosed to Loretta Young that many nights he crawled onto his mother's bed and cried himself to sleep—"me, a grown man!" When Miss Young asked the nature of the unhappiness that caused him to drink, he replied, "I don't know."

Some of Myron's close friends theorized that his sorrow stemmed from the complexity of being a Selznick in the movie industry.

"My brother is the only man in history to make a fortune from revenge," said David Selznick. Indeed, revenge had motivated Myron's drive for power in Hollywood. But now Myron had humbled the men who had ruined his father. What was left for him?

He did not enjoy the agency business. Beyond the wielding of power there was nothing creative in peddling other people's

David Selznick signs Shirley Temple to a contract.

talents. Those moments in Myron's youth when he was oversee-ing the production of five movie studios, when stars and direc-tors and writers were seeking his guidance and support—those were the golden times of Myron Selznick's life. Then he was cre-ating, building, seeking new vistas of entertainment. He was directing the destiny of his father's entertainment empire—and he failed.

Lewis J. Selznick had pushed his gamble too far, and Adolph Zukor and the other giants had closed in on him. Myron still har-bored the nagging thought that if he himself had managed pro-duction with greater brilliance, the name of Selznick might never have been dishonored.

The family name had been restored, but that had been largely the work of David. Myron was feared, even grudgingly respected in the film world. But he was an agent. David was the producer.

Myron became increasingly arrogant with the studios. When

Louis Mayer barred him from M-G-M in a moment of pique, Myron barred his client William Powell from M-G-M. Since Powell was starring in an important movie, Mayer quickly made peace.

Powell's contract with M-G-M came up for renewal, and studio negotiator Eddie Mannix asked Myron to come to the studio for discussions. "No, I've barred M-G-M," Myron replied. "Come to my office." He kept Mannix waiting in the outer office for half an hour. Myron spent the time having a drink with an assistant, Collier Young.

Myron sometimes became thick-tongued at the end of a day, but he rarely appeared drunk. He never seemed to lose command in negotiations. But his interest in the agency business was declining, and his clients were beginning to sense it. He was becoming less solicitous of his clients' concerns.

Three of his glamorous clients—Merle Oberon, Loretta Young, and Carole Lombard—were having problems with their studios and sought Myron's aid. He kept putting them off until he could do so no longer. He invited all three to dinner at his house. When each actress tried to present her problem, Myron changed the subject by rhapsodizing how beautiful she was and how he would like to have an affair with her.

When Miss Oberon attempted for the third time to discuss studio matters, he interrupted: "Merlie, you're so goddam gorgeous I can't stand it. I'd really like to get you in the hay."

Miss Oberon threw down her napkin and said: "All right, Myron, let's go upstairs right now. *Then* maybe you'll listen to what I have to say!"

"Now, Merlie, I was only kidding," said Myron. Her bluff worked, and he began listening to the actresses' problems.

Stars found it increasingly difficult to gain Myron's attention. Carole Lombard sued to end her contract with him. "I love the son of a bitch," she told a friend, "but Myron simply won't do anything for me."

His wife, Marjorie Daw, sued him for divorce and was granted a large settlement and custody of their daughter. In her suit she had estimated his wealth at $10,000,000, his monthly income $20,000.

Myron had built a showplace resort at Running Springs in the San Bernardino Mountains where he enjoyed taking friends for long weekends. Often he curled up in the windowseat of the mountain lodge at five in the afternoon and slept until ten at night, at which time his guests had dined and were ready for bed. Myron resumed drinking, oblivious of the others. As time went on, fewer guests were invited to the mountains. Myron sometimes disappeared from the office for a week.

Myron had kept his vow never again to take a partner after Frank Joyce died. He built up a highly competent staff and paid his agents handsome salaries; but Myron was complete boss. His underlings were understandably restive. Myron's absences became more frequent and prolonged; even when he paid visits to the Beverly Hills headquarters, he seemed distant and ineffectual.

Two of the leading agents in the office were delegated to make a pilgrimage to Running Springs. They found Myron drunk

Ginger Rogers and Joseph Cotten in I'LL BE SEEING YOU.

Jennifer Jones, THE SONG OF BERNADETTE.

but lucid. He listened attentively as they set forth their proposal: the top six men in the agency wanted a forty-nine percent share of the business. They pledged their continuing loyalty and stood ready to share the risks in the company. But in return they wanted to be consulted on policy matters and they wanted to participate in the profits.

Myron pondered a moment and made his reply: "_ _ __ _ you!" The interview was over.

Agents began leaving the Selznick Agency, sometimes taking clients along with them. Myron didn't seem to care.

In early 1944 he began suffering internal hemorrhages. He was rushed to Santa Monica Hospital where transfusions were administered, but his condition worsened. On March 23, he died at the age of forty-five.

David was inconsolable. He had to be supported by friends as he faltered down the aisle of Temple Israel for the funeral. Rabbi Max Nussbaum conducted the services, and William Powell read the eulogy by Gene Fowler:

"Here at Myron's side a mother sits, and in her sweet presence we can but say that she is a brave symbol of all the mothers who grieve in a world of present woe. Her tears are those of the mothers of all time. Still, today, they are shed for a son.

"Who was this man? And what was he, this man for whom a mother lived?

"'He was a little boy who never grew up,' she said in the hour of her great loss ...

"We knew his great place in the busy province of the motion picture. Indeed, many of us owe our good fortune to him. For he was both brilliant and wise, as was his great and adventurous father before him. Oh, yes, we knew, admired, loved—sometimes quarreled with him during the heat of battle—for we are volatile and impulsive in the arts. We remember that he was a loyal friend and an unbeatable foe during the days of crisis.

"'He had prejudices,' we say frankly, 'and he was not perfect.'

"He had moods. He could and did fight both with fist and brain. We loved him for his courage. We admired him for the quickest mind of anyone since the pioneer day of his great father, whose name he and his brother, David, perpetuated with energy and with honor.

"We may speak or write of all these things and more today, and again say them tomorrow. But how empty do our well-intentioned words seem in the presence of the mother's discerning summation:

"'He was a little boy who never grew up.'"

The decline and death of Myron brought further upset to the life of David Selznick. In the aftermath of *Gone With the Wind* he had been unable to direct his enormous energies to creative endeavor. He continued to maintain an active enterprise, making story purchases, preparing scripts, and signing performers to

On a movie set: Robert Walker, Jennifer Jones, David Selznick, and Shirley Temple.

contracts; one of his successful notions was introducing Shirley Temple as a grown-up actress.

But the picture projects he announced were never made, at least not by him. He prepared scripts for Alfred Hitchcock to direct, then sold them to the highest bidder. One package deal combined Hitchcock, Cary Grant, Ingrid Bergman, and a half-finished script of *Notorious* by Ben Hecht. He sold the package to RKO for $800,000 for almost triple his investment.

At one point he decided he wanted to make a picture of *Mein Kampf.* He studied newsreel footage of Adolf Hitler and the Nazi movement and assigned William Pereira to work on a production design. But the project died as abruptly as it had been conceived.

David realized he needed production to maintain his staff at a degree of efficiency, yet he could find nothing worthy of the Selznick name. So he devised the idea of a subsidiary company which could make use of the studio talent and facilities for inexpensive but worthwhile films. He formed Vanguard Productions with Dore Schary as producer. Schary had just left M-G-M where he had produced a number of impressive B pictures until his outspokenness had brought him into conflict with Louis B. Mayer.

"My father-in-law says you're a difficult man," David said to Schary. "But then, he said the same thing about me when I was at M-G-M. I think we'll get along."

David offered to give Schary complete freedom to make pictures, reserving only approval of story projects. Schary's first script derived from *Double Furlough,* a radio drama about the romance of a battle-fatigued soldier and a girl ex-convict. Within six weeks Schary submitted the completed script with the notation: "You wanted it quick, but I think it's also good."

Schary received a sixteen-page memo filled with Selznick scorn and lectures about screen writing. Schary, ill with influenza, answered with a memo accusing Selznick of unkept promises. Schary's memo concluded: "This letter carries my resignation—goodbye."

David insisted on visiting Schary that evening, despite Schary's illness. "I showed my memo and yours to Irene, and she said I was wrong," David admitted. "She's right. If I believed in what you did at M-G-M, I should leave you alone. Go ahead and do the picture. But I want no part of it."

He refused to allow Schary to cast Joseph Cotten for the lead and predicted: "You won't be able to get an important star to play either part." Schary bet $100 that he could. A few days later he announced that Ginger Rogers had accepted the film. The astonished Selznick handed over $100—and Joseph Cotten. He added Shirley Temple for the role of the sister, plus William Dieterle as director.

David began showering Schary with memos about Ginger's dresses, Shirley's hairdos, etc. Schary reminded him of their agreement about noninterference, and the memos ceased. When David saw the final version, he gave Schary a bearhug and said: "I don't know how the hell you did it; I never could see anything in the picture." David gave the picture an important release campaign and acquired the popular wartime song for the theme and

Robert Walker and Jennifer Jones in a love scene for SINCE YOU WENT AWAY.

Jennifer Jones receiving her Oscar for THE SONG OF BERNADETTE.

title: *I'll Be Seeing You.*

David Selznick issued the memo to all departments that hence-forth the contract player Phylis Isley would be known as Jennifer Jones.

His investment in her acting career paid off with gratifying swiftness. David knew that 20th Century-Fox was seeking an unknown actress for the leading role in *The Song of Bernadette*. He brought the new Miss Jones from New York to test for the part of the peasant girl whose visions at Lourdes led to her saint-hood. Henry King directed her in three tests and was impressed by her raw-boned naturalness. He also found her eager to work and to learn. She volunteered to act in the tests of other players being considered for roles in the film, and she played scenes opposite Lee J. Cobb, Charles Bickford, Anne Revere, and Roman

Bohnen. King put the footage together and showed the result to the producer, William Perlberg. "I think you'd better choose this girl," said the director. "If you go on testing other actresses, you'll end up confused and you'll settle for some star. That would be a mistake. This girl *is* Bernadette."

She proved to be a brilliant choice, embodying all the innocence and faith of Saint Bernadette. David Selznick was delighted to find himself with a brand-new star, created for him by another studio. He was perturbed to learn that Perlberg had invited her to attend the premiere of *The Song of Bernadette* with himself and his wife.

Unwilling to let 20th Century-Fox claim his star, David instructed her to tell Perlberg she was ill and couldn't go.

David recognized that Jennifer was colorless off-screen, a timorous, uncertain girl devoid of the attributes of a movie star. So he placed her under the tutelage of Anita Colby.

A woman of startling beauty and a talent for self-promotion, the famed Cover Girl had sold herself to Selznick as consultant to his growing list of female stars. She advised them in all matters, from how to pose for news photographers to how to handle Hollywood wolves. Among her instructions: "Bergman is so beautiful you must play it down; you cannot overpower her with clothes." "Make Fontaine smart, feminine, and refined." "Keep Shirley looking sweet sixteen with soft hair, pigtails, and girlish pinafores." "Give McGuire that sweater and skirt feeling."

Jennifer was a more complex challenge.

"Her clothes need the dressmaker, rather than the tailored look," Miss Colby analyzed. "I'd rather have them pretty than terribly chic. If you don't have the kind of dame who can give a fourteen-dollar dress a hundred-dollar look, you have to do something drastic about it."

Miss Colby steered Jennifer away from the simple, severe dresses she favored and tried to give her a soft, feminine look— "bouffant rather than sleek." To build up Jennifer's confidence, Miss Colby allowed her to buy her own clothes. After a few months of coaching, Miss Colby had to send back only one out of every four dresses.

David Selznick joins the United Artists team (left to right) Douglas Fairbanks, Jr., Charlie Chaplin, Samuel Goldwyn, John Hay Whitney, David Selznick, Walter Wanger, Jesse L. Lasky, Douglas Fairbanks, Sr., Roy Disney. Seated: Mary Pickford.

The advice extended to other matters besides clothes. Miss Colby taught Jennifer how to gaze directly at people's eyes, instead of averting her glance. "But I don't know what to say to people when they start telling me what a great actress I am!" Jennifer protested.

"Listen, darling," said her mentor, "just raise your eyebrows the next time that happens and say, 'Well, how have you been?'" Jennifer discovered that the device worked.

The marriage to Robert Walker was going badly. No longer were they the struggling couple sharing minor triumphs in the acting world; now both were stars. At the same time Jennifer was achieving fame in *The Song of Bernadette,* Walker was developing into a new star personality at M-G-M. He drew excellent notices as a cocky sailor in *Bataan,* then scored in the low-key comedy *See Here, Private Hargrove,* playing to perfection the hapless recruit of World War II.

Stardom seemed to underscore the mutual insecurities of Jennifer Jones and Bob Walker.

He had been a skinny, pimpled, and unattractive youth, and through his childhood he sought escape from the unappealing reality of his existence. Acting seemed to fill his need, and a rich aunt sent him to the American Academy of Dramatic Arts. There he met Phylis Isley, the quiet, apple-cheeked girl who also found in acting stimulating escape from the feelings of inadequacy. The struggle for livelihood and the arrival of two sons helped occupy their lives with common purposes. But their fragile temperaments were ill-prepared for the stresses of their double stardom.

Mary Pickford gives a "million-dollar kiss" to David Selznick after he bought into United Artists. At right, another United Artists partner, Charlie Chaplin.

Another disruptive influence in their lives was David Selznick.

In the beginning his relationship to Jennifer was the same as with his other leading ladies. He was domineering, persuasive, overpowering. He attempted to impose his will over her in all matters, from simple elements of grooming to the conduct of her everyday life. At first she was terrified, and she pleaded with studio acquaintances not to leave her alone with him. She was confused about her feelings toward him and his toward her.

For his own part, David was more intrigued with Jennifer than he had ever been with any other actress. She seemed deeper and more malleable, ever-changing in a thousand provocative ways. Bernadette had been only the beginning, he believed; there could be no limit to her versatility. To provide a vehicle for her, David Selznick ended his drought of film making.

David still felt frustration at having no meaningful role in the war. He decided to make a film that would show through the lives of a single family what changes the war had brought to America. For $30,000 he purchased a book by Margaret Buell Wilder, *Since You Went Away,* in which she described her experiences on the home front in letters to her husband overseas.

This time David said he would not rely on his usual corps of scenarists. He would write the script himself.

He began dictating to around-the-clock shifts of secretaries, amassing a mountainous script. He went back and edited the script to more reasonable size, then began adding scenes he felt were necessary. As he rewrote, the role to be played by Jennifer Jones grew larger.

Each role needed perfect casting. He was determined that Claudette Colbert would portray the compassionate mother, but she balked at playing mother to Jennifer Jones and Shirley Temple. David convinced Miss Colbert that her glamour would be unimpaired, and he paid her $150,000 to play the role.

David had written a fifteen-page speech about the war effort, and he hired the Broadway veteran Fred Stone to deliver it. The scene required three days of filming because Stone had difficulty remembering the disjointed lines. David was dissatisfied with the scene, which had cost $35,000.

"What's wrong with it?" he asked Dore Schary.

"The scene doesn't belong in the picture," Schary suggested.

"Yes, it does," David insisted. "It was miscast. I'll shoot it again."

He hired Charles Coburn to deliver the speech, paying him $10,000 for a single day's work. Later David discarded the entire sequence.

David decided he needed Ruth Gordon to play the role of the next-door neighbor. He importuned her with a nine-page telegram, but she preferred to remain in the East to star in the play she had written, *Over 21.* David continued his campaign, dispatching a contract with the money terms left blank—"fill in your own amount," he urged.

She returned it unsigned. He tried to persuade producer Max Gordon to postpone *Over 21* so Miss Gordon could appear in *Since You Went Away.* All his pleas failed, and he cast Agnes Moorehead in the role.

Also cast were Joseph Cotten, Monty Woolley, Lionel Barrymore, Hattie McDaniel, Nazimova, Keenan Wynn, Albert Basserman, Guy Madison, and Craig Stevens. For the role of Jennifer Jones's soldier boyfriend David borrowed Robert Walker from M-G-M.

Jennifer's role continued to grow as David produced new rewrites of the script. He instructed the director, John Cromwell, to take special pains with her scenes. When Cromwell became ill, David himself took over as director for three days.

As the filming neared an end, the involvement of producer and star became evident to other members of the company. Jennifer became more and more unstable, and her upset was especially noticeable when she was required to play an intimate love scene with Bob Walker in a haystack. She was scarcely able to continue with the scene.

Next came a railroad station sequence in which she was to bid a tearful farewell to Bob Walker as he went off to war. The station—the same one used for the long shot in *Gone With the Wind*—was packed with extras as Cromwell attempted to

Alfred Hitchcock directs Ingrid Bergman in SPELLBOUND.

rehearse the scene. Suddenly Jennifer burst into tears and ran to her dressing room.

David Selznick arrived on the set and disappeared inside Jennifer's dressing room. Later he emerged with Jennifer, and she appeared to have regained her composure. She rehearsed the dialogue with her husband, who remained glum and quiet. After several takes, they completed the scene, and Jennifer once more dashed to her dressing room.

Shortly afterward, she won an Academy Award for her performance in *The Song of Bernadette.* A day later, Jennifer Jones announced she was suing Robert Walker for divorce.

It should have been a triumphant evening for David Selznick.

At long last he had returned to production with *Since You Went Away,* which he proclaimed—and perhaps believed—to be a better picture than *Gone With the Wind.* The Hollywood

The Selznick Touch: a frontier cantina becomes a huge casino in DUEL IN THE SUN.

premiere was preceded by an immense advertising and publicity campaign, directed by David himself.[4] The entire list of Selznick players was bidden to the premiere and to a gala dinner afterward at the Scandia Restaurant.

The premiere performance failed to evoke the response that David had expected. There was scattered applause for certain scenes, but the audience failed to evidence the electric response that greeted a thoroughly engrossing film. Many of the premiere guests had been touched by the war in intimate and tragic ways, and to them the Selznick view of the home front seemed glossy and saccharine. The effusions after the premiere were in the traditional Hollywood style, but David had been around long

---

[4] Russell Birdwell had left Selznick after *Gone With the Wind* to open his own publicity office. He had been followed by a succession of Selznick publicity directors.

Gregory Peck, Joseph Cotten in DUEL IN THE SUN.

enough to detect the hollow tone.

He entered the Scandia with head high, acknowledging the applause of his employees. All were there—Ingrid Bergman, Joan Fontaine, Jennifer Jones, Joseph Cotten, Gregory Peck, Shirley Temple, Dorothy McGuire, etc., and they gathered at the large table over which David and Irene presided. The talk was effervescent and gay, and few noticed that David was drinking heavily. He ordered one drink after another, and his manner grew more irritable, especially toward Joan Fontaine, who was chattering at his side. As she sometimes did on social occasions, she lapsed into a British manner of speech.

Suddenly the gaiety was shattered by David's reproving

voice:

"Joan, you're full of _ _ _ _, Don't give me that _ _ _ _ ing British accent."

The guests fell into stunned silence. Ingrid Bergman whispered to her companion, publicist Joseph Steele, "Do you think we ought to leave?"

"No, that would just make it worse," Steele replied.

Quiet talk resumed at the table. The director Edmund Goulding smoothly changed seats with the shattered Joan Fontaine and began engaging David in conversation. The embarrassment passed, but the gaiety of the evening had been destroyed.

Since You Went Away was a damaging blow to David's ego, especially because he had taken sole credit for the screenplay. Some of the reviews offered fainthearted praise, but he realized from their tone that he had not achieved another *Gone With the Wind*.

The movie public was less critical. Attracted by the impressive cast and the intensive selling campaign, wartime audiences patronized *Since You Went Away* in large numbers, and many found its message profound and moving. The film, which had cost $2,900,000, collected world-wide rentals of $7,100,000, an impressive figure in view of the limited market in wartime. *Since You Went Away* was nominated for best picture of 1944 by the Academy of Motion Picture Arts and Sciences, but the award went to *Going My Way*.

The commercial success of *Since You Went Away* buoyed David's enthusiasm for film making, and once more he was brimming with grandiose plans.

"I feel it inevitable," he told *Time* reporter Dwight Whitney, "that three years hence I must be one of the real masters of the picture business."

David began devising plans by which to achieve that status. In time he expected to take over as the major power of United Artists, with which he had formed a new alliance in 1941. The contract had been signed with Mary Pickford, Charlie Chaplin, and their partner of that time, Alexander Korda, and Mary planted on David's cheek a "million-dollar kiss." Actually, the price David paid for a quarter interest in United Artists was $1,200,000. His partners became discontented as years passed and Selznick failed to produce films for United Artists release. In fact, Mary and Charlie grumbled that David had used a million-dollar loan to develop *Notorious, The Keys of the Kingdom, Claudia,* and other properties he sold to competing companies. The partners' discontent was partially placated when David finally delivered *Since You Went Away* and *I'll Be Seeing You,* both money-makers. David was convinced he could not only co-exist with Mary and Charlie but eventually gain dominance of United Artists from them.

When that time arrived, David expected to have the most modern, progressive production system in the industry. The major studios were hopelessly outdated, he concluded; a whole new approach to film making was needed.

He planned to build a studio bigger than his father-in-law's M-G-M, but not as unwieldy as that sprawling giant. He would call it Selznick City, and it would be planned for the ultimate in efficiency. The studio would be shaped like a wheel, with the set-building shops at the hub. Wedge-shaped stages would flare out from the center, and each would be a self-contained unit complete with dressing rooms, makeup rooms, etc. Around the outer edge would be the administration building and other offices. Immediately outside the studio would be a planned community where studio workers would live.

The studio would not be required to grind out product as the major companies did to meet release schedules. Facilities would be available to independent producers, who could follow their own schedules in the creation of quality films. David himself planned to produce no more than a film per year at his utopian studio.

Early-morning hours were occupied for weeks on end in the creation of memos outlining the studio of the future. David assigned William Pereira to draw tentative plans. Construction was not possible until the war ended and building restrictions were lifted. But David wanted to be ready when that time came, and he scouted locations for Selznick City.

David's executive vice president, Daniel O'Shea, had located a promising parcel of real estate on La Brea Avenue only a few miles from the Selznick studio. David couldn't find the time to look at it. Finally he agreed to an inspection after O'Shea warned that the property might be sold to others.

On a Saturday afternoon, O'Shea and the studio treasurer, Ernest Scanlon, rode in the Selznick limousine with David and his sons Danny and Jeffrey.

"Stop the car!" David commanded. The driver pulled over to the side of the road where a Good Humor truck was parked. David leaped out and began taking orders from his fellow passengers.

"What flavor will you have?" he asked, then he relayed the complicated order to the Good Humor man.

"Sorry, I only got vanilla and chocolate bars," the man replied.

"What about sundaes?" David inquired about the entire variety of ice cream and then returned to the limousine with the information.

"David, for God's sake, we've got to get to that property!" O'Shea insisted. "The sellers will be waiting for us."

"They can wait," David answered. "Now he's got a cup with vanilla ice cream and chocolate syrup . . ."

He finally took all the orders and purchased the ice cream. The limousine drove on to the property. Nibbling on his ice cream bar, David stepped out of the car and met the sellers. "What are the boundaries?" he asked.

One of the men pointed out the limits of the property.

"How much do you want for it?" David asked.

"Three million," was the answer.

"Okay, I'll take it. Let's go." He stepped back into the car.

The astonished owners could not believe that anyone could agree to a three-million-dollar purchase so quixotically. They decided to withdraw their proposal, and the property was sold to a less impulsive buyer. David lost interest in his vision of Selznick City.

David now discovered a new toy: psychoanalysis.

The years that had followed the creative explosion of *Gone With the Wind* had proved profoundly disturbing. He was unable to explain his fallow three years, when he could not bring himself to place a film in production. His personal life was becoming more unsettled. He remained deeply attached to Irene, and he valued her strength and judgment. She provided a stability that his life seemed to need.

Irene could be strong-minded, like her father. When David came home from the studio after a long day's work, she said: "Take those old clothes off, get into a tub, and dress. We have guests arriving in fifteen minutes."

More than once he tossed his clothes on the floor and trampled them. "David, pick those things up and put them away properly," she admonished. Louis B. Mayer knew about such scenes, and he sympathized with his son-in-law. "If I were married to Irene, I'd hit her," he told Hedda Hopper.

David began regular sessions with a female psychiatrist and he poured out his feelings about his work, his wife, his family, his protegee, Jennifer Jones. It was a strangely comforting experience for him, and he began recommending psychiatry to his friends and associates.

One concrete result came from David's adventure into psychoanalysis: *Spellbound.*

David decided he wanted to make a film which would show the film audience for the first time the real nature of psychiatry. He purchased a novel called *The House of Dr. Edwardes*, which concerned a madman who took charge of an insane asylum. Alfred Hitchcock was assigned to direct, and Ben Hecht, who had a wide acquaintance among psychiatrists, wrote the script. Ingrid Bergman was cast as a doctor at the asylum and Gregory Peck as the amnesiac who masqueraded as the asylum's new director.

Hitchcock sought to avoid the blurred photography that marked most dream sequences in films. He convinced Selznick to hire Salvador Dali to create backgrounds in his sharply

Before the explosion: David Selznick and King Vidor on the location of DUEL IN THE SUN.

detailed style. Some of the Dali designs were used; others proved impractical. For one scene he wanted to have a statue disintegrate and become infested with ants; then Ingrid Bergman would be revealed underneath, also covered with ants. Selznick vetoed the idea.

Spellbound proved to be less than a happy confluence of talents. Bergman said at the outset: "I won't do this movie. I don't believe the love story. The heroine is an intellectual woman, and an intellectual woman simply can't fall in love so deeply." Newcomer Peck was intimidated by the glacial attitude of Hitchcock. Hitchcock resented the constant interference of Selznick. The intimacy of the story was lost in one overproduced sequence after another, and the finished film was burdened with an electronic musical score.

Accompanied by the usual Selznick selling barrage, *Spellbound* was commercially successful ($7,900,000 world gross) and won an Academy nomination as best picture of 1945.

Next, *Duel in the Sun.*

Or, as the radio comedians called it, *Lust in the Dust.*

David had purchased the Niven Busch novel and assigned Oliver H. P. Garrett to fashion a screenplay in conjunction with King Vidor, who was to direct. "I want this to be an artistic little western," he instructed them. "You take it over and if you need any help, let me know. But it's your baby."

It was fanciful, of course, to expect that David Selznick could restrain himself from interference. Soon he was totally involved in *Duel in the Sun,* determined to make it the *Gone With the Wind* of the west.

From the artistic little western, *Duel in the Sun* grew to epic size. Eventually David took over the writing of the script, creating new sequences to enlarge its scope. Late one night he was pumping Dore Schary and Daniel O'Shea for suggestions to make the picture bigger.

"Why must it be bigger?" O'Shea asked.

"You'll just be adding to the cost, and you won't be contributing to the picture," said Schary.

David smiled. "You know what my problem is," he said. "I know that when I die, the stories will read, 'David 0. Selznick, producer of *Gone With the Wind,* died today.' I'm determined to leave them something else to write about."

He demonstrated his determination by spending more money than he had on *Gone With the Wind*—$5,000,000. *Duel in the Sun* took much longer to produce, being in various stages of production from March of 1945 to November of 1946. But the Selznick touch, painstaking and sure on *Gone With the Wind,* went awry on *Duel in the Sun.* His judgment was warped by the compulsion to top *Gone With the Wind.* Also, his personal emotions were involved, since *Duel in the Sun* was to star Jennifer Jones.

David surrounded her with a prestigious cast. For her evil

Jennifer Jones and Gregory Peck in the DUEL IN THE SUN *love scene.*

lover he chose Gregory Peck; it would be a stunning change of pace for Peck, who had heretofore appeared as stalwart and noble on the screen. Joseph Cotten completed the triangle as Peck's brother. The supporting cast included Lionel Barrymore, Herbert Marshall, Charles Bickford, Walter Huston, Harry Carey, Otto Kruger, Sidney Blackmer. He induced Lillian Gish to return to the screen as Barrymore's wife. Huston was needed only for a four-day sequence as a revivalist preacher, but his agent refused to allow him to work for less than his usual $40,000 fee. David exercised his privilege of keeping Huston available for ten weeks at $4000 a week—and then paid him more to remain overtime.

Authenticity became a passion with David. Every costume, every prop had to be checked and rechecked by the research department to make certain they existed in the West of the 1880s. One day King Vidor reported to the set and found a well-dressed man seated in a chair next to his. Vidor presumed him to be a banker who had invested in *Duel in the Sun*. The visitor stood nearby as Vidor directed a barroom scene. Becoming annoyed, Vidor asked members of the crew who the man was. None had ever seen him before. Vidor confronted the visitor and asked, "Would you mind telling me what you're doing here?"

"I'm a bartender," the man explained, "and last night I was working at a party in Beverly Hills. Mr. Selznick said he wanted to hire me as an expert for a barroom scene he was shooting today. He wants me to make sure that the whisky is poured correctly and that it's the right color."

Vidor, who detested technical experts, asked the man to stand out of the way.

David was especially meticulous in matters concerning Jennifer. Her costumes were redesigned again and again until he was satisfied with them. Her makeups and hair styles were tested with utmost care. David hired Josef von Sternberg to give Jennifer the same glamour treatment the director had supplied for Marlene Dietrich.

Selznick couldn't leave the script alone. Often he arrived on the set in mid-afternoon to show Vidor new versions of the sequences in progress.

"But, David, I'm almost finished with these scenes," the director protested.

"I know," said Selznick. "Would you show me what you've done so far?"

Vidor put the actors through the day's scenes, and David said eagerly, "Don't you think the new version is better?"

"Perhaps—a little," Vidor said. At Selznick's request, he began retakes on sequences which hadn't yet been completed.

When the *Duel in the Sun* company moved to locations in Arizona, David's behavior became more erratic and unpredictable. He hovered around the set, constantly making suggestions to Vidor about the shooting. If Vidor did not agree, David sometimes became loud and abusive. "Don't do that, David," Vidor said quietly. "I won't have you doing that in front of the company."

David apologized to the director. But his suggestions continued.

One evening during the Tucson location, David announced he wanted to gamble. Daniel O'Shea reminded him that gambling was illegal in Tucson, but David insisted, "You can always find a gambling spot in every town."

The sheriff helpfully supplied the address of a roadhouse which offered gambling, and David organized an expedition with Gregory Peck and Joseph Cotten and their wives and a few others.

A caravan of black limousines roared through the desert until it arrived at a wooden frame house with the shutters drawn. A knock on the door brought an obese, frightened-looking man who eyed his guests carefully before allowing them to enter. He donned a green eyeshade and turned on the light over a roulette table. David let out a joyful whoop and ordered drinks for everyone. The game began.

To the others, the rickety casino seemed quaintly squalid; to David it could have been Monte Carlo in August. He papered the board with ten-dollar bills and shouted gleefully when his numbers paid off. Peck and Cotten played with dollar bills and soon dropped out as losers. David continued playing—and winning. Soon the currency was stacked high before him, and the fat man with the green eyeshade was dripping with sweat. David was ahead $13,000.

He continued playing with zeal, taking large gulps of the house whisky. The others watched him with fascination; he roared with delight or groaned loudly as his fortune changed. But as the morning hours wore on, the fascination of the others turned to boredom, as well as embarrassment for the grimacing little man who was losing all to the rich producer from Hollywood.

Compulsively, irrepressively, David continued placing his bets on the numbers, and his stack of currency diminished. Then it was gone, but he played on, writing IOUs for his bets. At 5 A.M., Danny O'Shea said to him, "David, these people have to work today. We'd better leave."

David played one more roll and lost. "All right, that's all," he said. "What do I owe you?"

The fat man counted up the IOUs and gulped, "Thirty thousand dollars."

"Okay. But first I want to see all the moving parts."

The others stared at David incredulously. "You can't do that, David," O'Shea said.

"I'll pay him," David assured. "But first I want to inspect the mechanism."

Still sweating profusely, the fat man dismantled the wheel and placed all the parts in a row on the table. David looked at them and said to O'Shea, "Okay—pay him." David walked to his car.

The *Duel in the Sun* location continued for long weeks in the hot Arizona desert, and tempers grew short. It seemed to many of the company members that the picture would never be completed, because David wouldn't allow it to be. He came forth with new script pages to expand and modify existing scenes or he devised totally new sequences. More and more he encroached upon the prerogatives of the director. King Vidor's patience wore thin.

One day Vidor was directing the melodramatic climax to the

picture, in which Peck and Jennifer, having wounded each other mortally, crawled over the rocks toward each other. The scene was one of David's favorites, and he insisted that it be photographed exactly as he had conceived it.

As the two stars lay on the ground for the death scene, David decided they did not appear sufficiently wounded. He splashed Jennifer and Peck with makeup blood.

King Vidor closed his script and rose from his director's chair. Quietly he said to David, "You can take this picture and shove it."

As the entire company stared in awed silence, Vidor walked to his limousine and stepped inside. He instructed his driver to head back for Tucson. The black car started off on the long, dusty road across the desert. For almost eight miles the road stretched in the straight line, and the company members followed the limousine's progress as it continued on the dusty trip.

Finally the limousine disappeared over the brow of the next range of hills, and all eyes turned to David Selznick. "Well, that's all for today," he said to an assistant director. "Dismiss the company."

No amount of persuasion could induce King Vidor to return to *Duel in the Sun*. William Dieterle came from Hollywood to direct the remaining location scenes.

After the principal photography had been completed, David continued tinkering with the picture. He extended the story to show the beginnings of the troubled family. He shot an elaborate train wreck, perpetrated by Peck out of sheer cussedness. When he saw an early version of the film, King Vidor argued strenuously against the fatal train wreck, declaring the scene would alienate the audience, especially since Peck rode away from the scene merrily singing, "I've Been Working on the Railroad."

David refused to eliminate the sequence. "I want to make Lewt the worst son of a bitch that's ever been on the motion picture screen," he replied, "and I believe that train wreck will help me prove my point."

David was excessively demanding in his search for a score for

Duel in the Sun. Seven prominent composers of movie scores came to the Selznick studio and left, because their themes did not please him. His next candidate was the Russian-born Dimitri Tiomkin. "I like you, Dimitri," David said to him, "and I hope we can work together. But you understand that you come here on probation. I must hear your themes first."

"Dot I understand," said Tiomkin. I know that seven udder composers have been fired before me. I insist on vun thing only: if you like my themes, you give me a run-of-de-picture contract."

"Agreed," said David.

Tiomkin went home to contemplate the challenging assignment. Soon he received a lengthy memo from David detailing what he expected of the *Duel in the Sun* score. He declared that there had to be eleven separate themes: "Spanish theme, ranch theme . . . love theme, desire theme, and orgasm theme."

The composer was both amused and perplexed by the latter. "Love themes I can write," he mused. "Desire, too. But orgasm! How do you score an orgasm?"

"Try!" David urged him in a conference. He rarely used Yiddishisms, but he employed one for Tiomkin: "I want a really good *shtump*."

Tiomkin retired to his studio and labored for weeks over the eleven themes. The orgasm theme was the most difficult of all, but he finally hit upon a crescendo that seemed to comprise what Selznick had asked for. He rehearsed a dozen players as if they were the Philharmonic, then decided it was time to audition the themes for Selznick.

"Now boys, don't laugh; I vant you to be serious for Meestair Selznick," he instructed his orchestra. He ordered the lights in the recording studio turned down, then he informed Selznick's office that he was ready to play the score. The audition was scheduled for two in the afternoon. David arrived after midnight.

Tiomkin conducted with rare fervor, gazing over his shoulder at the Selznick secretaries, who in turn were gazing at David to determine how to react. They joined him in polite applause for the love theme. He applauded more loudly for the desire theme and seemed enthusiastic for the orgasm theme.

Joseph Cotten, Jennifer Jones in LOVE LETTERS.

David took the composer to his office and agreed to a run-of-the-picture contract. Tiomkin went to work on orchestrations, but little could be done until David finished editing *Duel in the Sun*. For six months Tiomkin polished the score, rehearsing with his orchestra at Goldwyn studio, where recording facilities were superior. The orchestra included forty-one drummers but no piccolos—he knew that David hated piccolos. A hundred-voice chorus joined the rehearsals.

A week before the recording was to begin, David arrived unexpectedly at the recording studio. He drew Tiomkin aside and said, "Dimmy, I'll tell you a secret. We ran the picture at a preview in New Jersey and it didn't go so well. Then we added canned music for a preview in New York, and that didn't help, either. So you can see that the music will need to contribute a

Alfred Hitchcock and Gregory Peck confer on the set of THE PARADINE CASE

great deal to the picture. Can you let me hear that love theme again? Just whistle it." Tiomkin whistled the love theme.

"I love it," said David. "Now would you please whistle the desire theme?" Again the composer whistled.

"Fine! Fine! Now the orgasm theme."

Tiomkin whistled, and David shook his head worriedly. "No, that isn't it. That's just not an orgasm."

Tiomkin returned to his studio and worked for weeks on the orgasm theme. By alternating flageolets and cellos and combining them with trombones, plus the rhythm of a handsaw cutting through wood, he believed he had achieved the effect. Now he had devoted six months to *Duel in the Sun* and was eager to accept two other assignments, *It's a Wonderful Life* for Frank Capra and *The Dark Mirror* for Nunnally Johnson.

The time arrived to play the theme for Selznick, and he arrived at the recording studio with his retinue. "Play me the orgasm theme," David requested, "and put the film on the screen so I can get the full effect."

The passionate love sequence with Jennifer Jones and

Gregory Peck appeared on the screen, and Tiomkin conducted the orchestra, playing the piano passages himself. When the sequence had finished, he gazed expectantly at David. David was smiling.

"I like it,"' said David. "Play it again."

Again the scene appeared on the screen, and the orchestra played the theme. This time Tiomkin was confident, and he improvised some jazz beats in his piano playing, ascending half a note as he did.

"Play it again," said David, and Tiomkin performed the theme the third time.

At the end David sighed and said, "Dimmy, you're going to hate me for this, but it won't do. It is too beautiful."

The Russian balanced between rage and despair. "Meestair Selznick," he cried, "vot is troubling you? Vot don't you like about it?"

"I like it, but it isn't orgasm music. It's not *shtump*. It's not the way I _ _ _ _."

"Meestair Selznick, you _ _ _ _ your way, I _ _ _ _ my way. To me, that is _ _ _ _ ing music!"

David collapsed in laughter. The orgasm theme was recorded as Tiomkin had written it.

Lewis J. Selznick's legacy to his son David included three basic tenets:
1. Profligacy in all things is a virtue.
2. Whether you win or lose, gambling is a pleasurable pursuit.
3. The movie bosses are the enemy.

For a decade, through boom years and fallow periods, David Selznick had thrived in the picture business under such a philosophy, continuing his highly independent course. But during the late 1940s, his father's teachings began a slow process of ruination. In peak times the system could work. But with the end of the war came abrupt shifts in entertainment patterns, and times began to change. So did the Selznick luck.

Through most of his career, David had been unable to rid himself entirely of the movie bosses his father had taught him to distrust. At Paramount, RKO, and M-G-M, he had worked for them. Even after he had struck out on an independent course, he was required to release his films through United Artists (with M-G-M forcing its way into *Gone With the Wind*). Although United Artists was the creature of two other independent spirits—Mary Pickford and Charlie Chaplin—David equated the company with the movie bosses, and he grumbled over the terms imposed upon him.

He became obsessed with the belief that the independent producer was victimized by the releasing company. He pictured these companies—and not without some truth—as hulking bureaucracies that charged immense fees for releasing films. He decided to form his own releasing organization, and he announced he would deliver no more films to United Artists.

Expectably, Mary and Charlie responded with anger, accusing David of misappropriating the million dollars they loaned him to develop film properties. Nonsense, replied David, the properties were his to dispose of as he wished. He accused Mary of having a compulsive urge to run the company and of harassing him to sell back his stock. He pointed out that he had contributed three profitable pictures for United Artists release—*Since You Went Away, I'll Be Seeing You,* and *Spellbound*—while Mary and Charlie had made none.

Asked how he felt about being pushed out of United Artists, David told a reporter: "Pushed, hell—I jumped!"

The extent of his leap was revealed with the announcement of the Selznick Releasing Organization which would release *Duel in the Sun* and all future Selznick films. Later he discussed the reasoning behind his move: "It enabled me to practice what I had long preached and to prove that the whole method of distribution was wasteful and completely outmoded. Within a matter of weeks I opened branch offices—not 'exchanges'—in thirty key cities and arranged for the physical distribution of films through existing nontheatrical channels on a per shipment basis. I thereby cut distribution costs sixty percent, even though I had extremely few pictures, and got far more efficient distribution. Moreover, it proved that it was unnecessary to make pic-

The Portrait of Jennie by "Eben Adams" (Robert Brackman)

tures no one wanted to see in order to absorb overhead, which in most cases was absurdly inflated."

The Selznick plan had merit, and it might have worked except for a series of tragedies. David hoped to attract other independent producers to S.R.O., and he made a deal with Mark Hellinger, who was preparing a series of pictures, some of them in partnership with Humphrey Bogart. David planned to release films produced by Dore Schary, who had produced three successful pictures which David had sold to RKO—*The Spiral Staircase, The Farmer's Daughter,*[5] and *The Bachelor and the Bobbysoxer.* David also enlisted M.J. Siegel to produce a series of lower-budget films to develop new talent. Both Hellinger and Siegel died suddenly. Then Charles Koerner, head of production at RKO, also died, and the post was offered to Dore Schary. David agreed to release Schary, in return for the rights to *The Farmer's Daughter* and *The Spiral Staircase*.

The loss of three potential producers for S.R.O. left only David 0. Selznick as the supplier of product. His rate of production was scarcely enough to warrant maintenance of a releasing company, and the very thing he had sought to avoid—overhead—began to drain his resources.

The release of *Duel in the Sun* was accompanied by the most intensive selling campaign in film history. The campaign was directed by a new Selznick publicity chief, Paul MacNamara, former managing editor of *Cosmopolitan*. MacNamara theorized that Hollywood publicity was mistakenly oriented to the columns of Louella Parsons, Hedda Hopper, and press outlets. Advertising and exploitation were more effective means of communicating with the mass audience, he argued.

"All right, you've got a million dollars to spend on the *Duel in the Sun* campaign," David told him. "Spend it any way you want."

MacNamara inserted an item in the Walter Winchell column

---

[5] Schary had prepared *The Farmer's Daughter*, based on a Finnish play, *Hulda Goes to Parliament,* as a vehicle for Ingrid Bergman. When Miss Bergman refused to appear in the comedy, Selznick sold it to RKO. Loretta Young played the leading role and won the Academy Award as best actress of 1947.

that he had a million dollars to spend and was looking for ideas. The response was enormous. Each idea was examined for (1) the number of people it would reach, and (2) the cost. A minimum rate of two dollars per thousand people was established. Ninety-three different proposals were purchased for use in the campaign.

One of the stunts involved purchase of a thousand war-surplus weather parachutes. Fifty important sports events, including the Kentucky Derby, were selected throughout the country, and the parachutes were dropped from airplanes, some of the chutes containing winning bets on the sports events.

MacNamara believed one of the best unexploited forms of publicity was word-of-mouth rumor. He instituted a test case in Hackensack, New Jersey. Forty bartenders were sent duplicate letters to be held for the arrival of a regular customer. The letter was purportedly from a brother in California who told of visiting the set of *Duel in the Sun* and discovering the action was so outrageous that armed guards had been posted to keep out the curious. Interviewers from the Gallup Poll visited the bars and verified the effectiveness of the rumor. The rumor reached the United Press, which checked them through its Hollywood bureau. David Selznick denied any knowledge of the incident, and his denial added fuel to the rumors.

The Hackensack rumor factory proved so effective that similar campaigns were conducted in twenty other areas of the United States.

MacNamara counseled David Selznick on the release of *Duel in the Sun:* "This is a lousy picture. The critics will knock the hell out of it, and the word-of-mouth will kill you. You've got to play it off as fast as you can."

Selznick was offended by his publicity man's evaluation of the picture, but his pride was not so great that he wouldn't listen to a practical proposal on how to make *Duel in the Sun* pay off. MacNamara pointed out that an average advertising campaign for the opening of a major motion picture in Manhattan would reach three to four million people. But if the picture was playing in the two-thousand-seat Astor Theatre, only four thou-

SELZNICK

sand items of merchandise could be sold daily to those millions. It would be far better, he argued, to make the movie available in all five boroughs at the same time and cash in on the saturation ad campaign before the adverse word-of-mouth that was certain to follow.

The saturation-booking device was adopted, and a record $2,000,000 was spent for exploitation. In the first five days of New York release, *Duel in the Sun* collected $750,000. The system was repeated in other parts of the country with phenomenal results. By systematic milking of the market, Selznick was able to wrest $17,000,000 from the first release of *Duel in the Sun*.

The campaign was helped when Archbishop John J. Cantwell of Los Angeles declared Catholics could not "with a free conscience attend *Duel in the Sun*." The archdiocese newspaper condemned the film for brutal killings and "immorality more than lightly suggested," adding that Jennifer Jones was "unduly, if not indecently exposed," and that Walter Huston portrayed a religious man as a comic figure.

Selznick reacted with hurt and dismay, commenting that the film's moral content had been approved by the industry's censor, Joseph Breen. After allowing the controversy to flourish for several days, David agreed to make a few cuts in *Duel in the Sun*, and the archbishop praised his voluntary action.

He had escaped the scorn of the Catholics, but David Selznick wasn't able to convince his peers in the film industry that *Duel in the Sun* was anything but a bald-faced attempt to make a buck. The most devastating comment came from the genteel producer-writer Charles Brackett, who provided his own capsule review. Howard Hughes's *The Outlaw* had recently been released amid cries that it was both pornographic and ludicrous, and Brackett termed *Duel in the Sun* "*The Outlaw* in bad taste."

During his years of immense productivity in films, David Selznick had been subject to personal influences that helped curb his instinct to excess and discipline his sometimes erratic talent. Now those influences were beginning to leave him.

Marcella Rabwin had been a devoted executive secretary since the RKO days. Her steady hand had long saved David's affairs from chaos. She smoothed over disputes between David and his employees, delaying the dispatch of angry memos until his temper had subsided. More than once she had snipped off infatuations by failing to transmit messages from actresses to David. The press of her own family duties prompted Mrs. Rabwin to leave the Selznick organization.

Raymond Klune had been another steadying influence. As production manager, he tried to keep budgets within reason, though he was often thwarted by last-minute changes by David. The break between the pair came at the end of *Since You Went Away.* Klune was hospitalized with pneumonia, and David sent him a furious memo because his telephone calls had not been answered by Klune.

David was astounded when Klune announced he was quitting. He offered to triple Klune's salary and give him a share of the profits and vowed: "Every time I write an angry memo I'll put it in a drawer overnight. Then I'll probably never send it." Klune was moved, but not enough to change his mind.

And then David lost Irene.

She adored David, exulted in his triumphs, comforted him in his defeats, encouraged his dreams, disciplined his childishness, tolerated his errors. She was never less than honest, often bluntly so. Her honesty could hurt, but it also helped David maintain a grasp on reality.

Irene had a Jewish wife's forbearance for David's romantic adventures. Her own mother had been through the same torment, as had Florence Selznick. All had believed the infatuations would pass and their straying husbands would return.

David had always been careful. There had been no real romances, merely physical conquests that satisfied his virility and his search for excitement. But this time it was different.

He became obsessed with Jennifer and her career. She was unlike any woman he had known before—enigmatic, enchanting, quintessentially feminine. He saw in her the limitless potential of a consummate actress. There was nothing she was incapable of, no role she could not play. He took complete charge of every aspect of her career. When he loaned her to other studios, as he did for *Love Letters* and *Cluny Brown,* he issued voluminous instructions concerning her makeup, wardrobe, etc.

David's extraordinary interest in the career of Jennifer Jones became standard gossip in Hollywood. There was no escape from it for Irene Mayer Selznick, who had pride in her position in the community. The hurt was deep and telling.

In addition, life with David had become almost intolerable. His personal affairs were in such a constant state of turmoil that even the orderly Irene could not maintain control. He arrived home in the early morning—or not at all. He expected everything to be done for him; he didn't even know the location of the light switch in his bedroom. Fifteen years of chaotic living had been too much for Irene; her own health and well-being were being threatened.

On the afternoon of April 29, 1945, David came home to find his suitcases in the front hall. Irene told him she could no longer live with him. David was astounded, but he accepted her decision, realizing that nothing he could say would make Irene change her mind. He picked up his bags and started to leave. Irene had planned to give him a ceremonious kick as he went out the door. But in typical fashion David caught his sleeve on the doorknob, and she had to help him get loose.

That evening Sam and Frances Goldwyn saw David at the bar of Romanoff's Restaurant and invited him to their table. "Irene threw me out," he said miserably. The Goldwyns took him to their house, and Frances made him a hamburger sandwich while he poured out his troubles.

Irene Mayer Selznick enjoyed a refreshing sleep that night; it was the first time in years she had been able to sleep without a sedative.

When he was producing films at M-G-M, David Selznick considered *The Paradine Case* as a vehicle for Greta Garbo. It was a novel by Robert Hichens, author of *The Garden of Allah,* and the plot concerned a respectable lawyer who fell in love with his client, an accused murderess. David left M-G-M before he could undertake the project. Years later, he remembered *The Paradine Case* when searching for a film for Alfred Hitchcock to direct. Hitchcock was between loan-outs and earning $5000 a week, hence an assignment for him was urgent. David purchased *The Paradine Case* from M-G-M for $60,000.

Hitchcock and his wife, Alma Reville, adapted the novel, and James Bridie, a Scottish playwright, wrote the script in England. David was dissatisfied with the result, and he took over the scriptwriting himself. That was only one of the things that went wrong with *The Paradine Case.*

David sent Hitchcock to England to photograph Old Bailey so that it could be reproduced with complete fidelity at the Selznick studio. Upon David's orders, the set was built like a fortress, with the result that side walls could not be removed for convenient camera angles.

Selznick's sure touch with casting turned faulty with *The Paradine Case.* He insisted on Gregory Peck as the defense attorney. Hitchcock argued for Laurence Olivier, Ronald Colman, or another English actor, but David remained firm. Peck was under contract and an important star.

Both Selznick and Hitchcock had hoped to lure Greta Garbo out of retirement to portray the defendant, but she declined. David decided he would create a new star, as he had done with Ingrid Bergman. He sent to Italy for an actress named Alida Valli, whom he had seen in a screen test. Unlike Bergman, she underwent a transformation to convert her to the Hollywood pattern. She was placed on a rigid diet to eliminate ten pounds. Her teeth were capped. She spent long hours with a speech coach to eliminate her heavy Italian accent. As a final indignity, her first name was eliminated. Midway through *The Paradine Case* she wailed: "I wish I could go back to Italy! I wish I could eat a big plate of spaghetti! I wish I had my teeth back!"

David chose another European for the important role of Mrs. Paradine's groom and lover. He was a young French actor, Louis Jourdan, to whom David had taken an immediate liking. Hitchcock was opposed to the casting of Jourdan, arguing that

Peck's degradation would be greater if Mrs. Paradine's lover had
been a rough-handed horse handler. David insisted on the suave,
handsome Jourdan. David also brought Ann Todd from England
to play Peck's wife, and he cast Charles Laughton, Ethel
Barrymore, Charles Coburn, and Leo G. Carroll in supporting
roles.

Never a facile writer, David fashioned *The Paradine Case*
script under troublesome conditions. His relationship to Jennifer
was in a turmoil. She felt guilt over the crackup that Bob Walker
had been undergoing since their divorce; he had been involved
in drunken scrapes with policemen. David spent hours arguing
with Jennifer, then tried to produce script changes he felt were
necessary. Production began without a completed script, and in
a few weeks Hitchcock had filmed everything that had been
written. Each morning new scenes came from Selznick's office.

The process was wastefully expensive and highly unsatisfactory to Hitchcock. He preferred to prepare each scene before
production began and to adhere to the script throughout; the
piecemeal methods of David upset him. Nor was David's dialogue in the Hitchcock style. David's lines were explicit and
melodramatic while Hitchcock preferred his characters to talk
obliquely about dramatic matters.

The cost of *The Paradine Case* mounted to $4,000,000, far
beyond the budget. This time the Selznick exploitation campaign
wasn't able to bring the customers in. The picture lost millions.
It was the first time David had experienced a big financial failure, and he was stunned. The basic elements of film making and
selling that he had learned from his father no longer seemed to
apply. The market was shifting in new and inexplicable ways.

Television was beginning to invade the living rooms of
America, and millions of customers stopped going to movies.
Foreign films, particularly those from postwar Italy, were exciting critics and selective moviegoers with fresh glimpses of reality. The handsomely mounted Hollywood films, such as those in
which David Selznick excelled, seemed passé and empty.
Audiences were seeking change.

One day when he was ill, David Selznick reached to his bed-
side table and chose a slender volume with a title that intrigued
him: *Portrait of Jennie*. It was a Robert Nathan fantasy about an
artist and his beautiful model, whom he suspected of being a spirit. It seemed like an ideal vehicle for Jennifer. David was disappointed to learn that M-G-M had already purchased the rights.

A year later, a friend at M-G-M called David with the news
that the studio was dropping the option on *Portrait of Jennie*.
The call came on David's birthday, and he was convinced that it
was a good omen. He bought the rights to film *Portrait of
Jennie*.

David decided to play the fantasy against a background of
reality, and he planned to film the picture in New York City and
Boston, photographing each season as the story progressed. The
climactic sequence would be filmed in an actual storm in Boston
harbor, he decided.

His staff members were aghast. They pointed out that filming
in the East during the various seasons would be enormously
expensive. Photographing a real storm would produce nothing
but gray film, they argued.

David remained firm. He went ahead with his production
plans and hired Paul Osborn to write the script and William
Dieterle to direct. One day David left for New York to make
arrangements for the start of filming. He had planned to be gone
from Hollywood for a weekend. He returned eighteen months
later.

The filming of *Portrait of Jennie* was beset with troubles.
The weather changed abruptly, making it impossible to match
previous scenes. Jennifer was in an emotional state and often
failed to appear. The script proved too fragile to be playable, and
David rewrote constantly. He stationed a camera crew in Boston
harbor to await a storm. After two weeks a storm arrived; the film
was useless.

As the New York filming neared an end, David suddenly
called a halt in production. "I've read this book many times," he
announced, "and now I think I understand it." He began com-
posing the new version. Jennifer, her co-star Joseph Cotten, and

others in the cast waited, on salary, in New York for nine months until David had produced another script. The film was almost completely remade in California.

By the time *Portrait of Jennie* was ready for release, the fragile little ghost story had cost almost $4,000,000, Most of the Selznick aides agreed that the picture was far from satisfactory. But they also realized that the project had bled the company's resources at a time when little revenue was coming into the Selznick Releasing Organization. It seemed mandatory to rush *Portrait of Jennie* into release, for whatever income it could provide.

Paul MacNamara arranged a benefit premiere in New York for Mrs. Millicent Hearst's pet charity, the Milk Fund, and the premiere and the party afterward received wide coverage in the Hearst newspapers. Predictably, the reviews were bad.

Selznick summoned his staff and announced: "I'm going to pull the picture. I was talked into releasing it before I had the right ending for it, and that's why we got poor reviews. I'm going back into production and reshoot the ending."

Neil Agnew, who headed the Selznick Releasing Organization, was dismayed. He had already made deals to release *Portrait of Jennie* in other parts of the country; after seeing the New York reviews, exhibitors would be certain to wriggle out of their agreements if the picture were withdrawn. Paul MacNamara pointed out that the publicity of the withdrawal would severely injure the picture.

Their arguments could not convince David to change his mind.

That weekend David was staying in the country with his good friends, the William Paleys. MacNamara telephoned David and pleaded: "I want you to come in town and study the audience watching *Portrait of Jennie.* You look at pictures in projection rooms, and you don't really know what the public's reaction is."

David agreed to return to New York on Sunday and accompany MacNamara to the theater. MacNamara instructed the manager to turn up the house lights as soon as the picture concluded. The theater was almost full, and David noticed that the patrons seemed pleased and entertained.

"Would those people understand two-foot cuts?" the publicity man argued. "Would it make any difference to them if you added a hundred and fifty thousand dollars' worth of scenes?"

David seemed convinced. He thanked MacNamara and said he would abide by the public's judgment.

At eight the following morning, MacNamara was awakened at his hotel by the Selznick chauffeur, who delivered a four-page memo. David wrote that he had been impressed by the MacNamara stunt, but he had returned to his previous decision. He was withdrawing *Portrait of Jennie,* and the film would go back into production.

"Even if nobody goes to the picture, I will know that I have done my best," David concluded.

He spent $250,000 on a new storm sequence, which he expanded to an oversized screen, adding stereophonic sound. The spectacle was out of harmony with the fragile story, and *Portrait of Jennie* fared badly with critics and audiences. The theater contracts had been lost, and the release brought scarcely a million dollars into the Selznick company.

Not even David's closest friends realized how the *Portrait of Jennie* debacle had upset him. That became apparent one evening at a dinner party that David and Jennifer gave at his home. David was especially proud of the Robert Brackman painting of Jennifer that had been used in the picture, and Joseph Cotten and Daniel O'Shea thought it would be a good basis for a prank on David. They ordered a photo-copy, and Cotten took it to the Selznick house on the night of the party. He entered through the service entrance and switched the copy for the original painting, which hung in a place of honor in the dining room.

The usual glittering assemblage gathered for cocktails in the living room, and no one noticed that David was more somber than usual. Dinner was announced, and he led the procession into the manorial dining room. Clare Boothe Luce and Henry Luce had come with Joseph Cotten and his wife and were apprised of the prank. Mrs. Luce was seated next to David, and she gazed behind her and commented, "What an unusual paint-ing!"

"Yes, isn't it beautiful?" David said proudly.

"But I find it a bit strange," Mrs. Luce commented.

David whipped his head around and stared at the portrait. A large black mustache had been drawn on it.

His face turned lobster-red. The room fell silent.

"Who would do such a thing?" David raged. "What vandal, what idiot would desecrate such a work of art? Who did it? I demand to know!"

Painfully aware that the joke had misfired, Cotten confessed that the original painting had been removed. David had always enjoyed pranks before, but he remained furious. "I don't think it's funny!" he declared, and his anger cast a pall on the rest of the evening.

By 1949 the Selznick empire had deteriorated to an alarming degree. *The Paradine Case* and *Portrait of Jennie* had caused a severe drain on the company's finances. Now the talent roster was beginning to shrink.

David's remarkable facility for selecting talent helped him maintain a star list as prestigious as some of the major studios. His attitude toward his performers had been paternal and pro-prietary, but now he seemed cavalier.

Gregory Peck, after a series of top-notch vehicles, found him-self loaned to Warner Brothers for a western potboiler, *Only the Valiant,* co-starring with Barbara Payton. When he protested to a Selznick aide, he was told: "David needs the money; he won't dis-cuss it." Peck received $60,000 for the picture; Selznick collect-ed $150,000.

David's relations with Ingrid Bergman had worsened. Her longtime ambition was to portray Joan of Arc, but he ignored her pleas. Instead, he had Ben Hecht prepare a script on the life of Sarah Bernhardt.

"But I am the complete opposite of Sarah Bernhardt," Miss Bergman protested.

"Who will know that in America?" David argued.

"I will know," she replied.

Leo McCarey, who had directed Miss Bergman in *The Bells of St. Mary's,* convinced her that she should attempt the Broadway stage, and the opportunity came with the Maxwell Anderson play *Joan of Lorraine.* David was violently opposed to her leaving Hollywood, but she was resolved.

Shortly before her departure, both appeared at a party, and David sulked in a corner, unwilling to speak to her. She walked over to him and said: "You must wish me good luck. I will not go unless I can go with your blessing." He relented and wished her luck.

Joseph Cotten, who remained a close personal friend of David's, nevertheless bridled at being loaned for such films as *Beyond the Forest,* which helped bring the end of Bette Davis' career as a leading lady. Some of David's stars, notably Dorothy McGuire, never appeared in a Selznick picture; they were merely kept under contract for lease to other producers.

Despite his disgruntlement over loan-outs to other studios, Alfred Hitchcock had been willing to sign again with David at the end of his seven-year contract. But he found David curiously distant whenever the matter of a new contract arose. For eighteen months, as the end of the contract approached, Hitchcock could get no decision.

"You'll have your deal; I want to renew," said David. "Let's shake on it."

"No, I don't want any handshake deal," the director insisted. "I want it in writing." But David never produced a concrete proposal, and Hitchcock left him to become an independent film maker.

The drain of Selznick loyalists continued. Hal Kern had made a valuable contribution to the Selznick features with his sure touch as editor. One day during the editing of *Portrait of Jennie,* David had wanted Kern to show some footage to Mary Pickford, but Kern had taken a rare day off. David told Kern afterward that the incident had humiliated him and he felt he could dispense with Kern's services. "That's all right with me," said the film editor, and their fifteen-year association came to an end.

David tried desperately to find quality product for the Selznick Releasing Organization, and in one case he succeeded. Alexander Korda and Carol Reed came to him with a proposal to participate in a film based on Graham Greene's novel *The Third Man*. David consented to supply part of the financing, plus services of Joseph Cotten and Alida Valli, in return for distribution rights and ownership of the film in the United States.

Reed agreed to consult with Selznick on the script, with the proviso that changes would be made by mutual consent. The director and Greene went to California for consultations but found David more concerned with a production of *Serena Blandish,* starring Jennifer, at the La Jolla Playhouse. Script conferences on *The Third Man* were held in David's office late at night, and he seemed distracted and nonresponsive. Reed went off to film the picture in Europe. David was impressed with the result and made no changes for the American release except to edit the final chase. The well-played suspense and the distinctive zither score helped make *The Third Man* a substantial moneymaker, keeping S.R.O. in operation for a few months longer.[6]

But the end was coming.

David's inattention to the new economic facts of the movie business, his willingness to take any gamble at outrageous odds, his alienation of trusted advisers who had helped build his empire, his increasing obsession with Jennifer and her career—these factors were combining to bring financial ruin. David found himself $12,000,000 in debt to the banks, with no immediate prospect of making restitution.

He was tired and confused. At forty-seven, he had accomplished more than most men could in a lifetime. Now he was at a crossroads, both in his career and in his personal life. The tie to Irene had been formally broken; she divorced him in January of 1948, and the action became final under California law a year later. He was a free man, and he was deeply in love with Jennifer.

---

[6] Selznick erred in refusing *Red River* for the Selznick Releasing Organization. He considered the Howard Hawks film a routine western. United Artists released *Red River,* which proved to be a highly profitable film.

Two courses were open to David in dealing with his overwhelming debt: he could file for bankruptcy, or he could somehow attempt to pay back the money. Bankruptcy was unthinkable. His father had been forced into it, and that had been the source of the family shame. "It was the one thing I never forgave my father," said David. To admit before the movie community and the world that the father's failure had been repeated by the son—that would have been more than David could bear. And so he began to make plans for liquidation.

The Selznick Releasing Organization, already in disarray, was shut down entirely. Daniel O'Shea prepared a book bound in red morocco; inside was a complete listing of the Selznick assets, ranging from stars like Gregory Peck and Shirley Temple to films like *Rebecca* and *Spellbound*. The book was ready to be peddled to the highest bidder.

David went first to Nicholas Schenck of M-G-M. O'Shea remained in the outer office while David spoke privately with Schenck. When David emerged, he said sheepishly "I couldn't do it." O'Shea understood. For David to sell out to the company of his former father-in-law would have been ignominious.

"Do you think you can sell it to Warners?" David asked, handing over the red book.

"Yes, I think so," said O'Shea.

O'Shea visited Harry Warner, president of Warner Brothers, at his ranch in the San Fernando Valley. Warner was interested, but he had to consult with his brother Jack, head of the studio operation. The Warners wanted the Selznick assets, but their offer was a half million short of the $2,900,000 David wanted.

The following week, David boarded the train for New York, taking with him the red book. He telegraphed O'Shea en route that Frank Freeman and other Paramount executives were on the train and asked if he should propose a deal. O'Shea replied in the affirmative, and David offered the red book to Paramount.

Negotiations continued for weeks. Then Selznick's tax attorneys advised disposing of the assets in parcels instead of a single package. The receipts totaled $5,000,000 instead of the $2,900,000 which David had expected.

For $1,500,000, Warner Brothers bought commitments with seven Selznick stars: Gregory Peck, Jennifer Jones, Shirley Temple, Joseph Cotten, Louis Jourdan, Betsy Drake, and Rory Calhoun. To Eagle-Lion went reissue rights to ten Selznick pictures. The entire physical assets of the Selznick studio, from *Gone With the Wind* costumes to David's own mahogany desk, were put up for public auction.

It was not quite like the auction which Lewis J. Selznick had undergone at the family's Park Avenue home. David had suffered a setback, but he hadn't been run out of the industry, as his father had. The name of Selznick still ranked high in Hollywood's pantheon; David's achievements could not be negated by temporary defeats.

He would sit back awhile, study the bewildering changes in the industry, look into the promise of filming in Europe. And he hoped to convince the wavering Jennifer to marry him. Her career, in which he had the most profound faith, would help restore his zest for film making. So he firmly believed.

VI

●●●●●●●●●●●●●●●●●●●●

WANDERINGS

●●●●●●●●●●●●●●●●●●●●

The Man Who Made
"Gone With the Wind"

David Selznick and Jennifer Jones

WHEN DAVID SELZNICK WAS FIFTY-TWO,
he attended a dinner party one evening
in the New York apartment of Vincent Astor.
He and Jennifer arrived late,
as was their custom.
At the sumptuous dinner table,
John Crosby overheard David remark to Lilli Palmer,
"My psychiatrist said I would always feel guilty
until I paid back the twelve million.
So I paid back the twelve million."
David took a swallow of soup and added,
"Of course I'm broke now.
But I don't feel guilty."

After the trying experience with *Portrait of Jennie,* David Selznick loaned Jennifer Jones for two more difficult pictures: *We Were Strangers* at Columbia and *Madame Bovary* at M-G-M. Her creative energies were depleted, and the turmoil in her personal life was becoming almost unbearable. David continued to dominate her life in an overwhelming manner. Both were ambivalent about marriage. They felt a strong physical tie, but they were wary of second marriages and the emotional adjustments that would be required. Both were aware of their emotional instability. The breakups of their marriages had left scars which caused both David and Jennifer to seek psychiatric aid.

Jennifer was disturbed by the erratic behavior of Bob Walker. He had become one of the screen's most engaging young actors and was earning $2000 a week from M-G-M. But the honors and riches were hollow rewards in view of the unhappiness he believed Hollywood had brought him. He plunged into fits of despair, when a single drink could send him on a rampage.

One drunken escapade brought Walker a suspended jail sentence of one hundred and eighty days and a $500 fine after he pleaded guilty to hit-and-run driving. He married Barbara Ford, daughter of John Ford, but they separated five weeks later. She divorced him, declaring that he had no intention of consummating the marriage.

Again Bob Walker was arrested on a drunk driving charge, and newspapers printed photographs of him in a bravado mood, then in drunken rage. When he saw the photographs, he realized he was mentally ill. He accepted the suggestion of M-G-M production boss Dore Schary that he submit to treatment at the Menninger Clinic.

After six months at the Topeka, Kansas, clinic, Bob Walker returned to Hollywood and talked freely about his mental problems. He admitted that the divorce from Jennifer had contributed to the upset of his equilibrium, but he felt he had achieved some inner calm. He resumed his career with greater success than before.

Hopeful that Bob Walker had solved his personal problems,

Jennifer Jones went off to Europe to seek an answer to hers.

She was still undecided about marrying David, and she felt that getting away from Hollywood would help her make up her mind. She went first to Ireland with her traveling companion, Anita Colby, who tried to convince her that the marriage would be a mistake. Jennifer was almost persuaded.

When she left for Europe in March of 1949, David had told the press that they planned to marry. "I don't know exactly when or where we will be married, but it will be some time before the end of summer, when we can get a breather from our work." He remained in Hollywood to liquidate his operations, then joined her in Zurich in midsummer.

Jennifer declared that she thought a marriage between them would be unwise. David was not prepared to accept that decision. He had already announced to the world that they would marry; if the wedding did not take place, he felt he would be ridiculed. Besides, he worshiped Jennifer and wanted to devote himself, now that he was freed from the burden of running a stu-

Vincente Minnelli, Jennifer Jones, and Louis Jourdan on the set of MADAME BOVARY.

Robert Walker snaps his fingers with unconcern for his arrest on drunk charges ...

... then expresses his fury over being held in custody.

dio, to the further glory of her career. As for Jennifer, she felt a deep attachment and a sense of gratitude to David, but she feared marriage to him. She had been greatly disturbed by the marriage to Bob Walker and the grief that followed it. She did not want to risk another emotional cataclysm.

David continued his campaign with customary persistence. He took Jennifer to the French Riviera and chartered a yacht, the thirty-three-ton *Manona*. They anchored offshore and basked in the Mediterranean sun while David applied his persuasion. One day Jennifer became so annoyed with his arguments that she leaped into the water and swam ashore.

David invited friends to join the cruise. He chose two married couples he knew would help further his cause: the Leland Haywards and the Louis Jourdans.

Said Jourdan: "We will go along if you promise to get married."

"Of course," David replied.

But now he himself was

Jennifer Jones is helped from the yacht Manona *following her marriage to David Selznick, who stands on deck.*

vacillating about the wisdom of his course; Jennifer's arguments were beginning to sway him. Both were concerned that the marriage might not be the best thing for their sons.

The *Manona* cruised along the Italian Riviera and down the boot of Italy. David's guests became playfully insistent that he get married. "If you don't," Jourdan warned, "Leland and I won't shave." The beards of Jourdan and Hayward grew for three days, and then David made up his mind. He delivered his final plea to Jennifer. This time she said yes.

David cabled his staff to make the necessary arrangements. When the Manona docked at Portofino, he learned that the marriage license had to be obtained in Genoa, thirty miles distant. David hired a car and raced over the mountain roads to Genoa, arriving at the bureau five minutes before closing time. Then he went to the cable office and dispatched a message to Irene. It consisted of one word: "David."

Laurence Olivier and Jennifer Jones pose on a bicycle built for two on the set of CARRIE.

At eight-thirty the following morning, July 13, 1949, Jennifer Jones (real name: Phylis Isley Walker), age thirty, and David O. Selznick, forty-seven, were married aboard the *Manona* by the British captain of the vessel. The witnesses were Mr. and Mrs. Leland Hayward and Mr. and Mrs. Louis Jourdan. Members of the press were not present, but photographs were taken of the bride and Selznick as they left the Manona at noon to board the yacht of Prince Pignatelli. They sailed to nearby Rapallo, where they attended a wedding reception given by an Italian millionaire, Rudi Crespi. To assure the legality of the marriage, a second ceremony was performed at the Genoa city hall.

David was jubilant. He was more than ever certain of the wisdom of his marriage to Jennifer, and he was determined to make her life happy and fulfilled. In her he had found the cause to which he would devote the remaining years of his life.

The ensuing years were unsettled ones for David Selznick. He remained in Europe and became involved with Alexander Korda in a vehicle for Jennifer, *Gone to Earth*. Michael Powell and Emeric Pressburger adapted the gypsy story, and the result displeased David. He took the two and a half hour film to Hollywood and edited it down to thirty-five minutes. Then he brought the English actors to Hollywood, and Rouben Mamoulian directed additional scenes to return the film to feature length. The film was released in the United States as *The Wild Heart*, and it was poorly received.

David loaned Jennifer to Paramount to play the title role in *Carrie*, William Wyler's adaptation of the Theodore Dreiser novel *Sister Carrie*. Jennifer co-starred with Laurence Olivier in the prestigious film, which fell short of popular appeal.

Jennifer was loaned to co-star with newcomer Charlton Heston in *Ruby Gentry*, to be directed by King Vidor. Remembering his experience on *Duel in the Sun,* Vidor insisted on a contract provision that David could not visit the set or view rushes. But the terms did not preclude the writing of memos.

David, who was making his headquarters in New York, sent memo after memo to Vidor in Hollywood instructing him on the treatment of Jennifer in *Ruby Gentry*. Vidor was too busy to reply, and David stormed that he would not allow Jennifer to appear in the picture unless his memos were acknowledged.

Vidor wearily agreed to do so. He pored over the Selznick memos for five hours with a secretary and writer. They discovered that Selznick's later memos negated all his earlier suggestions, and Vidor wrote David that he had found nothing to reply to.

David continued managing his remaining assets to pay off his debts. His pride required that he pursue a lone course in this, and he turned down offers of help from friends. Once he was visiting Darryl Zanuck at his home in Palm Springs. The 20th Century-Fox boss was aware of David's straits, and as David was leaving Zanuck remarked, "I'm not too rich, but if you want two hundred and fifty thousand dollars, I'll go in the house and sign the check right now."

The gesture touched David, but he replied: "No, thanks, Darryl. I don't need it now. But if I do need it, I'm glad to know that I can call on you."

David did a masterful job of milking the commercial possibilities of what he owned. He released his pictures abroad and to television, he peddled story properties to other producers, he sold commitments to players. He traveled widely, preferring to make his deals in person.

When she wasn't engaged in film making in Hollywood, Jennifer accompanied David on his journeys. During the summer of 1951, she went with him to Europe, leaving sons Michael and Robert with their father.

Robert Walker appeared to have conquered his troubles, and his career was in full flower. That summer was a joyful one for him. He worked all day at the studio, then returned to his Malibu home to romp on the sand with his sons. Only after the boys had gone to bed did the old phantoms return.

On the night of August 28, Walker had been drinking and was in an emotional state. His psychiatrist and an assistant arrived to calm him, but persuasion didn't help. Walker became more unmanageable, and the psychiatrist administered a sedative, sodium amytol. Walker's respiration failed. By the time a physician arrived, Walker was dead.

Jennifer canceled her plans to attend the Venice Film Festival and flew to Hollywood. Walker's parents had planned a funeral at nearby Forest Lawn Memorial Park, but Robert and Michael, eleven and ten years old, asked that their father be taken home for burial. Robert Walker was buried in a Mormon cemetery at Ogden, Utah, near the fields where he had played as a boy.

David was convinced that work was the proper antidote for Jennifer's grief over the death of Bob Walker. Impressed by the postwar Italian films, he sought a liaison that would allow Jennifer to be the first important American star to participate in that vital new school of cinema. He formed a partnership with Vittorio de Sica, famed for his accomplishments with *Shoeshine* and *The Bicycle Thief.* The project was a disaster from the start.

The original title was *Terminal Station,* and the entire action was to take place in Rome's handsome new railroad station. Jennifer was cast as an American wife suffering through a separation with her American-Italian lover, Montgomery Clift.

The clash of the two cultures proved violent. De Sica spoke almost no English and was accustomed to shooting off-the-cuff with a minimum crew. Selznick spoke no Italian and was the master of the heavily supervised Hollywood style of production. While he did not function as producer on the film, he made his presence felt. He hired a procession of writers to work on the script: Truman Capote, Carson McCullers, Alberto Moravia, Paul Jarrico. None could breathe life into the fragmentary tale.

David returned to Hollywood with the finished film. By the time he had eliminated hundreds of feet of film in which De Sica lingered his camera on the architectural features of the Rome station, he had a sixty-minute feature—too short for commercial presentation. He began tinkering with it.

One of his additions was an insert in which Jennifer penned a farewell note to Clift. Since Jennifer's own handwriting was unsuitable, he assigned his studio publicity chief, Ann McCall, to be her write-in. For three days, David directed Miss McCall's handwriting before a camera. Her performance didn't suit him. "You're not acting!" he complained.

"But all you asked me to do was write a letter," she replied.

"But I want you to act! You're leaving this man. Doesn't that mean anything to you?"

"No, I've got writer's cramp," she replied.

David agonized over a new title for the film. For a while he favored *Assignation at Terminal Station.* He asked each member of his staff to submit twenty-four titles per day. He discarded them all and chose his own title: *Indiscretion of an American Wife.*

Arthur P. Jacobs, whose publicity firm David had hired to help promote his interests, protested that it was a cheap title not befitting such talents as De Sica, Jennifer, and Clift.

"I know more about titles than anyone else in the business,"

David replied flatly. He would not be swayed. Nor would he listen to Jacobs' criticism of a prologue in which Patti Page sang a sentimental song related to the picture. *Indiscretion of an American Wife* was released by Columbia at a spare sixty-three minutes to a minimum of popular and critical response.

The streak of ill fortune seemed to end in 1954. In the early part of the year, Jennifer appeared opposite Humphrey Bogart in the European-made *Beat the Devil.* Although the film's obtuse humor baffled audiences—it was to be cherished by later film students as an early example of black comedy—*Beat the Devil* helped re-establish Jennifer as an important star. The picture was directed by John Huston, who was the inevitable recipient of voluminous memos cabled from David in New York. After the third memo, Huston sent back his answer, numbering the sections "Page 1," "Page 2," and "Page 4." The rest of David's correspondence with Huston was largely concerned with the question "What happened to Page 3?"

By mid-1954, David had paid off the entire indebtedness of

Jennife Jones (left), INDISCRETION OF AN AMERICAN WIFE.

$12,000,000, and he began contemplating full-scale production once more. His return to films would necessarily be something vaster in scope that *Gone With the Wind*. The choice seemed obvious: *War and Peace.*

"A large percentage of critics the world over regard *War and Peace* as the greatest novel ever written," he declared in his public announcement. "It contains many of the things to be found in its American counterpart, *Gone With the Wind:* its great love story, and its complete portrait of an era and of a vanished civilization—that of pre-Communist Russia. Its opportunities for spectacle are magnificent, including Napoleon's advance upon and retreat from Russia, and the burning of Moscow."

But before taking on Tolstoy, David decided to follow the advice of CBS boss William Paley and venture into television. He was hired by the electrical industry to produce a two-hour television spectacular, *Light's Diamond Jubilee,* to celebrate on all three networks the seventy-fifth anniversary of Thomas A. Edison's invention of the incandescent lamp.

David leaped into the assignment with his old-time zeal. He induced King Vidor, William Wellman, and Norman Taurog to work for him again in directing filmed segments of the show. He hired his favorite writer, Ben Hecht, to produce the script, and both retired to the Beverly Hills Hotel to get the job done. Hecht worked night and day to meet the deadline for presentation of the script to the network executives. David was conferring with them when Hecht, wearing a four-day growth of beard, walked dramatically into the hotel bungalow and tossed the thick script on David's desk.

"There it is," Hecht said triumphantly.

"Ben—you're interrupting!" David chided.

The script was bright and original and it was well played by a cast of Hollywood names.[1] Also on the show was the President of the United States. David had telephoned his friend, Dwight D. Eisenhower, who accepted the invitation to make a speech for

---

[1] *Light's Diamond Jubilee* featured a little-known comedian, George Gobel. His monologue proved highly effective, helping him win his own television series.

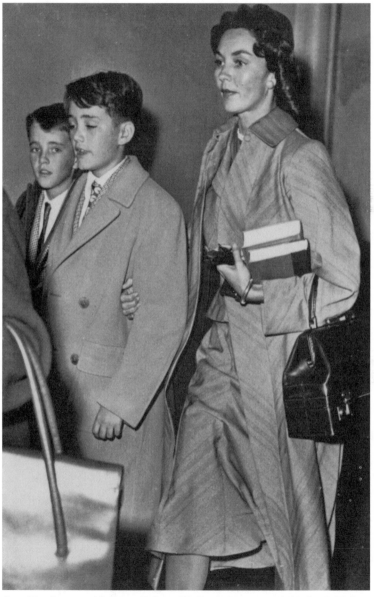

Jennifer Jones with sons Robert Walker, eleven, and Michael Walker, twelve, in Paris en route to the boys' school in Switzerland.

Light's Diamond Jubilee. David himself wrote the speech, rewrote it sixteen times, then flew to Denver to direct the President's performance.

The success of *Light's Diamond Jubilee* portended a bright career in television for David Selznick. He wasn't interested. "In TV there is a fixed return for what you create," he said. "I like the film business, where you can profit by making things better. I always worked on the theory that if you make your picture one percent better, you might improve your take ten percent." Television, with its exacting schedules and its lack of the big gamble, held no appeal for him.

The year 1954 brought an event of unsurpassing joy for David: the birth of a daughter, Mary Jennifer Selznick, on August 12. He idolized the girl unstintingly to the end of his life.

Following the birth of Mary Jennifer, David decided that Jennifer should demonstrate her versatility by starring on the Broadway stage. He selected Henry James's *Portrait of a Lady,* adapted by William Archibald and directed by José Quintero. The play lasted only a week in New York.

David suffered another disappointment with *War and Peace.* M-G-M had agreed to finance and release his project. But then the freewheeling Mike Todd announced he was planning a film based on *War and Peace.* And Italy's Dino de Laurentiis declared he was preparing his own version of *War and Peace,* to be backed by Paramount.

The American companies had long kept a gentleman's agreement to respect each other's story properties, and the Motion Picture Producers Association maintained a Title Registration Bureau for that purpose. David Selznick had registered *War and Peace* first and hence had precedence for the title. But he learned to his dismay that the rulers of film companies no longer behaved like gentlemen. Paramount declared that it was going ahead with the De Laurentiis *War and Peace,* releasing it under a different title if necessary.

David's cries of foul play were to no avail. M-G-M boss Nicholas Schenck asked David if his *War and Peace* could beat the Italian version to the theaters. David admitted that his mode

John Huston, Jennifer Jones and Peter Lorre on the set of BEAT THE DEVIL.

of producing precluded such a possibility. Schenck regretfully canceled the project.

Two more years of frustration and disappointment.

A contract to produce two large-scale pictures for M-G-M was announced with ostentation. But again David could not reach agreement with Nick Schenck on subjects, and the deal fell quietly in limbo.

Daniel O'Shea had become president of RKO, now a subsidiary of the General Tire and Rubber Company, and he reasoned that his old boss could provide the magic to resuscitate the failing RKO. In 1955, Selznick signed a three-year contract to provide top-quality films at RKO expense. It was expected that David would eventually take charge of all the studio's production, as he had a quarter century before.

David declared he would start three pictures for RKO the following winter, and he talked of later producing movies specifically for television. He emphasized that he intended to maintain his independent course:"I'm concerned with the building of the Selznick Company, not with RKO primarily . . . I'll be working on a program of production for the Selznick Company to establish it as an important producing factor in the motion picture industry."

Brave words, but they became hollow when RKO's fortunes worsened. The O'Neil family, owners of General Tire, grew wary of partnership with Hollywood's most profligate producer. The deal was canceled, and the O'Neils retired from film making, selling RKO studio to Lucille Ball and Desi Arnaz.

David next decided he would plunge into television, in a manner befitting the Selznick tradition. His subject: the entire Bible.

It was a revolutionary concept: to produce three hundred hours of film depicting the major events of the Bible. Each segment would occupy an hour of network time every Sunday night. Such a grandiose scheme obviously needed important backing, and David began at the top: General Motors. The automobile executives were impressed with his proposal and entered negotiations for a contract. But upon reconsidering, General Motors decided the plan was unfeasible, and David experienced another disappointment.

During this vexing period of irresolution, David suffered an affront to his reputation that sent his temper flaring.

The new management of M-G-M studio under Dore Schary — Louis B. Mayer had been deposed in 1951 — marshaled its stars to appear on a special broadcast of Ed Sullivan's *Toast of the Town* television show for a salute to the company's thirtieth year. The review of the studio's achievements, narrated by Schary himself, omitted any mention of Louis B. Mayer and failed to state that David 0. Selznick had produced *Gone With the Wind.*

Both Mayer and Selznick issued public complaints, and David's was the most vitriolic. He was especially incensed that his onetime protege, Schary, should be guilty of such ingratitude.

"I'm not concerned with seeking personal credit so much as preventing those who aren't entitled to it from taking credit,"

David grumbled to the press. He said he was shocked "by the startling and, in my opinion, disgraceful and inexcusable attempt on the part of Dore Schary to present *Gone With the Wind* as an M-G-M production and, what is worse, to claim by implication that it was a picture produced by the present production team of that studio."

Schary issued a statement that attempted to smooth the ruffled egos of Mayer and Selznick. Nothing came of David's threat of a lawsuit. When he and Schary met in a restaurant a year later, David smiled and said he wasn't angry any more.

Jennifer's career remained active. She appeared opposite William Holden in *Love Is a Many-Splendored Thing,* a sentimental tale about an American war correspondent in love with a Eurasian lady doctor. The film was a money-maker, its popularity aided by the much-played title song, an Academy Award winner of 1955. The bestselling novel by Frances Gray Patton, *Good Morning, Miss Dove,* provided Jennifer with the strong characterization of a spinster schoolteacher in a New England hamlet. Another best-seller, *The Man in the Gray Flannel Suit,*[2] cast her again with Gregory Peck. It was a popular film. Less successful was *The Barretts of Wimpole Street,* filmed in England with John Gielgud and Bill Travers. It was a mistake to refilm the picture when the excellent Norma Shearer-Charles Laughton-Fredric March version was still fresh in the memories of many filmgoers.

David was pleased that Jennifer was in demand to appear in pictures for other producers, but he believed that none of them realized her true potential as a romantic star. In each film he discovered elements which he as a producer could have improved,

---

[2] The producer of *The Man in the Gray Flannel Suit* was the Georgia wit, Nunnally Johnson. He was flooded with the customary memos from David Selznick on how Jennifer should be treated in the film. Johnson replied succinctly: "Thank you very much, David. I have passed your notes on to Mr. Zanuck." Darryl F. Zanuck was production chief at 20th Century-Fox.

On another occasion, Johnson wrote Selznick: "In case your wife is too modest to tell you, I want you to know that she did a scene today that was absolutely marvelous. P.S. Don't answer this."

and his memos of correction too often went unheeded. Only he, David O. Selznick, understood Jennifer's inordinate skill as an actress. Therefore it was imperative that he return to production.

It all began because Warner Brothers wanted Judy Garland to appear in a musical remake of *A Star Is Born.*

Warners had purchased the remake rights from a producer who had bought them during the dissolution of Selznick International. But David Selznick, the canny trader, had retained certain rights, and he called Jack Warner to announce, "You won't be able to sell your picture to television or in several countries."

Having already committed himself with Miss Garland, Warner asked David for a solution. "You give me *A Farewell to Arms*[3] and I'll give you my rights to *A Star Is Born,*" David proposed.

Warner protested that the trade was not equitable, so David agreed to pay $25,000 for *A Farewell to Arms.* He was delighted. He considered the Hemingway novel one of the great love stories of the century and hence a fitting vehicle for Jennifer.

"Don't do it, David," counseled Sam Goldwyn. "It's a mistake to remake a great picture, because you can never make it better. Better you should find a picture that was done badly and see what can be done to improve it."

David remained firm. It didn't matter that Paramount had produced a memorable film of the Ernest Hemingway novel with Helen Hayes and Gary Cooper in 1933, nor that Warner Brothers filmed a less creditable version as *Force of Arms* with William Holden and Nancy Olson in 1951. David was convinced that neither had captured the full scope of the war theme nor the intrinsic beauty of the love story.

Arthur Jacobs was instructed to make the announcement that Ernest Hemingway's *A Farewell to Arms* would be filmed in Italy starring Jennifer Jones; it would be David O. Selznick's successor to *Gone With the Wind.* The news did not receive the

---

[3] Warner Brothers had acquired the rights to *A Farewell to Arms* in a trade with Paramount, which wanted Warners' property *A Connecticut Yankee* as a Bing Crosby vehicle.

attention David expected, and he fired off a four-page memo chiding Jacobs. Among other things, David questioned how the New York *Times* dared to refer to his new production as a "remake." He urged a full-scale publicity campaign and agreed to give interviews, including those he had promised to Tom Pryor of the New York *Times* and Philip Scheuer of the Los Angeles *Times.*

His broadside was answered in a frank, seventeen-page memo by Jacobs, who pointed out that the New York *Times* could not be told what to call the film, which certainly was a remake, no matter what David chose to call it—"in fact, the Warner Brothers version can be seen on television this week." As for Pryor and Scheuer, both suggested delaying interviews until David was ready to disclose concrete plans.

"The truth is, David, that you have announced too many projects that never happened," Jacobs said bluntly. The publicist advocated trade-paper ads which would state: "In six months, production will start on *A Farewell to Arms* . . ." He further advised eliminating all references to the film's being Selznick's successor to *Gone With the Wind.*

David agreed to Jacobs' suggestions. Now David immersed himself in the production process, as he had not done since *A Portrait of Jennie* eight years before. He assigned Ben Hecht to write the screenplay, and together they produced nine different scripts. David decided to hire John Huston as director.

"Don't do it, David," cautioned Ray Klune, his one-time production manager. "It would be a great mistake."

"Why?" David asked.

"Because you'll kill each other. It's the old law of physics about an immovable object and an irresistible force."

Despite Klune's predictions, the initial meetings between Selznick and Huston went smoothly. Together with Hecht, they worked on the script in New York and Hollywood, and their relations were cordial. David and John had long been social acquaintances, and it had been at David's house that Huston had met his wife, Ricky Soma.

As his meetings with David continued, Huston became more

apprehensive about the project. The director's original enthusiasm had been based on his desire to interpret Hemingway on the screen. But with each rewrite of the script, Huston realized that David was not interested in filming the Hemingway novel but in providing a love story for Jennifer Jones.

Huston attempted to remove parts of the script that had not been in the novel and to add portions of the Hemingway original. In some instances David agreed. But he argued it would be impossible to please the author since Hemingway disliked any changes in dramatizations of his work. David declared that he was being more faithful to *A Farewell to Arms* than he had been to *Gone With the Wind,* "with which not only a couple of hundred million people but Margaret Mitchell herself were delighted."

David completed arrangements for 20th Century-Fox to finance and distribute *A Farewell to Arms.* Rock Hudson, one of the most important box-office stars, was borrowed from Universal to co-star with Jennifer. For production manager David chose Arthur Fellows, who had risen in the Selznick organization from office boy in 1935. Fellows began setting up production facilities in Rome, and David arrived to take charge in early 1957.[4]

The memos flew. To Art Fellows: precautions must be taken to prevent any loss of life during filming. To Rock Hudson: practice rowing, if necessary, so you will seem professional in the lake sequence. To Ben Hecht: the script should be polished so that *A Farewell to Arms* will be remembered as long as *Gone With the Wind.* To the cameraman: instructions on how to photograph Jennifer (twenty pages).

To Arthur Jacobs in New York, David sent a memo criticizing the publicist's preparation for the *Farewell to Arms* campaign. When rolled out, the cable extended down the hallway of the

---

[4] Before leaving for Italy, David Selznick interviewed actors for *A Farewell to Arms* with the intention of rebuilding his list of contract players. Rod Steiger was invited to the Selznick mansion and he expressed his eagerness to appear in *A Farewell to Arms.* But the young actor balked at David's insistence on a contract for future film commitments. David was offended, and he terminated the interview. He was displeased to learn that others in the new generation of actors refused to sign term contracts with a studio or producer, even David O. Selznick.

Robert Stack, Jennifer Jones, Bill Elliott, GOOD MORNING MISS DOVE.

Jennifer Jones, William Holden, LOVE IS A MANY SPLENDORED THING.

John Gielgud, Jennifer Jones, Bill Travers, THE
BARRETTS OF WIMPOLE STREET.

Selznick office, and Jacobs read it on his hands and knees. When Jacobs reached the peroration, he read: "On s e c o n d thought, I take back every-thing I said. Proceed as you suggested."

To John Huston went m e m o s o f increasing testiness. The two men continued to clash over the script, Huston seeking more fidelity to the Hemingway original. They argued over a variety of matters, including the cut of Rock Hudson's hair. Huston wanted it to be in the severe style of World War I; David accused Huston of trying to ruin Rock's sex appeal.

Finally on March 19, David dictated the memo that was to be the coup de grâce. He declared that he was desperately unhappy with how things were going; that their differences would not help the picture, as Huston had suggested; that he, David, knew damn well he could prepare a better picture than could Hemingway; that he was not asking Huston to resign but telling him the conditions under which they could continue working together; that they were both individualists but on *A Farewell to Arms* only one individualist could prevail, and that was David Selznick.

David instructed Art Fellows to deliver the memo to Huston at the location site in the Dolomite mountains, where filming was to begin in two days. Fellows telephoned the director and said: "I've got something to give you, and I don't think you'll like it. I think he's nuts, and you'll hit the ceiling when you read it."

Huston read half of the voluminous memo and telephoned Fellows:

"I not only hit the ceiling; I'm stuck up there." Within half an hour Huston had packed his belongings and left the location.[5]

The departure of Huston caused a flurry of headlines, and David played the story with the skill of a master publicist. He issued a widely quoted remark: "In Mr. Huston, I asked for a first violinist and instead got a soloist."

David and Jennifer flew from Rome to California to be with his seventy-eight-year-old mother, who was undergoing an operation. En route, David told reporters there was no truth in reports Huston had quit because of differences over Jennifer's portrayal.

"I am the producer and must produce," he declared. "When differences arose, I gave Huston the choice of either carrying out his contract and verbal agreements or leaving. He chose to leave." He added that he was usually an easy man to get along with and had changed directors only three times in thirty years—on *Viva Villa, Gone With the Wind,* and *Duel in the Sun.*

To sensitive observers of the patterns of movie history, David's treatment of Huston represented the *dernier cri* of the old-time producer, which Selznick epitomized. As with others of his breed, David brooked no challenge to his will. His own taste and judgment had to prevail. Opposing him was Huston, one of the new kind of film makers who contended that the director was the prime creative force. This was a concept that David Selznick could never accept.

David moved quickly to avoid delay in production. Art Fellows first took over direction of the location scenes which Huston had planned. Andrew Marton, an expert in spectacle, arrived to

---

[5] David Selznick and John Huston met once again, two years later in the lobby of the St. Regis Hotel in New York. Both gazed at each other to detect signs of hostility. Seeing none, they shook hands, exchanged a few words and parted. Later, in Hollywood, Jennifer invited Huston to a party at the Selznick house. Huston declined, saying, "I'm still sore."

direct the mountain scenes, which involved eighty-five hundred soldiers from the Italian army.

To replace Huston, David chose Charles Vidor,[6] a director accustomed to survival with an autocratic producer; he had endured a sometimes productive, often violent relationship with Harry Cohn at Columbia.

Vidor now became the recipient of the outpouring of memos. One of them conveyed David's concern over the effectiveness of a forthcoming scene in which the Hemingway hero, Frederic Henry, was to meet Catherine Barkley in a Milan hospital. Jennifer had asked for a "business appointment" with David to discuss her disquiet over the scene. All of her arguments were sound, he added, since she was a very creative actress. He advised Vidor to allow Jennifer to play the scene her way first, so he could benefit from her creativity and her long study of the role. Then Vidor could re-direct as he saw fit.

David wrote to Ben Hecht that the picture was becoming an increasing obsession to him and he could think about nothing else. That was apparent in David's attitude on the set. One day Rock Hudson observed the producer, deep in contemplation, walk into a wall.

Once during an intimate love scene with Jennifer, Hudson looked behind the camera to see Selznick whispering in Vidor's ear. "David!" the actor chided. "Oh, sorry—sorry," David replied absent-mindedly.

The memos, some of which were later excerpted in *Life* with David's permission, continued. He was concerned about the number of umbrellas in the Orsino retreat; he himself had cut them down during the filming. Having fought Huston's "slavishness" to the book, he now combated Vidor's contention that *A Farewell to Arms* was not the Bible. Vidor became more argumentative, declaring that David wanted not a first violinist as a director, but a piccolo player. The Hungarian-born Vidor exploded after David had dispatched a memo suggesting that the long stirring of gruel in the breakfast scene would become a bore.

6 Charles Vidor was unrelated to a previous Selznick director, King Vidor.

Gregory Peck, Jennifer Jones, THE MAN IN THE GREY FLANNEL SUIT.

Vidor fired back a telegram:

I RECEIVED YOUR MEMO REGARDING THE KITCHEN SCENE STOP
IN THE LIGHT OF MY PAST PERFORMANCE ON THIS PICTURE
ALONE I FIND IT IDIOTIC AND I THINK THAT BY THE LIGHT OF
MONDAY MORNING YOU WILL TOO STOP THE MEMO INDICATES
THAT YOU THINK YOU HAVE ON YOUR HANDS A HOPELESSLY INEX-
PERIENCED DIRECTOR STOP IF YOU DON'T STOP I WILL THINK
THAT I AM STUCK WITH A TOTALLY INEXPERIENCED PRODUCER
STOP FOR HEAVEN'S SAKE LET ME FUNCTION OR ELSE COME
DOWN AND SHOOT IT YOURSELF.

VIDOR

David responded in a hurt tone, suggesting that their previous relationship did not warrant such a message. He proposed
having lunch together and getting on with the show. Columnist
Art Buchwald, then based in Paris, went to Rome to cover the
filming of *A Farewell to Arms.* He filed this dispatch:

David Selznick and Rock Hudson on the location of A FAREWELL TO ARMS.

ROME—THERE IS A LEGEND IN ROME THAT IF YOU THROW A MEMORANDUM BY DAVID O. SELZNICK INTO THE FOUNTAIN OF CINECITTA STUDIOS, YOU WILL NEVER WORK ON *A FAREWELL TO ARMS* AGAIN.

THE PEOPLE WHO HAVE SAID FAREWELL TO *A FAREWELL TO ARMS* NOW NUMBER IN THE HUNDREDS AND INCLUDE ONE DIRECTOR, JOHN HUSTON, ONE CHIEF OF PHOTOGRAPHY WHO QUIT TWO WEEKS AGO, THREE ART DIRECTORS, A FILM EDITOR, A SPECIAL EFFECTS DIRECTOR, FOUR CHAUFFEURS, AND THE ENTIRE STAFF OF THE VILLA WHERE MR. AND MRS. SELZNICK WERE STAYING.

MOST OF THE PEOPLE CLAIM IT WAS NOT MR. SELZNICK BUT HIS MEMORANDUMS THAT GOT THEM DOWN.

MR. SELZNICK, WHO IS PRODUCING HIS FIRST FILM IN NINE YEARS, IS PROBABLY THE GREATEST MEMORANDUM WRITER IN THE MOTION-PICTURE INDUSTRY. HIS MEMOS, WHICH TOUCH ON EVERY PART OF PRODUCTION FROM MAKE-UP TO LIGHTING, HAVE BEEN KNOWN TO RUN UP TO 25 SINGLE-SPACED TYPEWRITTEN PAGES.

SINCE HE DICTATES THEM AT NIGHT TO THREE SECRETARIES WHO WORK IN SHIFTS, MR. SELZNICK HAS NO TIME TO READ THEM ONCE THEY ARE TYPED UP. THIS OCCASIONALLY LEADS TO MISUNDERSTANDINGS BETWEEN THE PRODUCER AND HIS HELP AND MOST EVERYONE ON THE PICTURE KEEPS A BAG PACKED IN CASE HE WANTS TO LEAVE ROME IN A HURRY.

MR. SELZNICK'S MEMORANDUMS ARE WRITTEN ON YELLOW PAPER (HE IS THE ONLY ONE ALLOWED TO USE YELLOW PAPER ON THE PRODUCTION) AND EVERYONE BUT THE ACTORS AND ACTRESSES CAN EXPECT TO RECEIVE THEM.

PEOPLE ON *A FAREWELL TO ARMS* COLLECT SELZNICK MEMORANDUMS LIKE OTHER PEOPLE COLLECT STAMPS. THE MEMO WRITTEN TO JOHN HUSTON WHICH CAUSED HIM TO QUIT IS WORTH

David Selznick commanding the troops for A FAREWELL TO ARMS.

THREE MEMOS THAT SELZNICK WROTE TO THE CAMERAMAN ABOUT PHOTOGRAPHING JENNIFER JONES. ONE PERSON IN THE COMPANY HAS A COLLECTOR'S ITEM, A SELZNICK MEMORANDUM OF ONE LINE. HE HAS BEEN OFFERED 50,000 LIRE FOR IT, BUT REFUSES TO SELL IT.

EACH PERSON REACTS DIFFERENTLY TO A SELZNICK MEMO. ONE DEPARTMENT HEAD WHO IS NO LONGER THERE THOUGHT HE WOULD FIGHT FIRE WITH FIRE AND SO WHEN HE RECEIVED A MEMO FROM SELZNICK HE SENT HIM BACK A MEMORANDUM OF THE SAME LENGTH. BUT HE GOT A MEMO THE NEXT DAY FROM SELZNICK SAYING PLEASE DON'T SEND HIM ANY MEMOS ANY MORE BECAUSE HE DOESN'T HAVE TIME TO READ THEM.

ANOTHER PERSON WHO WAS UPSET ABOUT HIS MEMOS WENT TO VITTORIO DE SICA, WHO IS ACTING IN FAREWELL BUT DIRECTED A SELZNICK PICTURE, TERMINAL STATION, AND ASKED WHAT HE DID WHEN HE RECEIVED A MEMORANDUM FROM SELZNICK.

DE SICA SAID: "I TORE THEM UP."

AS A JOKE DE SICA RECENTLY WROTE SELZNICK A LONG MEMO DISCUSSING THE FACT THAT ITALIAN CIGARETTES WERE DIFFERENT FROM AMERICAN CIGARETTES AND POINTED OUT HE WOULD BE HOLDING THE CIGARETTE DIFFERENTLY IN A SCENE, AND WANTED SELZNICK TO KNOW ABOUT IT.

MR. SELZNICK IMMEDIATELY SENT BACK A LONG MEMORANDUM THANKING DE SICA FOR POINTING IT OUT AND DISCUSSING AT LENGTH HIS THOUGHTS ON CIGARETTES AND THEIR RELATION TO *A FAREWELL TO ARMS.*

NOT ALL MR. SELZNICK'S MEMORANDUMS ARE SENT BY HAND. SOMETIMES, WHEN HE IS ON LOCATION, THEY ARE SENT BY TELEGRAM.

ONE TELEGRAM WHICH MR. SELZNICK SENT FROM NORTHERN ITALY COST $750. AN ITALIAN PRODUCTION MAN WHO SAW IT BEING SENT SAID TEARFULLY TO A FRIEND: "BEFORE THE WAR WE COULD MAKE A PICTURE FOR WHAT THAT TELEGRAM IS COSTING."

MR. SELZNICK, ACCORDING TO HIS DETRACTORS, HAS A TENDENCY TO KEEP REFERRING TO
GONE WITH THE WIND WHEN TRYING TO MAKE A POINT IN A MEMORANDUM. HE WAS SO INTENT ON
MAKING *A FAREWELL TO ARMS* AS BIG A SUCCESS THAT HE INSISTED THAT ALL OF THE TECHNICAL
STAFF ATTEND A SPECIAL SCREENING OF *GWTW.*

AN OUTSIDER WHO ATTENDED THE COMMAND PERFORMANCE CAME UP AFTER IT WAS OVER AND
SAID: "WHAT IS SELZNICK WORRIED ABOUT? THE RUSHES LOOK GREAT TO ME."

Buchwald also interviewed Selznick, asking if he considered
himself a tough producer.

"Sure I am," David replied. "Who the hell doesn't insist on
having his own way if he is in charge. Why is this a criticism? I
have a different concept of producing than other producers.
Some producers are simply money men, others entrepreneurs,
and others just lieutenants. But to me to produce is to make a
picture."

Why didn't he direct the picture himself?

"There is no mystery to directing. I don't have time. Frankly
it's easier to criticize another man's work than to direct myself.
As a producer, I can maintain an editorial perspective that I
wouldn't have as a director. I consider myself first a creative producer, then a showman, and then a businessman. You need all
three things to succeed in the movie business today."

Buchwald asked David about reports that he protected his
wife in the film.

"Ask Ingrid Bergman and Vivien Leigh that question," David
replied. "I have always protected my stars and I make no difference between her and any other star."

Tempers wore thinner as the filming of *A Farewell to Arms* continued through the hot Italian summer and into autumn. Finally
it appeared that production would conclude with night scenes
at Lake Maggiore. But as the end approached, David was dissatisfied.

He told his new plan to his production manager, Art Fellows:
"This picture has got to be Love, Love, Love, and there isn't
enough in it yet."

"You've lost your perspective," Fellows argued. "You're not
making *A Farewell to Arms;* you're making a love story between

Rock and Jennifer."

"I've made up my mind," David announced. "I'm going to shut down the company until new love scenes can be written. The company can stay here while the rewriting is done, then we'll move everything to Switzerland and finish the picture there."

"That could cost a million dollars!" Fellows protested. "Be reasonable. You're on your budget right now. Finish the picture. You're in trouble; you can't get money for pictures because everybody thinks you spend too much. But if you bring this picture in at a reasonable cost, you'll be able to re-establish yourself in the industry."

David had his mind set on expanding the romance of the story, no matter what the cost.

The following night was meant to be the end of filming. It was a miserable evening on the water, chill and misty, and everyone on the set was tired and edgy. Fellows was trying to line up a shot of a German patrol boat roaming the lake as Rock and Jennifer attempted to row to safety. Fellows wanted to stage the scene at the "magic hour," the period of twilight when the camera could capture a luminous quality. But the patrol boat's searchlight would not cast a beam at that hour, and David argued that the scene should be filmed in darkness. Fellows countered that the film would then record nothing more than the spotlight.

The entire company, including Rock and Jennifer, awaited the decision. As Fellows was telephoning to the camera barge on the lake, David bustled over.

"If you had any sense, you'd call the Army," David snapped. "They could light up the lake with searchlights."

"David," Fellows said disgustedly, handing over the receiver, "why don't you call the Army?"

David slapped Fellows across the face. Fellows instinctively struck back, smashing his fist against David's face and crushing his glasses.

The others in the company watched the exchange of blows with astonishment. David's face was streaming with blood from the cut glass, some of which had entered his eyes. Jennifer screamed and leaped up to attack Fellows. She was restrained, and Fellows was hurried from the set.

David staggered about. "Don't open your eyes, David, don't open your eyes!" someone shouted. Jennifer rushed to David's side and helped him to an ambulance. He was taken to a Milan hospital, where the glass was removed. By that time Fellows was flying back to the United States.

A reporter for the London *Express* broke the story of the slugging, and the publicity added to the reputation of *A Farewell to Arms* as a troubled picture. But when David returned to the United States, he was brimming with confidence.

The troubles on the picture, he said, were magnified by two segments of the Italian press that hated him: the communists, because he wouldn't employ any communist labor; and the fascists, neofascists, and monarchists who thought the Hemingway story denigrated Italy's conduct in World War I. He dismissed the Huston dispute with Ben Hecht's comment: "It was the case of two Caesars and one Alp."

Selznick added: "Actually, I don't think John is the kind of director who can work with a producer. The producers he has had have pretty much given him the rein. I feel the producer must have a real participation in the film. Not many operate that way any more. I think Sam Goldwyn and I are the only ones left."

The lake scenes were completed on a studio tank. David still considered returning to production. He had wanted to include the character of Count Greffi, who appeared briefly in the novel to encourage Frederic Henry in his love for Catherine. He proposed the role to Alfred Lunt, Leopold Stokowski, Bertrand Russell, and Frank Lloyd Wright, then abandoned the idea because the film ran too long.

Twentieth Century-Fox's fortunes were at a low ebb in 1957, and the sales organization was clamoring to add *A Farewell to Arms* to the release schedule. David was reluctant to hurry into release. His publicity chief, Mervin Houser, advised gradual openings in California, followed by selected showings in other regions. But the Fox people were eager for the revenue of a New York release. They showered David with compliments about *A*

David Selznick, Jennifer Jones, and their daughter Mary Jennifer return to the United States on the Queen Elizabeth after the filming of A FAREWELL TO ARMS.

Farewell to Arms and advised opening in New York before the end of the year to qualify for the New York Film Critics Awards. David saw the value of possible awards, as well as attractive Christmas trade, but he was concerned about the unpredictability of the New York critics.

In the end David succumbed to the blandishments of the Fox salesmen; *A Farewell to Arms* was scheduled for New York release in December. Confident of the film's success, David took Jennifer to Jamaica for a holiday. The New York reviews were devastating, terming the picture old-fashioned, overproduced, poorly acted, and ineffective.

"Why? Why?" cried David as he studied the reviews helplessly.

Returning to Culver City, David summoned Mervin Houser to his office. The publicity man found Selznick pacing the floor with his shoes off, as was his custom. He stared at the carpet, the smoke from his cigarette curling around his head.

"The picture hasn't come off; you know that," said David.

"Yes," Houser replied.

"The thing that bothers me is that I don't know why. God knows I gave it everything I could. And yet it didn't come off. Maybe my kind of picture is out of style. Maybe I'm an anachronism. I just can't figure it out."

"What are you going to do now?"

"I think I'll take some time off. I don't owe anyone anything, and the picture will make some money. I can afford to do nothing for a while. I need some time to think."

Everything about *A Farewell to Arms* seemed to have gone wrong, even David's grandiose gesture to the author. Hemingway had long before signed away his movie rights to the book, but Jennifer insisted to David that the novelist should receive some compensation. After finishing the film, David announced to the press that he would voluntarily pay Hemingway $50,000 from the picture's profits.[7] He cabled his decision to Hemingway, who was revisiting Pamplona in Spain.

Hemingway, who disliked David, dictated a reply in which he deprecated the chances of a profit on the remake in which the forty-one-year-old Mrs. Selznick[8] portrayed the twenty-four-year-old Catherine Barkley. If such a miracle did occur, Hemingway added, Selznick could change the $50,000 into nickels at the local bank and shove them up his ass until they came out of his ears.

David Selznick was devastated by the failure of *A Farewell to Arms*. His distress was caused not only by the adverse critical response; he had received bad reviews before. What hurt him most was the feeling that he had failed Jennifer. He had intended *A Farewell to Arms* to be the crowning achievement of her career, but the picture fell far short of that goal. His confidence

---

[7] Selznick had once before made such a gesture. After the immense success of *Gone With the Wind,* he sent Margaret Mitchell $50,000, doubling her return from the movie rights.

[8] Jennifer was actually thirty-eight while filming *A Farewell to Arms.*

shattered, David Selznick never produced another film.

He and Jennifer traveled, always in the most luxurious style. "David claims to be broke," mused a friend, "but David's being broke is not like the ordinary person's being broke." During an extended stay at the St. Regis Hotel in New York, David ordered fresh flowers for Jennifer every day; the monthly florist bill amounted to a thousand dollars.

When in California, the Selznicks lived in the Tower Grove Road home once owned by John Gilbert. The place had been rebuilt, with new rooms added for Jennifer's two sons and young Mary Jennifer. David had schooled Jennifer to live in the Selznick manner. She would wear stockings and gloves only once, then discard them. Hair stylist George Masters came daily to the Selznick mansion both before lunch and before dinner to style Jennifer's hair.

David and Jennifer often traveled to Europe and appeared at film festivals to receive or give awards. He adopted the stance of elder statesman of the film industry and issued pronouncements deploring the trend of events. He responded to Hedda Hopper's invitation to diagnose the ills of Hollywood:

"The men who make movies have been digging their own graves . . . This miserable situation has occurred mainly because of a lack of discipline. Agents couldn't exist with the power they have if discipline had been maintained . . . When this industry gets into trouble now, the lack comes from weakness of the men who run it. They'll put up with anything for a transient advantage. They have no long-term concern because they're busy getting dollars for the next statement, watching the effect that statement will have on the company's stock."

David deprecated the ascending power of agents and actors and cited two "movies of desperation"—*Mutiny on the Bounty* and *One-Eyed Jacks,* both of which soared over-budget, allegedly because of the temperament of Marlon Brando.

"I don't mind spending money," said David Selznick, "but there's no more reason to believe that Marlon Brando is a producer than Karl Malden is. We always had difficulties, but actors used to accept discipline. I've called Jack Barrymore into my office for not knowing his lines; he was contrite and apologetic. I had to speak to Leslie Howard, who was embarrassing Vivien Leigh by not being prepared for a scene. But you never had to speak again. They recognized their fault and corrected it. Garbo was never once late but was considered demanding when she wanted to know who would produce, who would co-star, and who direct. She insisted on a closed set but always knew her dialogue."

When Mrs. Hopper suggested action to curb the excesses of actors, David replied dourly: "The Hollywood situation has got to get worse before it gets better."

David turned his restless energies to other matters. He advised Republican chieftains on strategy. An unsatisfactory flight caused a voluminous memo to the airline president about how to improve treatment of passengers. Poor service in a restaurant brought the owner a Selznick memo on how to please customers.

David Selznick Jennifer Jones, and Rock Hudson at the Hollywood Premiere of A FAREWELL TO ARMS, *December 18, 1957.*

David Selznick and Jennifer Jones attend a film premiere with Mr. and Mrs. Louis Jourdan.

He began toying with the notion of producing again. Warner Brothers made him a two-picture offer, and David seemed interested. He began negotiating for a contract with his customary zeal, but the talks stretched on for weeks as he repeatedly made counterproposals. Finally Warner Brothers agreed to his terms, but the contract remained on his desk.

"I can't bring myself to sign it," he admitted to a close friend.

In a conversation with his former associate, John Houseman, David mused, "If I were to decide what to do in show business, I'd say,'_ _ _ _ pictures!' and I'd go into television. I'm bored with making pictures."

"But why?" asked Houseman.

"Because I've made *Gone With the Wind* and I don't think I

can do any better."

In 1961 M-G-M planned a Civil War centenary re-release of *Gone With the Wind,* including another premiere in Atlanta. Howard Strickling, the studio publicity chief, telephoned David.

"Yes, I know what you want," said Selznick. "It's about the premiere in Atlanta. Well, I'm not going."

Strickling realized that Selznick wanted to be persuaded. The publicity chief appealed to David's pride of family: it would honor the Selznick tradition for him to attend the premiere.

"That damned picture!" David muttered. "When I go they'll put on my tombstone, 'Here lies the man who made *Gone With the Wind.'*"

"That's right, David," said Strickling. "You produced the greatest picture ever made. Is that bad?"

David was persuaded.

Olivia de Havilland accompanied him on the airplane journey from California to Georgia. She had not seen David for some time, and she was disturbed by his lassitude. Although he was only fifty-nine, he seemed old and spent. His curly hair was almost white, his face pale and lined.

At Atlanta they were joined by the other surviving star of *Gone With the Wind,* Vivien Leigh.[9] She was no longer the youthful Scarlett of twenty-two years before. The ravages of ill health showed in her face.

David's lethargy continued during the festivities that surrounded the Atlanta premiere. Then came the evening when *Gone With the Wind* would be shown again. Once more the Loew's Grand Theatre was converted to the facade of a Southern mansion. Atlantans cheered as the Hollywood notables arrived at the theater.

The onstage ceremonies seemed to have little effect on David. After a number of speeches had been delivered, the master of ceremonies, George Murphy, introduced "the producer of *Gone With the Wind,* David O. Selznick."

---

[9] Clark Gable had died of a heart attack in 1960.

David padded onto the stage, slue-footed as always, his shoulders hunched over. Suddenly he found himself enveloped in the mighty noise of a theaterful of people applauding wildly. He stood at center stage, at first bewildered and then deeply affected by the roaring tribute. Olivia de Havilland noticed that for the first time since they had left California, David stood with his head high and his eyes clear. His whole being seemed infused by the electricity of the applauding crowd.

If he could not escape *Gone With the Wind,* David would make it work for him. He decided to invade Broadway with the greatest musical in the history of the theater: *Gone With the Wind.*

First, he had to secure the rights. Ironically, this put him in negotiation with the woman who had hounded him to buy the film rights to *Gone With the Wind,* Kay Brown. Now an agent, she represented the estate of Margaret Mitchell. The deal was made, and David began scouting the musical talent to create the production he envisioned. He started with Richard Rodgers and Oscar Hammerstein II. They rejected the assignment, reasoning that their version would be unfavorably compared to the movie. Harold Rome and other Broadway composers also declined.

David offered the musical to Dimitri Tiomkin, who had scored *Duel in the Sun* and *Portrait of Jennie.* Tiomkin was reluctant because David himself planned to write the libretto.

"Then I'll get Ben Hecht to help me," said David.

"Dot won't help," said Tiomkin. "Ben only does vot you vant him to do."

Next David turned to Leroy Anderson, who agreed to accept the assignment. David began to envision the physical aspects for the musical. He outlined his plans one night to Garson Kanin and Ruth Gordon. The production would be so long that a dinner intermission would be needed. He would stage the burning of Atlanta and other spectacle scenes in a manner never seen before in the theater.

"But there isn't a theater in New York that could hold that kind of a production," Kanin observed.

"Then I'll have to build one," David replied.

Vivien Leigh and David Selznick sign autographs at the Civil War Centennial premiere of GONE WITH THE WIND *in Atlanta.*

David retained the option on the *Gone With the Wind* musical for three years, ever hopeful that he could put together the elements that would make it the biggest success of theater history. But his efforts ended in failure, and he sadly allowed the option to lapse.[10]

Jennifer's career remained uppermost in David's mind, and he was constantly looking for vehicles that would further her glory. Encountering Josh Logan one night at a party, he said, "You're doing *Picnic,* aren't you? You really ought to consider Jennifer to play the girl."

"But we're starting the picture tomorrow," Logan protested.

---

[10] In 1966, a stage spectacle based on *Gone With the Wind* proved an enormous success in Tokyo.

"And Kim Novak is already cast as the girl."

"Oh, there's still time to change," David said.

David had long owned the film rights of F. Scott Fitzgerald's brilliant, flawed *Tender Is the Night,* and he now viewed it as an ideal vehicle for Jennifer. He engaged Ivan Moffat to write the script with him, and David considered it one of the best he had ever created. But he hesitated producing it himself. He did not want to risk another crushing disappointment like *A Farewell to Arms.* Besides, British theater organizations threatened a boycott of his future releases because he had sold his features to television. Loss of the all-important English market would have made financing difficult. So David sold *Tender Is the Night*, together with Jennifer Jones as star, to 20th Century-Fox.

Henry Weinstein was assigned to produce the film. David strove to oversee all phases of the production, especially those which affected Jennifer. When the company was on location in Zurich and on the French Riviera, he talked to her every night on the transatlantic telephone. He also telephoned the director, Henry King, to register his suggestions for filming.

David's advice was not always taken. When he viewed a preview of *Tender Is the Night* in Riverside, he was furious. He accused 20th Century-Fox of violating his contract, which called for approval of casting and script changes. His memo went unheeded.

The critical reaction to *Tender Is the Night* was mixed, many reviewers terming the film as unrealized as the Fitzgerald novel. Some praised Jennifer's portrayal of the neurotic Nicole, some accused her of overacting. The film was not a financial success.

Angered by his experience with *Tender Is the Night,* David decided once more to return to production. He convinced the new management of M-G-M of his intention, and discussions were held with the company president, Joseph Vogel. David made suggestions for projects, but he could get no decisions. After fifteen months of aching frustration, he called off the deal. It was another devastating blow to David.

"In shallow waters the dragon becomes the joke of the shrimp."

Jennifer Jones, Jason Robards in TENDER IS THE NIGHT.

Dore Schary applied the proverb to the last days of David 0. Selznick. The Selznick luck had turned sour, and many in Hollywood were quick to make him an object of ridicule. His memos, his profligacy, his preoccupation with the career of Jennifer Jones—such things provided humor for those who neglected to remember the towering achievements of David Selznick.

Some remembered. David wanted to speak with Elia Kazan about a picture for Jennifer, and the director readily agreed to a meeting.

"Why go?" said one of Kazan's associates. "The guy's a has-been; you wouldn't want to do a picture with him."

"Maybe not," Kazan replied. "But Selznick was one of the giants of films. He deserves to be listened to."

Kazan drove up to the Tower Grove Road mansion for the appointment. He was received by a maid who asked him to wait while she informed Mr. Selznick of his arrival. Kazan could hear the maid announcing him to David, who was in the patio. Kazan also heard David's reply: "Oh, yes, yes. Show him in . . . No, wait a minute. Turn on the fountain first."

Another film maker who was bidden to the Selznick home was Arthur Jacobs, David's onetime publicity man and now a producer. David congratulated Jacobs on his new career.

"I'm proud of you; if you were my own son, I couldn't be more proud," said David warmly. "I have a proposal for you. I own forty screen properties, most of which I'll never make. I want you to look them over, and maybe you'll find something you'd like. We'll make a deal."

Jacobs agreed, and he studied the forty film stories. Each of them was a vehicle for Jennifer.

Paul MacNamara, another in David's succession of publicity men, brought a quartet of well-heeled Texans to the Selznick house to discuss financing a picture about Winston Churchill. David was in good form, and throughout the afternoon he kept the Texans enthralled with his visions of how monumental the Churchill film could be. But the project collapsed because no major company was willing to risk a Selznick epic.

In the summer of 1964, David and Jennifer went to Cap d'Antibes with their close friends, the Louis Jourdans. David seemed weary and energyless. He was still going through the motions of preparing films, and he invited James Baldwin to visit him and discuss writing a picture based on *Blues for Mr. Charlie.* Nothing came of the project.

The organizational skill he employed for creating pictures was now applied to little things. He planned a party for the tenth birthday of Mary Jennifer, attending to the smallest details. He even organized the games, and while jumping onto a boat he fell and broke his ankle. For two weeks he lay abed, occupying himself with Chinese checkers and other games he played with visitors.

Later that summer, the Selznicks and the Jourdans cruised on the yacht of Irwin Shaw. One night after the others had retired, David and Louis lingered on deck, enjoying the star-filled Riviera night and their own conversation. They decided to spend the night on deck. For hours they talked quietly, and David was unusually reflective. "I'm ready to go," he said. "Everything is settled. My only thought now is for my wife, my daughter, and my sons; they're all I care about. I want them to enjoy the best after I have gone."

David had taken out a million-dollar insurance policy on his life, with Jennifer as the beneficiary. When he returned to California, he decided that the premiums were more than he could handle, since his income now was limited. He had to undergo a physical examination before he could reduce the amount of the policy. It was then that he discovered he had a serious heart condition.

He told no one—except Irene.

The relationship between David and his former wife had become one of deep understanding. Irene had not remarried; she lived in New York and had produced *A Streetcar Named Desire, Bell, Book and Candle,* and other plays. Her devotion to David continued, and she often consulted him about their sons Jeffrey and Daniel and her own business matters. When Louis B. Mayer died in 1957, Irene sought David's counsel on the funeral. Irene helped console David when his mother died in 1959.

Irene was present when David had his first heart attack. Both were attending a gay dinner party at the New York apartment of the Arthur Hornblows. David had come alone, since Jennifer was in Florida with a play. He appeared to be in good form, and he engaged in a lively argument with Mrs. Bennett Cerf. Later Leland Hayward entered one of the bedrooms to find David stretched out on a bed. Hayward called for Irene, who immediately sent for a doctor. David was advised not to move, but he insisted on returning to his apartment in the Waldorf Towers. As he entered the hotel, he suffered a second heart attack. He was taken to a hospital and confined for ten days.

Some of David's vigor seemed to return when he went back to California, and he resumed management of his business affairs. In March of 1965, the Producers Guild was planning a testimonial dinner for Alfred Hitchcock, and David Selznick was invited to be among the speakers.

The great names of Hollywood came to the Beverly Hilton Hotel for the dinner. Seated with David on the dais were Samuel Goldwyn, Jack L. Warner, Jules Stein, Maureen O'Hara, Elke Sommer, James Stewart, Cary Grant, and others. The speeches were warm and humorous. David himself laughed when Hitchcock remarked, "When I first arrived in this country, David Selznick sent me one of his famous memos. I wanted to make it into a film titled, *The Longest Story Ever Told.*"

There was an air of expectancy as David was introduced by the master of ceremonies, Dick Van Dyke. David had long been absent from the Hollywood scene, and many were curious to hear him speak. Some of the dinner guests had known and worked with David during his period of greatness in Hollywood. But to many of the more recent members of the industry, David O. Selznick was a distant and faintly humorous figure.

David began talking. He lashed out at the industry powers for allowing the drain of Hollywood's talent and resources while building up production abroad. His message struck a responsive note with many members of his audience who were concerned about "runaway production."

Then he began to ramble. He made the same points over and over again, the words pouring out with the profusion of one of his lengthy memos. His audience began to fidget, and conversations started at some of the tables. Still David continued talking, pleading with those who controlled the film business to return Hollywood to its onetime greatness. He spoke with force and emotion, out of love for the business he had first learned from his father. But he spoke too long.

David slumped in his chair amid scattered applause. "He spoke like a man who was dying," said Garson Kanin.

David Selznick's champion in his declining years was his one-time competitor, Samuel Goldwyn. Like David, Goldwyn had long cherished his independence as a motion picture producer. Goldwyn felt it was a loss to the industry for a man of David's creativeness to remain unproductive.

Goldwyn repeatedly pressed his friends among the major companies to provide film deals for David. Often Goldwyn's persuasion was effective, and the companies made overtures to David, only to be discouraged by his excessive demands. He would settle for nothing less than complete autonomy; he would not allow the new masters of the industry to pass judgment on his decisions.

David was chided by Goldwyn for being unreasonable.

"Sam, I'll tell you the truth," David said wearily. "The only one I've told it to is Irene. I have a heart ailment, and I could go at any time. So you can see that I'm not going to make any more pictures."

David could no longer keep his secret from Jennifer. Now she devoted herself to keeping his life as free from stress as possible. She realized that David needed to see his friends, and they sometimes entertained with small dinner parties. But as soon as she detected a sign of attack, she maneuvered the guests out of the house. None was aware that David was ailing.

He spent more and more time at the Tower Grove house, taking leisurely swims in the ninety-degree pool and dictating the usual stream of memos. The delight of his life was Mary Jennifer, now a lively eleven-year-old. One afternoon Jennifer came home to find Mary Jennifer in ballet costume with train and David in white tie and tails. They were performing to the record album of *The Sound of Music.* "She didn't like my costume, so I changed," David explained.

In May of 1965, Russell Birdwell began running a series of advertisements in the *Hollywood Reporter,* reminiscing about the great old times at the Selznick studio, when he and Carole Lombard raised hell with the boss, when he hired the former G-man to guard the ideas in the Selznick vault, when the nation was engrossed in the search for Scarlett O'Hara. The ads puzzled the film community, which suspected that they presaged a renewal of activity by David 0. Selznick. Actually they were inspired solely by Birdwell's spontaneous notion that his old boss should return to film production.

The series of ads ended on June 22 with ten columns of type in which Birdwell cited the achievements of Selznick. Birdwell ended with the message: "Come home, DOS, the industry needs you."

Then he reported one recent memo from his old boss. David wrote that he would have responded before, but he didn't realize the series of columns was going to last so long—"and I am now fearful that it's going to stretch into 'Ozzie and Harriet.'" David added that he hoped Birdwell would make it clear that he, not Selznick, was paying for and sponsoring the ads.

On the morning that the last Birdwell ad appeared, David Selznick decided to visit the office of his attorney, Barry Brannan. Jennifer tried to dissuade him, but David insisted that he had important papers to sign.

As David was discussing business matters with his attorney, he said, "Mind if I sit down?"

Brannan noticed David seemed ill and said, "No, of course not. We can finish this later."

"I'd rather finish it now," David replied. He sat down on the couch. Then, as the pain increased, he lay down. Brannan noticed his paleness and telephoned for an ambulance. He notified Jennifer.

The ambulance rushed David to Mount Sinai Hospital three miles away, and he was taken immediately to the intensive care unit. Jennifer arrived at the hospital shortly afterward, but she was not permitted inside the room where doctors strove to save her husband's life. She watched sobbingly through a window as his life flickered out. He had arrived in the hospital at 1 P.M. At 2:22, he was pronounced dead. The cause of death was a coronary occlusion. He was sixty-three years old.

Word of his passing swept through the studios. The news brought shock, because few had been aware that he had been ailing. It was the same shock that came from the deaths of other vital, long-famous figures—and David Selznick had been a leader in Hollywood for thirty-five years. At once the failure of his later years was dismissed, and the greatness of his legacy was remembered: *David Copperfield, Dinner at Eight, Anna Karenina, A Tale of Two Cities, A Star Is Born, Nothing Sacred, Rebecca, Gone With the Wind* ...

The mourners converged. Jock Whitney and William Paley flew in from New York. Katharine Hepburn, Louis Jourdan, Sam and Frances Goldwyn, Lauren Bacall, Joseph Cotten, and other close friends came to the Tower Grove Road house to give their sympathy to Jennifer. Plans were formulated to make the funeral a fitting tribute to a man of David Selznick's stature—despite his oft-expressed wish for a simple ceremony. The third generation of the Selznick dynasty, Jeffrey and Daniel Selznick, took charge and made their wishes felt. Overcome by grief, their mother, Irene Mayer Selznick, remained in New York.

The funeral was held on a misty, mournful day in the Church of the Recessional at Forest Lawn Memorial Park. Joseph Cotten spoke the main eulogy, remarking, "Greatness in a man makes him larger than life. This was not true of David Selznick. He was very much a part of life."

William Paley had written his feelings about David, but he was too upset to deliver the speech. It was spoken by Cary Grant, who said in part, "I cannot help but think that our world will never be the same—nor will heaven. And if we are lucky enough to get there too, David will see that all the arrangements are made."

Katharine Hepburn recited Kipling's *If,* a selection which had been requested by Jennifer. George Cukor added words written by Truman Capote, among them: "We have lost an irreplaceable individualist who was as tender as he was tenacious, as courageous as competitive, as inventive as ingenious, as sensitive as stalwart."

Many times in his late years, David had remarked out of pride and weary resignation that his epitaph should read, "Hear lies David 0. Selznick, who produced *Gone With the Wind.*" But his burial place was marked only by his proud signature and the dates of his life: 1902-1965.

The tributes poured in. The newly elected Senator George Murphy said from Washington that David Selznick was one of the first persons who urged him to go from the New York stage to Hollywood and added, "I will miss David very much." Olivia de Havilland appeared on the NBC *Today* telecast and called David "an extraordinary man of astonishing achievement; his death was a frightful loss to all the industry." Bosley Crowther in the New York *Times* observed that Selznick's contribution to American films "was his taking on and giving meaning and importance to the role of creative producer, which is peculiar to Hollywood."

Jock Whitney's New York *Herald Tribune* editorialized: "David 0. Selznick was one of that small band of film giants of whom it can truly be said that Hollywood—at its best—is their monument. A fierce attention to detail; a passionate devotion to his tasks; an unshakeable faith that better pictures were worth making, and worth whatever effort was needed to make them better; all these contributed to the Selznick legend and to the Selznick legacy."

Time termed him the Producer Prince and recalled Lewis J. Selznick's advice to his sons concerning money: "Throw it around! Give it away! Always remember to live beyond your means."

On another film location in Italy ten years after the blowup over

A Farewell to Arms, John Huston shared some mellow reflections of David: "There was a kind of innocence that he had. Like all boys, he loved to play games, and there was a quality of game-playing in everything he did. He loved to dress up and to entertain, to play the host. He was kind of high and handsome; he couldn't do enough for his guests.

"He had a childish, young approach to picture making as well. Even the memos were a sign of his playfulness. He was playing at the game of being the producer."

David Selznick had no illusions about permanence in Hollywood. In 1959, when Tara was dismantled for shipment to Atlanta, he commented: "Once photographed, life here is ended. It is almost symbolic of Hollywood. Tara had no rooms inside. It was just a facade."

But, although he sometimes begrudged its dominance over his professional life, David Selznick at the age of thirty-seven had, with *Gone With the Wind,* created for himself a kind of permanence in the transitory world of film. Every seven years as fresh audiences experience the sorrows and elations of Scarlett and Rhett and Melanie and Ashley, the achievement of the Producer Prince will be remembered.

APPENDIX A

Credits of Major Films Produced by David O. Selznick

Selznick's earlier films included *Will He Conquer Dempsey?*, 1923 (a brief film of Luis Firpo in training), and *Rudolph Valentino and his 88 American Beauties*, 1923 (a beauty contest short). The following are feature films produced by David O. Selznick.

Tim McCoy (center) SPOILERS OF THE WEST.

WYOMING

ROULETTE
Selznick-1924

PRODUCER David O. Selznick
DIRECTOR S. E. V. Taylor
AUTHOR William McHarg
SCREENPLAY Lewis Allen
CAST: Montagu Love, Norman Trevor, Maurice Costello, Edith Roberts,
Mary Carr, Effie Shannon, Walter Booth, Flora Finch, Dagmar Godowsky,
Henry Hull

SPOILERS OF THE WEST
M-G-M-1927

EXECUTIVE PRODUCER David O. Selznick
DIRECTOR W. S. Van Dyke
AUTHOR John Thomas Neville
SCREENPLAY Madeleine Ruthven, Ross B. Willis
CAST: Tim McCoy, Marjorie Daw, William Fairbanks

WYOMING
M-G-M-1928

EXECUTIVE PRODUCER David O. Selznick
DIRECTOR W. S. Van Dyke
AUTHOR W. S. Van Dyke
SCREENPLAY Madeleine Ruthven, Ross B. Wilson
CAST: Tim McCoy, Dorothy Sebastian, William Fairbanks, Bert Henderson,
Blue Washington, Charles Bell

FORGOTTEN FACES
Paramount-1928

EXECUTIVE PRODUCER David 0. Selznick
DIRECTOR Victor Schertzinger
AUTHOR Richard Washburn Child
SCREENPLAY Oliver H. P. Garrett
CAST: William Powell, Clive Brook, Baclanova, Jack Luden, Fred Kohler

FOUR FEATHERS
Paramount-1929

EXECUTIVE PRODUCER David 0. Selznick
DIRECTORS Merian C. Cooper, E. B. Schoedsack, Lothar Mendes
AUTHOR A. E. W. Mason SCREENPLAY Howard Estabrook, Hope Loring
CAMERAMEN Merian C. Cooper, E. B. Schoedsack, Robert Kurrle
CAST: Richard Arlen, Fay Wray, William Powell, Clive Brook, Theodore von
Eltz, Noah Beery, Zack Williams, Noble Johnson, Harold Hightower,
Philippe de Lacey, Edward J. Ratcliffe, George Fawcett, Augustine Symonds

STREET OF CHANCE
Paramount-1930
EXECUTIVE PRODUCER David 0. Selznick
DIRECTOR John Cromwell
AUTHOR Oliver H. P. Garrett
SCREENPLAY Howard Estabrook
CAMERAMAN Charles Lang
CAST: William Powell, Jean Arthur, Regis Toomey, Kay Francis, Stanley
Fields, Brooks Benedict, Betty Francisco, John Risso, Joan Standing,
Maurice Black, Irving Bacon

STREET OF CHANCE, *Kay Francis, William Powell, Regis Toomey*

HONEY
Paramount-1930

EXECUTIVE PRODUCER David 0. Selznick
DIRECTOR Wesley Ruggles
AUTHOR Alice Duer Miller, A. E. Thomas (from "Come Out of the Kitchen")
SCENARIST Herman J. Mankiewicz
CAMERAMAN Henry Gerrard
CAST: Nancy Carroll, Stanley Smith, Skeets Gallagher, Lillian Roth, Harry Green, ZaSu Pitts, Mitzie Green, Jobyna Howland, Charles Sellon

SARAH AND SON
Paramount-1930

EXECUTIVE PRODUCER David 0. Selznick
DIRECTOR Dorothy Arzner
AUTHOR Timothy Shea
SCENARIST Zoe Akins
CAMERAMAN Charles Lang
CAST: Ruth Chatterton, Fredric March, Doris Lloyd, Philippe de Lacey, Fuller Mellish, Jr., Gilbert Emery

MANSLAUGHTER
Paramount-1930

EXECUTIVE PRODUCER David 0. Selznick
DIRECTOR George Abbott
AUTHOR Alice Duer Miller
SCENARIST George Abbott
CAMERAMAN A. J. Stout
CAST: Claudette Colbert, Fredric March, Emma Dunn, Natalie Moorehead, Richard Tucker, Hilda Vaughn, Ivan Simpson, Stanley Fields, Irving Mitchell, G. Pat Collins, Gaylord Pendleton

Four Feathers, *Fay Wray, Richard Arlen*

Sarah and Son, *Ruth Chatterton*

THE TEXAN
Paramount-1930

EXECUTIVE PRODUCER David 0. Selznick
DIRECTOR John Cromwell
AUTHOR 0. Henry (from "A Double-Dyed Deceiver")
SCENARIST Oliver H. P. Garrett, Daniel Rubin
CAMERAMAN Victor Milner
CAST: Gary Cooper, Fay Wray, Emma Dunn, Oscar Apfel, James Marcus, Donald Reed, Edward J. Brady

ROAR OF THE DRAGON
RKO-1932

EXECUTIVE PRODUCER David 0. Selznick
DIRECTOR Wesley Ruggles
AUTHORS George Kibbe Turner, Merian C. Cooper, Jane Bigelow (from Passage to Hong Kong)
SCREENPLAY Howard Estabrook
CAMERAMAN Edward Cronjager
CAST: Richard Dix, Gwili Andre, Edward Everett Horton, Arline Judge, ZaSu Pitts, Dudley Digges, C. Henry Gordon, Arthur Stone. William Orlamond

WHAT PRICE HOLLYWOOD?
RKO-1937

EXECUTIVE PRODUCER David 0. Selznick
DIRECTOR George Cukor
AUTHOR Adela Rogers St. Johns Hyland
SCREENPLAY Gene Fowler, Rowland Brown
CAMERAMAN Charles Rosher
CAST: Constance Bennett, Lowell Sherman, Neil Hamilton, Gregory Ratoff, Brooks Benedict, Louise Beavers, Eddie Anderson

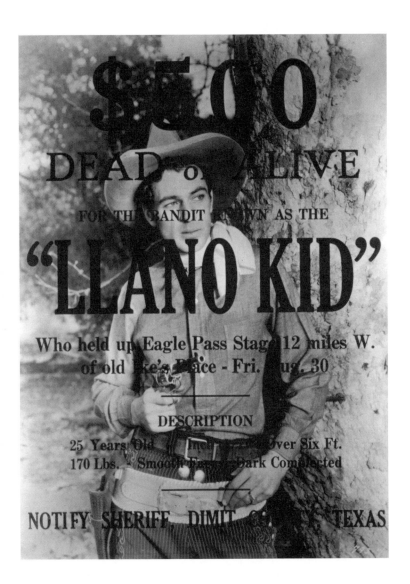

Gary Cooper as the Llano Kid in THE TEXAN.

ROADHOUSE MURDER
RKO-1932

PRODUCER David O. Selznick
DIRECTOR J. Walter Ruben
AUTHOR Laszo Bus Fekeete (from "Lame Dog Inn")
SCREENPLAY J. Walter Ruben
CAMERAMAN J. Roy Hunt
CAST: Eric Linden, Dorothy Jordan, Bruce Cabot, Phyllis Clare, Roscoe Ates, Purnell Pratt, Gustav von Seyffertitz, David Landau, Roscoe Karns

STATE'S ATTORNEY
RKO-1932

PRODUCER David O. Selznick
DIRECTOR George Archainbaud
AUTHOR Louis Stevens
SCENARISTS Gene Fowler, Rowland Brown
CAMERAMAN Leo Tover
CAST: John Barrymore, Helen Twelvetrees, Jill Esmond, William Boyd, Mary Duncan, Oscar Apfel, Raul Roulien, Ralph Ince, Frederick Burton, Ethel Sutherland, Leon Waycoff, C. Henry Gordon

WESTWARD PASSAGE
RKO-1932

PRODUCER David O. Selznick
DIRECTOR Robert Milton
AUTHOR Margaret Ayer Barnes
SCREENPLAY Bradley King
CAMERAMAN Lucien Andriot
CAST: Ann Harding, Laurence Olivier, Irving Pichel, Juliette Compton, ZaSu Pitts, Irene Purcell, Florence Roberts, Emmett King, Ethel Griffies, Bonita Granville

LOST SQUADRON
RKO-1932

EXECUTIVE PRODUCER David 0. Selznick
DIRECTOR George Archainbaud
AUTHOR Dick Grace
SCREENPLAY Wallace Smith
CAMERAMEN Leo Tover, Edward Cronjager
CAST: Richard Dix, Mary Astor, Erich von Stroheim, Joel McCrea, Dorothy
Jordan, Hugh Herbert, Robert Armstrong, Ralph Ince, Arnold Grey, Dick
Grace, Art Goebel, Frank Clark, Leo Nomis

YOUNG BRIDE
RKO-1932

PRODUCER David 0. Selznick
DIRECTOR William Seiter
AUTHOR Hugh Stanislaus Stange (from "Veneer")
CAMERAMAN Arthur Miller
CAST: Helen Twelvetrees, Eric Linden, Arline Judge, Rosco Ates, Polly
Walters, Cliff Edwards, Blanche Friderici, Allen Fox

SYMPHONY OF SIX MILLION
RKO-1932

EXECUTIVE PRODUCER David 0. Selznick
DIRECTOR Gregory La Cava
AUTHOR Fannie Hurst
SCREENPLAY Bernard Schubert, J. WalterRuben
CAMERAMAN Leo Tover
CAST: Ricardo Cortez, Irene Dunne, Anna Appell, Gregory Ratoff, Lita
Chevret, Noel Madison, Helen Freeman, John St. Polis

LITTLE ORPHAN ANNIE
RKO-1932

EXECUTIVE PRODUCER David 0. Selznick
DIRECTOR John Robertson
AUTHORS Harold Grey, Al Lowenthal
SCENARISTS Wanda Tuchock, Tom McNamara
CAMERAMAN Jack MacKenzie
CAST: Mitzi Green, Buster Phelps, May Robson, Kate Lawson, Matt Moore,
Sidney Bracey, Edgar Kennedy

AGE OF CONSENT
RKO-1932

EXECUTIVE PRODUCER David 0. Selznick
DIRECTOR Gregory La Cava
AUTHOR Martin Flavin (from "Crossroads")
SCREENPLAY Sarah Y. Mason, Francis Cockrell
CAMERAMAN Roy Hunt
CAST: Dorothy Wilson, Richard Cromwell, Eric Linden, Arline Judge, John
Halliday, Aileen Pringle, Reginald Barlow

HOLD 'EM JAIL
RKO-1932

EXECUTIVE PRODUCER David 0. Selznick
DIRECTOR Norman Taurog
AUTHORS Tim Whelan, Lew Lipton
SCREENPLAY S. J. Perelman, Walter De Leon, Mark Sandrich, Albert Ray
CAMERAMAN Len Smith
CAST: Bert Wheeler, Robert Woolsey, Edna May Oliver, Roscoe Ates, Edgar
Kennedy, Betty Grable, Paul Hurst, Warren Hymer, Robert Armstrong

HONEY, *Stanley Smith, Nancy Carroll*

WHAT PRICE HOLLYWOOD, *Lowell Sherman and Constance Bennett*

A BILL OF DIVORCEMENT, *Katharine Hepburn, Billie Burke, and John Barrymore.*

A BILL OF DIVORCEMENT
RKO-1932

EXECUTIVE PRODUCER David 0. Selznick
DIRECTOR George Cukor
AUTHOR Clemence Dane
SCREENPLAY Howard Estabrook, Harry Wagstaff Gribble
CAMERAMAN Sid Hickox
CAST: John Barrymore, Katharine Hepburn, Billie Burke, David Manners, Bramwell Fletcher, Henry Stephenson, Paul Cavanagh, Elizabeth Patterson, Gayle Evers

BIRD OF PARADISE, *Dolores Del Rio*

BIRD OF PARADISE
RKO-1932

EXECUTIVE PRODUCER David 0. Selznick
DIRECTOR King Vidor
AUTHOR Richard Walton Tully
SCREENPLAY Wells Root
CAMERAMAN Clyde De Vinna
CAST: Dolores Del Rio, Joel McCrea, John Halliday, Creighton Chaney (Lon Chaney, Jr.), Richard "Skeets" Gallagher, Bert Roach, Sophie Ortego, Agostino Borgato

THE PHANTOM OF CRESTWOOD
RKO-1932

EXECUTIVE PRODUCER David 0. Selznick
DIRECTOR J. Walter Ruben
AUTHOR Bartlett Cormack, J. Walter Ruben
SCREENPLAY Bartlett Cormack
CAMERAMAN Henry Gerrard
CAST: Ricardo Cortez, Karen Morley, Anita Louise, Pauline Frederick, H. B. Warner, Sam Hardy, Mary Duncan, Skeets Gallagher, Robert McWade, Gavin Gordon, Robert Elliott, Ivan Simpson, Hilda Vaughn, George E. Stone, Matty Kemp, Tom Douglas, Clarence F. Wilson, Eddie Sturgis

HELL'S HIGHWAY
RKO-1932

EXECUTIVE PRODUCER David 0. Selznick
DIRECTOR Rowland Brown
AUTHORS Rowland Brown, Samuel Ornitz, Robert Tasker
SCENARISTS Rowland Brown, Samuel Ornitz, Robert Tasker
CAMERAMAN Edward Cronjager
CAST: Richard Dix, Tom Brown, Rochelle Hudson, Louise Carter, C. Henry Gordon, Oscar Apfel, Warner Richmond, Sandy Roth, Charles Middleton, Clarence Muse, Stanley Fields, Jed Kiley, Fuzzy Knight, Bert Starkey, Bob Perry, Harry Smith, Edward Hart, John Lester Johnson

THE CONQUERORS
RKO-1932

EXECUTIVE PRODUCER David 0. Selznick
DIRECTOR: William A. Wellman
AUTHOR Howard Estabrook
SCREENPLAY Robert Lord
CAMERAMAN Edward Cronjager
CAST: Richard Dix, Ann Harding, Edna May Oliver, Guy Kibbee, Julie
Haydon, Donald Cooi, Harry Holman, Skeets Gallagher, Walter Walker, Wally
Albright, Marilyn Knowlden, Jed Prouty, Robert Grie

RENEGADES OF THE WEST
RKO-1932

EXECUTIVE PRODUCER David 0. Selznick
DIRECTOR Casey Robinson
AUTHOR Frank Richardson Pierce
SCREENPLAY Albert Shelby La Vino
CAMERAMAN Al Seiger
CAST: Tom Keene, Betty Furness, Rosco Ates, Rockliffe Fellowes, Carl
Miller, Jack Pennick, Max Wagner, James Mason, Joseph Girard, Josephine
Ramous, Roland Southern, Bill Franey

THIRTEEN WOMEN
RKO-1932

EXECUTIVE PRODUCER David 0. Selznick
DIRECTOR George Archainbaud
AUTHOR Tiffany Thayer
SCENARIST Bartlett Cormack
CAMERAMAN Leo Tover
CAST: Ricardo Cortez, Irene Dunne, Myrna Loy, Jill Esmond,
Florence Eldredge, Kay Johnson, Julie Haydon, Harriet Hegman,
Mary Duncan, Peg Entwistle, Elsie Prescott, Wally Albright, C.Henry
Gordon, Ed Pawley, Blanche Friderici, Kenneth Thomson, Leon Waycoff,
Edward Le Saint, Clarence Geldert, Violet Seaton

MEN OF AMERICA
RKO-1932

PRODUCER David 0. Selznick
DIRECTOR Ralph Ince
AUTHORS Humphrey Pearson, Henry McCarty
SCREENPLAY Samuel Ornitz, Jack Jungmeyer
CAMERAMAN J. Roy Hunt
CAST: Bill Boyd, Charles (Chic) Sale, Dorothy Wilson, Ralph Ince,
Henry Armetta, Inez Palange, Theresa Maxwell Conover, Alphonse
Ethier

THE HALF-NAKED TRUTH
RKO-1932

PRODUCER David 0. Selznick
DIRECTOR Gregory La Cava
AUTHORS Ben Markson, H. N. Swanson (from "Phantom Fame" by Harry
Reichenbach)
SCREENPLAY Bartlett Cormack, Corey Ford
CAMERAMAN Bert Glennon
CAST: Lupe Velez, Lee Tracy, Eugene Pallette, Frank Morgan, Bob McKenzie,
James Donlon, Shirley Chambers, Charles Dow Clark

THE ANIMAL KINGDOM
RKO-1937

EXECUTIVE PRODUCER David 0. Selznick
DIRECTOR Edward H. Griffith
AUTHOR Philip Barry
SCREENPLAY Horace Jackson
CAMERAMAN Lucien Andriot
CAST: Ann Harding, Leslie Howard, Myrna Loy, Neil Hamilton, Wilham
Gargan, Henry Stephenson, Ilka Chase, Leni Stengel, Donald Dillaway

THE ANIMAL KINGDOM, *Ann Harding and Leslie Howard*

TOPAZE, *John Barrymore and Myrna Loy*

TOPAZE
RKO-1933

EXECUTIVE PRODUCER David O. Selznick
DIRECTOR Harry D'Arrast
AUTHOR Marcel Pagnol
SCREENPLAY Ben Hecht
CAMERAMAN Lucien Andriot
CAST: John Barrymore, Myrna Loy, Albert Conti, Luis Alberni, Reginald
Mason, Jobyna Howland, Jackie Searle, Frank Reicher

NO OTHER WOMAN
RKO-1933

EXECUTIVE PRODUCER David O. Selznick
DIRECTOR J. Walter Ruben
AUTHORS Eugene Walter, Owen Francis
SCREENPLAY J. Walter Ruben
CAMERAMAN Edward Cronjager
CAST: Irene Dunne, Charles Bickford, Gwili Andre, Eric Linden, Buster
Miles, Leila Bennett, Christian Rub, J. Carroll Naish, Hilda Vaughn, Brooks
Benedict, Joseph E. Bernard, Frederick Burton, Theodore von Eltz,
Edwin Stanley

THE MONKEY'S PAW
RKO-1933

PRODUCER David O. Selznick
DIRECTOR Wesley Ruggles
AUTHOR W. W. Jacobs
SCREENPLAY Graham John, Louise M. Parker
CAMERAMAN Leo Tover
CAST: C. Aubrey Smith, Ivan Simpson, Louise Carter, Bramwell Fletcher,
Betty Lawford, Herbert Bunston, Winter Hall

King Kong, *Fay Wray*

KING KONG
RKO-1933

EXECUTIVE PRODUCER David O. Selznick
PRODUCERS AND DIRECTORS Merian C. Cooper, Ernest B. Schoedsack
AUTHORS Edgar Wallace, Merian C. Cooper
SCREENPLAY James Creelman, Ruth Rose
CAMERAMAN Edward Linden
CAST: Fay Wray, Robert Armstrong, Bruce Cabot, Frank Reicher, Sam Hardy,
Noble Johnson, Steve Clemento, James Flavin, Victor Wong

DINNER AT EIGHT, *Grant Mitchell, waiter, Louise Closser Hale, Jean Harlow, Wallace Beery, Edmund Lowe, Karen Morley, and Billie Burke*

DINNER AT EIGHT
M-G-M-1933

PRODUCER David O. Selznick
DIRECTOR George Cukor
AUTHORS George S. Kaufman, Edna Ferber
SCREENPLAY Frances Marion, Herman J. Mankiewicz
CAMERAMAN William Daniels
CAST: Marie Dressler, John Barrymore, Wallace Beery, Jean Harlow, Lionel Barrymore, Lee Tracy, Edmund Lowe, Billie Burke, Madge Evans, Jean Hersholt, Karen Morley, Louise Closser Hale, Phillips Holmes, May Robson, Grant Mitchell

NIGHT FLIGHT, *John Barrymore and Lionel Barrymore*

NIGHT FLIGHT
M-G-M-1933

EXECUTIVE PRODUCER David O. Selznick
DIRECTOR Clarence Brown
AUTHOR Antoine de St. Exupéry
SCREENPLAY   Oliver H. P. Garrett
CAMERAMAN Oliver T. Marsh
AERIAL PHOTOGRAPHY Elmer Dwyer, Charles Marshall
CAST: John Barrymore, Helen Hayes, Clark Gable, Lionel Barrymore,
Robert Montgomery, Myrna Loy, William Gargan, C. Henry Gordon, Leslie
Fenton, Harry Beresford, Frank Conroy, Ralf Harolde

MEET THE BARON
M-G-M-1933

EXECUTIVE PRODUCER David 0. Selznick
DIRECTOR Walter Lang
AUTHORS Herman J. Mankiewicz, Norman Krasna
SCREENPLAY Allen Rivkin, P. J. Wolfson
CAMERAMAN Allen Siegler
CAST: Jack Pearl, Jimmy Durante, ZaSu Pitts, Ted Healy, Edna May Oliver,
Ben Bard, Henry Kolker, William B. Davidson, Moe Howard, Larry Fine

DANCING LADY
M-G-M-1933

PRODUCER David 0. Selznick
DIRECTOR Robert Z. Leonard
AUTHOR James Warner Bellah
SCREENPLAY Allen Rivkin, P. J. Wolfson
CAMERAMAN Oliver T. Marsh
SONGS Burton Lane, Harold Adamson, Richard Rodgers, Lorenz Hart,
Jimmy McHugh, Dorothy Fields
CAST: Joan Crawford, Clark Gable, Franchot Tone, May Robson, Winnie
Lightner, Fred Astaire, Robert Benchley, Ted Healy, Gloria Foy, Art Jarrett,
Grant Mitchell, Maynard Holmes, Nelson Eddy, Sterling Holloway, Moe
Howard, Jerry Howard, Larry Fine (the 3 Stooges), and (unbilled) Eve
Arden, Lynn Bari

DANCING LADY, *Joan Crawford and Fred Astaire*

SWEEPINGS
RKO-1933

EXECUTIVE PRODUCER David O. Selznick
DIRECTOR John Cromwell
AUTHOR Lester Cohen
SCREENPLAY Lester Cohen, Howard Estabrook, H.W. Hanneman
CAMERAMAN Edward Cronjager
CAST: Lionel Barrymore, Alan Dinehart, Eric Linden, William Gargan,
Gloria Stuart, Gregory Ratoff, Lucien Littlefield, Helen Mack, George
Meeker

OUR BETTERS
RKO-1933

EXECUTIVE PRODUCER David O. Selznick
DIRECTOR George Cukor
AUTHOR W. Somerset Maugham
SCREENPLAY Harry Wagstaff Gribble, Jane Murfin
CAMERAMAN Charles Rosher
CAST: Constance Bennett, Gilbert Roland, Charles Starrett, Anita
Louise, Phoebe Foster, Grant Mitchell, Hugh Sinclair, Alan Mowbray,
Minor Watson, Violet Kemble Cooper, Tyrrell Davis, Virginia Howell, Walter
Walker, Harold Entwhistle

VIVA VILLA
M-G-M-1934

PRODUCER David O. Selznick
DIRECTORS Jack Conway, Howard Hawks
AUTHORS Edgcumb Pinchon, O. B. Stade
SCREENPLAY Ben Hecht, Charles MacArthur
CAMERAMEN James Wong Howe, Charles G. Clarke
CAST: Wallace Beery, Leo Carrillo, Fay Wray, Stuart Erwin, Donald Cook,
Henry B. Walthall, Joseph Schildkraut, Katherine De Mille, George E. Stone,
Philip Cooper, Frank Puglia, Francis X. Bushman, Jr.

VIVA VILLA, *Stuart Erwin and Wallace Beery*

MANHATTAN MELODRAMA, *Myrna Loy and William Powell*

MANHATTAN MELODRAMA
M-G-M-1934

PRODUCER David 0. Selznick
DIRECTOR W. S. Van Dyke
AUTHOR Arthur Caesar
SCREENPLAY Oliver H. P. Garrett, Joseph L. Mankiewicz
SONG Richard Rodgers, Lorenz Hart
CAMERAMAN James Wong Howe
CAST: Clark Gable, William Powell, Myrna Loy, Leo Carrillo, Nat Pendleton, Isabel Jewell, Muriel Evans, Thomas Jackson, Claudelle Kaye, Frank Conroy, Noel Madison, Jimmy Butler, Mickey Rooney

DAVID COPPERFIELD, *W.C. Fields and Frank Lawton (center)*

DAVID COPPERFIELD
M-G-M-1935

PRODUCER David O. Selznick
DIRECTOR George Cukor
AUTHOR Charles Dickens
SCREENPLAY Howard Estabrook
ADAPTATION Hugh Walpole
CAMERAMAN Oliver T. Marsh
CAST: W. C. Fields, Lionel Barrymore, Maureen O'Sullivan, Madge Evans, Edna May Oliver, Lewis Stone, Freddie Bartholomew, Frank Lawton, Elizabeth Allan, Roland Young, Basil Rathbone, Elsa Lanchester, Jean Cadell, Jessie Ralph, Lennox Pawle, Violet Kemble Cooper, Una O'Connor, John Buckler, Hugh Williams, Ivan Simpson, Herbert Mundin, Fay Chaldecott, Florine McKinney

Vanessa, Her Love Story, *Robert Montgomery, Helen Hayes, Otto Krager*

VANESSA, HER LOVE STORY
M-G-M-1935

PRODUCER David 0. Selznick
DIRECTOR. William K. Howard
AUTHOR Hugh Walpole
SCREENPLAY Lenore Coffee, Hugh Walpole
CAMERAMAN Ray June
CAST: Helen Hayes, Robert Montgomery, Otto Kruger, May Robson, Lewis
Stone, Henry Stephenson, Violet Kemble Cooper, Donald Crisp, Jessie
Ralph, Agnes Anderson, Lionel Belmore, Lawrence Grant, Crawford Kent,
Howard Leeds, Ethel Griffies, Elspeth Dudgeon, Mary Gordon,
George K. Arthur

RECKLESS, *William Powell, Jean Harlow, Henry Stephenson, Franchot Tone, Leon Waycoff (Ames) (foreground)*

RECKLESS
M-G-M-1935

PRODUCER David 0. Selznick
DIRECTOR Victor Fleming
AUTHOR Oliver Jeffries
SCREENPLAY P. J. Wolfson
MUSIC AND LYRICS Jerome Kern, Oscar Hammerstein II, Con Conrad, Herbert Magdison, Jack King, Edwin Knopf, Harold Adamson
CAMERAMAN George Folsey
CAST: Jean Harlow, William Robert Light, Rosalind Russell, Henry Stephenson, Louise Henry, James Ellison, Leon Waycoff (Leon Ames), Man Mountain Dean, Farina (Allen Hoskins), Allan Jones, Carl Randall, Nina Mae McKinney

ANNA KARENINA, *Greta Garbo, May Robson, Fredric March*

ANNA KARENINA
M-G-M-1935

PRODUCER David 0. Selznick
DIRECTOR Clarence Brown
AUTHOR Leo Tolstoy
SCREENPLAY Clemence Dane, Salka Viertel, S. N. Behrman
CAMERAMAN William Daniels
CAST: Greta Garbo, Fredric March, Basil Rathbone, Freddie Bartholomew,
May Robson, Reginald Owen, Reginald Denny, Phoebe Foster,Gyles Isham,
Maureen O'Sullivan, Buster Phelps, Ella Ethridge, Joan Marsh, Sidney
Bracey, Cora Sue Collins, Olaf Hytten, Joe E.Tozer, Guy D'Ennery, Harry
Allen, Mary Forbes, Constance Collier

A TALE OF TWO CITIES, *Isabel Jewell and Ronald Colman (left foreground)*

A TALE OF TWO CITIES
M-G-M-1936

PRODUCER David 0. Selznick
DIRECTOR Jack Conway
AUTHOR Charles Dickens
SCREENPLAY W. P. Lipscomb, S. N. Behrman
CAMERAMAN Oliver T. Marsh
CAST: Ronald Colman, Elizabeth Allan, Edna May Oliver, Reginald Owen, Basil Rathbone, Blanche Yurka, Henry B. Walthall, Donald Woods, Walter Catlett, Fritz Leiber, H. B. Warner, Mitchell Lewis, Claude Gillingwater, Billy Bevan, Isabel Jewell, Lucille Laverne, Tully Marshall, Fay Chaldecott, Eily Maylon, E. E. Clive, Lawrence Grant, Robert Warwick, Ralf Harolde, John Davison, Tom Ricketts, Donald Haines, Barlowe Borland

LITTLE LORD FAUNTLEROY, *Freddie Bartholomew (center)*

LITTLE LORD FAUNTLEROY
United Artists-1936

PRODUCER David 0. Selznick
DIRECTOR John Cromwell
AUTHOR Frances Hodgson Burnett
SCREENPLAY Hugh Walpole
CAMERAMAN Charles Rosher
CAST: Freddie Bartholomew, C. Aubrey Smith, Guy Kibbee, Dolores
Costello, Mickey Rooney, Jessie Ralph, Jackie Searle, Helen Flint, Una
O'Connor, E. E. Clive, Ivan Simpson

THE GARDEN OF ALLAH, *Charles Boyer and Marlene Dietrich*

THE GARDEN OF ALLAH
United Artists-1936

PRODUCER David 0. Selznick
DIRECTOR Richard Boleslawski
AUTHOR Robert Hichens
SCREENPLAY W. P. Lipscomb, Lynn Riggs
CAMERAMAN W. Howard Greene
CAST: Marlene Dietrich, Charles Boyer, Basil Rathbone, C.Aubrey Smith,
Tilly Losch, Joseph Schildkraut, John Carradine, Alan Marshall, Lucile
Watson, Henry Brandon, Helen Jerome Eddy, Charles Waldron, John Bryan,
Nigel De Brulier, Pedro De Cordoba, Ferdinand Gottschalk, Adrian Rosely,
"Corky," Robert Frazer, David Scott, Andrew McKenna, Bonita Granville,
Marcia Mae Jones, Betty Jane Graham, Ann Gillis

A STAR IS BORN
United Artists-1937

PRODUCER David O. Selznick
DIRECTOR William Wellman
AUTHORS William Wellman, Robert Carson
SCREENPLAY Dorothy Parker, Alan Campbell, Robert Carson
CAMERAMAN W. H. Greene
CAST: Janet Gaynor, Fredric March, Adolphe Menjou, May Robson,
Andy Devine, Lionel Stander, Elizabeth Jenns, Edgar Kennedy, Owen
Moore, J. C. Nugent, Clara Blandick, A. W. Seweatt, Peggy Wood, Adrian
Rosley, Arthur Hoyt, Guinn "Big Boy" Williams, Vince Barnett, Paul Stanton,
Franklin Pangborn, Dennis O'Keefe

THE PRISONER OF ZENDA
United Artists-1937

PRODUCER David O. Selznick
DIRECTORS John Cromwell, W. S. Van Dyke (uncredited)
AUTHOR Anthony Hope
SCREENPLAY John Balderston
ADAPTATION Wells Root
ADDITIONAL DIALOGUE Donald Ogden Stewart
CAMERAMAN James Wong Howe
CAST: Ronald Colman, Madeleine Carroll, Douglas Fairbanks, Jr.,
Raymond Massey, Mary Astor, C. Aubrey Smith, David Niven, Montagu Love,
William von Brincken, Philip Sleeman, Torben Meyer, Byron Foulger,
Lawrence Grant, Ian McLaren, Ralph Faulkner, Howard Lang, Ben Webster,
Evelyn Beresford, Boyd Irwin, Emmett King, Al Shean, Charles Halton,
Francis Ford, Spencer Charters

A STAR IS BORN, *Janet Gaynor, Fredric March, Adolphe Menjou, Lionel Stander and Vince Barnett*

THE PRISONER OF ZENDA, *Douglas Fairbanks, Jr. and Ronald Colman*

NOTHING SACRED, *Carole Lombard, Charles Winninger*

NOTHING SACRED
United Artists-1937

PRODUCER David O. Selznick
DIRECTOR William A. Wellman
AUTHOR James A. Street
SCREENPLAY Ben Hecht
CAST: Carole Lombard, Fredric March, Charles Winninger, Walter Connolly, Frank Fay, Sig Rumann, Maxie Rosenbloom, Aileen Pringle, Margaret Hamilton, Troy Brown, Hedda Hopper, John Qualen, Olin Howland, Art Lasky, Monty Woolley, Jinx Falkenberg

THE ADVENTURES OF TOM SAWYER, *Walter Brennan, Tommy Kelly, Jackie Moran*

THE ADVENTURES OF TOM SAWYER
United Artists-1938

PRODUCER David 0. Selznick
DIRECTOR Norman Taurog
AUTHOR Mark Twain
SCREENPLAY John V. A. Weaver
CAMERAMAN James Wong Howe
CAST: Tommy Kelly, Jackie Moran, Ann Gillis, May Robson, Walter Brennan, Victor Jory, David Holt, Victor Kilian, Nana Bryant, Olin Howland, Donald Meek, Charles Richman, Margaret Hamilton, Marcia Mae Jones, Mickey Rentschler, Cora Sue Collins, Philip Hurlie, Spring Byington

THE YOUNG IN HEART, *Billie Burke, Minnie Dupree, Roland Young, Janet Gaynor*

THE YOUNG IN HEART
United Artists-1938

PRODUCER David 0. Selznick
DIRECTOR Richard Wallace
AUTHOR I.A.R. Wylie (from "The Gay Banditti")
SCREENPLAY Paul Osborn, Charles Bennett
CAMERAMAN Leon Shamroy
CAST: Janet Gaynor, Douglas Fairbanks, Jr., Paulette Goddard, Roland
Young, Billie Burke, Richard Carlson, Minnie Dupree, Henry Stephenson,
Lawrence Grant, Walter Kingsford, Eily Malyon, Tom Ricketts, Irvin S. Cobb,
Lucile Watson, Margaret Early

MADE FOR EACH OTHER, *James Stewart, Carole Lombard*

MADE FOR EACH OTHER
United Artists-1939

PRODUCER David 0. Selznick
DIRECTOR John Cromwell
SCREENPLAY Jo Swerling
CAMERAMAN Leon Shamroy
CAST: Carole Lombard, James Stewart, Charles Coburn, Lucile Watson,
Eddie Quillan, Alma Kruger, Ruth Weston, Donald Briggs, Harry Davenport,
Esther Dale, Renee Orsell, Louise Beavers, Ward Bond, Olin Howland, Fern
Emmett, Jackie Taylor, Mickey Rentschler, Ivan Simpson

GONE WITH THE WIND
M-G-M-1939

PRODUCER David O. Selznick
DIRECTORS Victor Fleming, Sam Wood, George Cukor
AUTHOR Margaret Mitchell
SCREENPLAY Sidney Howard
CAMERAMAN Ernest Haller
CAST: Clark Gable, Leslie Howard, Olivia de Havilland, Vivien Leigh,
George Reeves, Fred Crane, Hattie McDaniel, Everett Brown, Zack
Williams, Thomas Mitchell, Oscar Polk, Barbara O'Neil, Victor Jory, Evelyn
Keyes, Ann Rutherford, Butterfly McQueen, Howard Hickman, Alicia Rhett,
Rand Brooks, Carroll Nye, Marcelia Martin, Laura Hope Crews, Harry
Davenport, Leona Roberts, Jane Darwell, Albert Morin, Mary Anderson,
Terry Shero, William McClain, Eddie Anderson, Jackie Moran, Cliff Edwards,
Ona Munson, Ed Chandler, George Hackathorne, Roscoe Ates, Eric Linden,
John Arledge, Tom Tyler, William Bakewell, Lee Phelps, Paul Hurst, Ernest
Whitman, William Stelling, Louis Jean Heydt, Isabel Jewell, Robert Elliott,
George Meeker, Wallis Clark, Irving Bacon, Adrian Morris, J. M. Kerrigan,
Olin Howland, Yakima Canutt, Blue Washington, Ward Bond, Cammie King,
Mickey Kuhn, Violet Kemble Cooper

INTERMEZZO: A LOVE STORY
United Artists-1939

PRODUCER David O. Selznick
DIRECTOR Gregory Ratoff
AUTHORS Gosta Stevens, Gustav Molander
SCREENPLAY George O'Neil
CAMERAMAN Gregg Toland
CAST: Leslie Howard, Ingrid Bergman, Edna Best, John Halliday, Cecil
Kellaway, Enid Bennett, Ann Todd, Douglas Scott, Eleanor Wellehoeft, Maria
Flynn

GONE WITH THE WIND *Vivien Leigh, Clark Gable, and Olivia de Havilland*

INTERMEZZO, *Leslie Howard and Ingrid Bergman*

REBECCA, *Laurence Olivier and Joan Fontaine*

REBECCA
United Artists-1940

PRODUCER David 0. Selznick
DIRECTOR Alfred Hitchcock
AUTHOR Daphne du Maurier
SCREENPLAY Robert E. Sherwood, Joan Harrison
CAMERAMAN George Barnes
CAST: Laurence Olivier, Joan Fontaine, Judith Anderson, George Sanders, Nigel Bruce, Reginald Denny, C. Aubrey Smith, Gladys Cooper, Florence Bates, Melville Cooper, Leo G. Carroll, Leonard Carey, Lumsden Hare, Edward Fielding, Philip Winter, Forrester Harvey

SINCE YOU WENT AWAY, *Robert Walker, Jennifer Jones, Shirley Temple, and Claudette Colbert*

SINCE YOU WENT AWAY
United Artists-1944

PRODUCER David O. Selznick
DIRECTOR John Cromwell
SCREENPLAY David O. Selznick
CAMERAMEN Stanley Cortez, Lee Garmes
CAST: Claudette Colbert, Jennifer Jones, Joseph Cotten, Shirley Temple, Monty Woolley, Lionel Barrymore, Robert Walker, Hattie McDaniel, Nazimova, Keenan Wynn, Gordon Oliver, Lloyd Corrigan, Jane Devlin, Agnes Moorehead, Albert Basserman, Guy Madison, Craig Stevens, Jackie Moran, Anne Gillis, Robert Anderson, Irving Bacon, Aileen Pringle, Charles Williams, Wallis Clark, Nella Hart, Leonide Mostovoy, Dorothy Garner, James Carlisle, George Chandler, John A. James, Mary Anne Durkin, Joyce Horn, Ruth Valmy, Grady Sutton, Buddy Gorman, Patricia Peters, Andrew McLaglen, Addison Richards

SPELLBOUND, *Ingrid Bergman and Gregory Peck*

SPELLBOUND

United Artists-1945

PRODUCER David O. Selznick
DIRECTOR Alfred Hitchcock
AUTHOR Francis Beeding (Hilary St. George Saunders and John Palmer)
SCREENPLAY Ben Hecht
ADAPTATION Angus McPhail
CAMERAMAN George Barnes
DREAM SEQUENCE Salvador Dali
CAST: Ingrid Bergman, Gregory Peck, Jean Acker, Rhonda Fleming,
Donald Curtis, John Emery, Leo G. Carroll, Norman Lloyd, Steven Geray,
Paul Harvey, Erskine Sandford, Janet Scott, Victor Kilian, Bill Goodwin, Art
Baker, Wallace Ford, Regis Toomey, Teddy Infuhr, Addison Richards, Dave
Willock, George Meader, Matt Moore, Harry Brown, Clarence Straight, Joel
Davis, Edward Fielding, Richard Bartell, Michael Chekhov

DUEL IN THE SUN, *Walter Hutton, Joseph Cotten, Jennifer Jones, Gregory Peck, and Lionel Barrymore*

REWARD UNLIMITED
U. S. Public Health Service-1944

A short subject supervised by David O. Selznick, featuring Dorothy McGuire, Aline MacMahon, and James Brown

DUEL IN THE SUN
Selznick Releasing Organization-1946

PRODUCER David O. Selznick
DIRECTOR King Vidor
AUTHOR Niven Busch
SCREENPLAY David O. Selznick
ADAPTATION Oliver H. P. Garrett
CAMERAMEN Lee Garmes, Hal Rosson, Ray Rannahan

CAST: Jennifer Jones, Joseph Cotten, Gregory Peck, Lionel Barrymore, Herbert Marshall, Lillian Gish, Walter Huston, Charles Bickford, Harry Carey, Butterfly McQueen, Otto Kruger, Charles Dingle, Tilly Losch Scott McKay, Sidney Blackmer, Don White, Joan Tetzel

THE PARADINE CASE, *Gregory Peck and Charles Laughton*

THE PARADINE CASE
Selznick Releasing Organization-1947

PRODUCER David O. Selznick
DIRECTOR Alfred Hitchcock
AUTHOR Robert Hichens
SCREENPLAY David 0. Selznick
ADAPTATION Almia Reville
CAMERAMAN Lee Garmes
CAST: Gregory Peck, Ann Todd, Charles Laughton, Ethel Barrymore,
Charles Coburn, Louis Jourdan, Alida Valli, Leo G. Carroll, John
Goldsworthy, Isobel Elsom, Lester Matthews, Pat Aherne, Colin Hunter,
John Williams, Joan Tetzel

PORTRAIT OF JENNIE, *Jennifer Jones and Joseph Cotten*

PORTRAIT OF JENNIE
Selznick Releasing Organization-' 949

PRODUCER David 0. Selznick
DIRECTOR William Dieterle
AUTHOR Robert Nathan
SCREENPLAY Paul Osborn, Peter Berneis
CAMERAMAN Joseph August
CAST: Jennifer Jones, Joseph Cotten, Ethel Barrymore, Lillian Gish, Cecil
Kellaway, David Wayne, Albert Sharpe, Henry Hull, Florence Bates, Felix
Bressart, Clem Bevans, Maude Simmons, Esther Somers, John Farrell,
Robert Dudley

A FAREWELL TO ARMS, *Rock Hudson and Jennifer Jones*

A FAREWELL TO ARMS
20th Century-Fox-1957

PRODUCER David 0. Selznick
DIRECTOR Charles Vidor
AUTHOR Ernest Hemingway
SCREENPLAY Ben Hecht
CAMERAMEN Piero Portalupi, Oswald Morris
CAST: Rock Hudson, Jennifer Jones, Vittorio de Sica, Alberto Sordi, Kurt
Kasznar, Mercedes McCambridge, Oscar Homolka, Elaine Stritch, Leopoldo
Trieste, Franco Interlenghi, Jose Nieto, Georges Brehat, Memmo
Carotenuto, Guido Martufi, Umberto Spadaro, Umberto Sacripanti, Victor
Francen, Joan Shawlee, Alberto D'Amario

APPENDIX B

Academy Recognition of Selznick Films

Academy of Motion Picture Arts and Sciences
nominations in major
categories for films produced by
David O. Selznick
(winners denoted by asterisk):

1929-30

ACTRESS Ruth Chatterton, *Sarah and Son*
WRITER Howard Estabrook, *Street of Chance*

1931-32

WRITER (ORIGINAL STORY) Adela Rogers St. Johns, *What Price*
Hollywood?

1934

PICTURE: *Viva Villa*
WRITER (ADAPTATION) Ben Hecht, *Viva Villa*
WRITER (ORIGINAL STORY) Arthur Caesar,* *Manhattan Melodrama*

1935

PICTURE *David Copperfield*

1936

PICTURE *A Tale of Two Cities*

1937

PICTURE *A Star Is Born*
ACTOR Fredric March, *A Star Is Born*
ACTRESS Janet Gaynor, *A Star Is Born*
DIRECTOR William Wellman, *A Star Is Born*
WRITERS (ORIGINAL STORY) William Wellman,* Robert Carson,* *A Star Is Born*
WRITERS (ADAPTATION) Alan Campbell, Robert Carson, Dorothy Parker, *A Star Is Born*

1939

PICTURE *Gone With the Wind**
ACTOR Clark Gable, *Gone With the Wind*
ACTRESS Vivien Leigh,* *Gone With the Wind*
SUPPORTING ACTRESS Hattie McDaniel,*   Olivia de Havilland, *Gone With the Wind*
DIRECTOR Victor Fleming,* *Gone With the Wind*
WRITER (SCREENPLAY) Sidney Howard,* *Gone With the Wind*
THALBERG AWARD David O. Selznick

1940

PICTURE *Rebecca**
ACTOR Laurence Olivier, *Rebecca*
ACTRESS Joan Fontaine, *Rebecca*
DIRECTOR Alfred Hitchcock, *Rebecca*
WRITER (SCREENPLAY) Robert E. Sherwood, Joan Harrison, *Rebecca*

1944

PICTURE *Since You Went Away*
ACTRESS Claudette Colbert, *Since You Went Away*
SUPPORTING ACTOR Monty Woolley, *Since You Went Away*
SUPPORTING ACTRESS Jennifer Jones, *Since You Went Away*

1945

PICTURE *Spellbound*
SUPPORTING ACTOR Michael Chekhov, *Spellbound*

1946

ACTRESS Jennifer Jones, *Duel in the Sun*
SUPPORTING ACTRESS Lillian Gish, *Duel in the Sun*

1947

SUPPORTING ACTRESS Ethel Barrymore, *The Paradine Case*

APPENDIX C

Printed Sources

BOOKS

BROWNLOW, KEVIN, The Parade's Gone By, Knopf, New York, 1968.

CROWTHER, BOSLEY, Hollywood Rajah, The Life and Times of Louis B. Mayer, Henry Holt, New York, 1960.

_ _ _ _, The Lion's Share, E. P. Dutton, New York, 1957.

FOWLER, GENE, Myron Selznick, Charlemagne Press, Los Angeles, 1944.

GRAHAM, SHEILAH and GEROLD FRANK, Beloved Infidel, Henry Holt, New York, 1951

HAYS, WILL H., The Memoirs of Will Hays, Doubleday, Garden City, N.Y., 1955.

HECHT, BEN, A Child of the Century, Simon and Schuster, New York, 1954.

HOPPER, HEDDA, The Whole Truth and Nothing But, Doubleday, Garden City, N.Y., 1963

HOTCHNER, A. E., Papa Hemingway, Random House, New York, 1966.

JOBES, GERTRUDE, Motion Picture Empire, Archon Books, Hamden, Conn., 1966.

LASKY, JESSE L., I Blow My Own Horn, Doubleday, Garden City, N.Y., 1957.

MAYER, ARTHUR, Merely Colossal, Simon and Schuster, New York, 1953.

MIZENER, ARTHUR, The Far Side of Paradise, Houghton, Mifflin, New York, 1951.

RAMSAYE, TERRY, A Million and One Nights, Simon and Schuster, New York, 1964

SCHUMACH, MURRAY, The Face on the Cutting Room Floor, William Morrow, New York, 1964.

STEELE, JOSEPH HENRY, Ingrid Bergman, David McKay, New York, 1959.

TAYLOR, ROBERT LEWVIS, W.C. Fields, His Follies and Fortunes, Doubleday, Garden City, 1949

TRUFFAUT, FRANCOIS, Hitchcock, Simon and Schuster, New York, 1967

TURNBULL, ANDREW, Scott Fitzgerald, Scribner's, New York, 1962. _ _ _ _,editor, The Letters of F. Scott Fitzgerald, Scribner's, New York, 1963

VIDOR, KING, A Tree Is a Tree, Harcourt, Brace, New York, 1952.

PERIODICALS

BARTLETT, RANDOLPH, "A Believer in Brains," *Motion Picture Magazine*, October, 1919.

BEHLMER, RUDY, and HENRY HART, "David 0. Selznick," *Films in Review*, June-July, 1963.

DOYLE, NEIL, "Jennifer Jones," *Films in Review*, August-September, 1962.

HENAGHAN, JIM , "The Tragedy of Robert Walker," *Redbook*, November, 1951.

JOHNSTON, ALVA, "The Great Dictater," *Saturday Evening Post*, May 16, 1942.

_ _ _ _, Russell Birdwell Profile, *The New Yorker*, August 19, 26, September 2, 9, 1944.

LIFE, "Making a Movie," March 17, 1958.

REYNOLDS, QUENTIN, "The Amazing Selznicks," Collier's, May 28 and June 4, 1938.

SELZNICK, DAVID 0., "Why I Started Making Movies Again," Los Angeles *Times,* December 1, 1957

SMITH, FREDERICK JAMES, "The Youngest Film Magnate," Motion Picture Classic, September, 1920.

Also: various editions of New York *Times,* New York *Herald Tribune, Time, Life,* Los Angeles *Times, Motion Picture Herald, Variety, Hollywood*

Reporter, Daily Variety, Associated Press, New York Journal-American, Motion Picture Almanac.

PHOTOGRAPH CREDITS

Columbia Pictures Corporation — *260*

Larry Edmunds Bookshop — *10*

Alwin Johnson — *199*

M-G-M — *2, 26, 31, 40, 55, 57, 58, 59, 60, 61, 62, 64, 66, 67, 68, 69, 70, 72, 73, 74, 86, 126, 138, 144, 148, 149, 150, 154, 155, 156, 157, 160, 253, 270, 320, 321, 323, 325, 326, 327, 328, 329, 330, 331, 333, 341*

Motion Picture Classic — *17*

Motion Picture Magazine — *5, 14*

Ken Murray — *29, 34*

Paramount — *38, 39, 46, 47, 48, 229, 256, 300, 303, 305, 307, 311*

RKO General — *53, 311, 312, 313, 317, 319*

Selznick International — *51, 68, 95, 112, 119, 170, 178, 185, 186, 195, 200, 202, 207, 216*

Selznick Releasing Organization — *215, 221, 223, 230, 233, 345, 346, 347*

Ray Stuart — *12, 192*

20th Century-Fox — *203, 270, 274, 275, 276, 283, 284, 289, 317, 348*

United Artists — *91, 100, 104, 106, 108, 210, 214, 332, 335, 336, 337, 338, 339, 341, 342, 343, 344*

Universal — *6*

Wide World — *40, 43, 92, 205, 208, 254, 255, 262, 264, 280, 287*